EMMA GOLDMAN
AND THE
AMERICAN LEFT

"Nowhere at Home"

TWAYNE'S TWENTIETH-CENTURY AMERICAN BIOGRAPHY SERIES

John Milton Cooper, Jr., General Editor

EMMA GOLDMAN AND THE AMERICAN LEFT

"Nowhere at Home"

Marian J. Morton

Twayne Publishers • New York
Maxwell Macmillan Canada • Toronto
Maxwell Macmillan International •
New York   Oxford   Singapore   Sydney

Twayne's Twentieth Century
American Biography Series No. 14

Twayne Publishers
Macmillan Publishing Company
886 Third Avenue
New York, New York 10022

Maxwell Macmillan Canada, Inc.
1200 Eglinton Avenue East
Suite 200
Don Mills, Ontario M3C 3N1

Macmillan Publishing Company is part of the Maxwell Communications Group of
Companies.

10 9 8 7 6 5 4 3 2 1 (hc)
10 9 8 7 6 5 4 3 2 1 (pb)

The paper used in this publication meets the minimum requirements of American National
Standard for Information Sciences—Permanence of Paper for Printed Library Materials,
ANSI Z39.48-1984.

Printed and bound in the United States of America.

Library of Congress Cataloging-in-Publication Data

Emma Goldman and the American Left : "Nowhere at home" / Marian J. Morton.
    p.   cm.—(Twayne's twentieth-century American biography series ; no. 14)
Includes bibliographical references and index.
ISBN 0-8057-7794-6 (hard : alk. paper).—ISBN 0-8057-7795-4 (pbk. : alk. paper)
1. Goldman, Emma, 1869–1940. 2. Anarchists—United States—Biography.
I. Goldman, Emma, 1869–1940. Nowhere at home. II. Title. III. Series.
HX843.7.G65M67 1992
335'.83'092—dc20
[B]   92–31335
                                                                        CIP

To the memory of my mother, Jean Inglis Lincoln

CONTENTS

PREFACE

I feel so cast out, pursued by the furies, and nowhere at home.[1]

When she wrote this, sometime in the 1920s, Emma Goldman was in exile from her adopted homeland, the United States, and she was a refugee from the country of her birth, Russia, which was then under Bolshevik rule; she was a woman without a country. In many ways she had always been "nowhere at home": outside of and at odds with the mainstream and Main Street, estranged sometimes from her closest political comrades and even from her beloved Alexander Berkman. Yet just as often, Goldman found her home within or alongside the political left, whose dreams and causes, fortunes and misfortunes she shared. To many Americans, the anarchist "Red Emma" was not only at home on the left, she *was* the American left.

Anarchism was one response to the growing size and power of the economic and political institutions that accompanied nineteenth-century industrialization, when large corporations, large factories, large government threatened to dwarf and stifle the individual. In 1840 Pierre-Joseph Proudhon became the first political thinker to use the term *anarchism* in a positive sense to describe his own belief that the state should be replaced by small, voluntary associations. Later anarchists attacked the state, the church, social conventions, and, with less unanimity, private property. In the best of all possible anarchist worlds, they believed, such artificial restraints would be removed, and each person would be free to develop to his or her fullest potential. Individuals would be governed only by associations that they chose to join, such as communes, trade unions, or workers' collectives. The vision of a free, just, and harmonious society was compelling. Its libertarianism had antecedents in the Enlightenment's distrust of established institutions and in the Romantic era's worship of the individual, as well as in the antistatism of some varieties of religious and non-Western thought.[2]

Anarchists advocated free speech, free thought, sometimes free love, and, occasionally, violence as necessary to overthrow the state and accomplish the anarchist revolution. By the early twentieth century, however, most anarchists rejected the individual act of violence—the *attentat,* or propaganda by deed—advocating instead revolution achieved through the education of the masses by the intelligentsia, or through direct action by trade unions. Nevertheless, most Americans continued to identify all anarchists with terrorism.

In fact there were three schools of anarchist thought in the United States, differentiated chiefly by their ideas about the management of economic resources.[3] Individualist anarchists—most often American-born—like Voltairine de Cleyre and Benjamin Tucker denounced the state and the church but usually endorsed private property. Individualist anarchists had emotional but not political affinities with the property-centered individualism of nineteenth-century American liberals and twentieth-century American conservatives. They believed, however, that an activist state should preserve but not regulate property. Most European-immigrant anarchists of the mid- to late-nineteenth century, disciples of Peter Kropotkin and Michael Bakunin, were communist anarchists. Communist anarchists thought that property should be owned communally not privately, and that communes and collectives should distribute goods and services "to each according to his needs." Emma Goldman belonged to this group, although she leaned toward the individualism of the American anarchists. The third school, anarcho-syndicalism, also rejected private property. Anarcho-syndicalists maintained that trade unions or workers' organizations should first lead the anarchist revolution and then run the economy. In the United States, anarcho-syndicalism was best represented by the Industrial Workers of the World, with which Goldman cooperated on a number of occasions.

Drawing connections between personalities and political philosophies is always problematic, but anarchism does seem either to have attracted men and women of a strongly individualistic—not to say eccentric—bent, or to have encouraged them in that direction. In either case, because it cut its adherents loose from institutional restraints, anarchism was a lonely philosophy. The exhilarating freedom from country, creed, and sometimes family was often accompanied by the frightening realization of solitude. Not surprisingly anarchists often felt, as Goldman did, "nowhere at home." Voltairine de Cleyre, for example, wrote, "I never feel at home anywhere. . . . I feel like a lost or wandering creature that has no place, and cannot find anything to be at home with." And here is the Spanish anarchist Francisco Ascaso, banished in 1932 to an African penal colony for leading an insurrection in Catalonia: "We are going away. . . . [D]eparture has always been a symbol of life. Constantly on the march, perpetually on the road like eternal Jews without a country; outside a society in which we find no environment in which to live . . . without any place in the world."[4]

But for an anarchist, this can be as much a boast as a lament, as much a political pose as a psychological reality. An anarchist is *supposed* to be at home nowhere. There was a rough—but unhappy—justice at work when in the last two decades of Goldman's life, her political persona became political reality.

Although she was better known as a dynamic public speaker, Goldman was also a prolific writer. Almost everything she wrote was political: her earliest published lectures, her *Mother Earth* editorials, her two books on Russia, her later letters collected in Richard and Anna Marie Drinnon's *Nowhere at Home: Letters from Exile of Emma Goldman and Alexander Berkman*, and her last essays in David Porter's *Vision on Fire: Emma Goldman on the Spanish Revolution*. I have used these to trace the uneasy and sometimes unhappy evolution of her political philosophy not because she was an original or systematic thinker but precisely because her ideas were often personal, contradictory responses to her changing political context.[5]

Because it was written with such drama and energy, I have relied heavily on Goldman's autobiography, *Living My Life*, even though it bears the unmistakable imprint of the circumstances in which it was written, during the years 1928 to 1930, when she was in political and spiritual exile. In her autobiography, Goldman wished to persuade her readers that she had lived her life "nowhere at home." In reality, however, the autobiography also shows us that she lived much of her life with others on the left, finding among them intellectual inspiration, political and sexual camaraderie, financial and moral support, and emotional solace.[6]

This, therefore, is a political biography and a story of the American left. I do not wish to deny Goldman's individuality—indeed that would be almost impossible—but to connect her personal story to her politics, because that is what she did. Emma Goldman is interesting and important today because of the political life she led and the political times in which she lived it.

ACKNOWLEDGMENTS

Thanks first to Lois Scharf, who encouraged me to write this book.

Thanks to John Carroll University for the George Grauel Fellowship that enabled me to work on the manuscript.

Thanks to colleagues Jim Krukones, Russell Duncan, Brenda Wirkus, Robert Kolesar, David Robson, and especially Margaret Berry, for reading the manuscript.

Thanks to archivist Anne Okey of the Labadie Collection at the University of Michigan for extraordinary help in finding photographs.

Special thanks to my great great-aunt Agnes Inglis, first curator of the Labadie Collection and friend of Emma Goldman, without whose archives this and other books about Goldman would not have been possible.

1

JEWISH ROOTS: RUSSIAN
RADICALISM, 1869–1885

"No-one would take her for a Jewess, this Gretchen, with her grey-blue eyes, brown hair, and undetermined features," commented Emma Goldman's biographer Frank Harris in 1924.[1] Goldman herself remained deeply ambivalent about her Jewish roots. In conflict with her stifling religious traditions and the repressive tsarist anti-Semitism, Goldman found freedom, self-expression, and her first political home in Russian radicalism.

Emma Goldman was born on 27 June 1869 in Kovno, Lithuania, the child of Abraham and Taube Goldman, both Lithuanian Jews. Lithuania was then part of the Russian empire, and Kovno (now Kaunas) was within the Jewish Pale of Settlement. The empress Catherine II had established the Pale at the end of the eighteenth century after the annexation of Poland brought large numbers of Jews into the empire. The Pale, stretching from the Baltic Sea to the Black Sea, included parts of Poland, Lithuania, Byelorussia, and the Ukraine, and was home to almost five million Jews, 94 percent of all Jews living within imperial Russia.

The Russian Jewish author Mary Antin, a later immigrant to the United States, recalled her own childhood within this Jewish ghetto: "In Russia lived the Czar, and a great many cruel people; and in Russia were the dreadful prisons from which people never came back. . . . My father and mother and friends and all other people like us . . . must not be found outside the Pale, because we were Jews. So there was a fence around Polotzk [Antin's home town]. . . . The world was divided into Jews and Gentiles."[2]

Jews were among the dozens of ethno-cultural groups including Armenians, Ukrainians, and Georgians, living within the empire. Languages, cultures, and religions varied widely, making the business of governing difficult. A large bureaucracy administered a multitude of rules and regulations for commerce, education, residence, and marriage that were intended to impose uniformity upon this diversity. Yet even within this heterogeneous population, the Jews were set apart by their dress, dialect, and, especially, religion. Among orthodox Christians, Jews were detested as the killers of Christ. Doubly vulnerable because they did not have an historic homeland within the empire, Jews became special targets of both the imperial regime and its inhabitants.

The official goal of the tsars was assimilation. They compelled Jews to abandon Yiddish for Russian, Judaism for Christianity, peddling and commerce for farming and manufacturing. To this end, tsarist persuasion alternated with outright oppression. Alexander I (1801–1825) encouraged Jews to establish farming colonies and opened special government schools for Jewish children. Nicholas I (1825–55) was openly and fiercely anti-Semitic, censoring Hebrew and Yiddish books and instituting harsh conscription laws that forced Jewish boys, ages 12 to 18, into cantons so that they would become both Russian soldiers and Russian Christians.[3] By contrast, the early reforms of Nicholas's successor, Alexander II (1855–81), brought hope to many groups. The emperor emancipated the serfs and reformed the Russian judiciary and local governments. Jews especially were encouraged when he abolished juvenile conscription and eased requirements for Jewish residence and government service. Certain classes of Jews—those with wealth or education—received special privileges throughout Alexander's reign. Yet he refused to abolish the Pale, even though some of his advisers recommended it. Pogroms in 1871 were officially ignored, and most schools for Jewish children were closed in 1873.

Encouraged by the anti-Semitism of official imperial policies, non-Jewish Russian peasants found Jews ready scapegoats for their own destitution. Antin recalled with terror the peasant pogroms: "The Gentiles made the Passover a time of horror for the Jews. . . . The stupid peasants would . . . fill themselves with vodka and set out to kill the Jews. They attacked them with knives and clubs and scythes and axes, killed them or tortured them, and burned their houses."[4]

Even earning a living was perilous for the Jews. Barred from many occupations and burdened by extra taxes, their economic fortunes may actually have worsened after midcentury. Alexander II's emancipation of the serfs in 1863 encouraged Russian landowners to sell their own products, pushing Jews out of their traditional jobs as middlemen. Prevented from owning land themselves, Jews moved continuously within the Pale from the village *shtetls* into the swarming, suffocating urban ghettos. Here they competed bitterly for jobs as artisans and small traders, knowing that they could not go elsewhere. The beginnings of industrialization also put them at a disadvantage. Without sufficient capital to purchase machinery, they owned or worked in small, labor-intensive and technologically backward factories, especially in textiles.

Most Russian Jews followed the Orthodox faith of their fathers. As they awaited the imminent coming of the Messiah, they followed age-old laws and rituals: "We lived by the Law that had been given us through our teacher Moses. How to eat, how to bathe, how to work, especially the study of the Torah," recalled Antin.[5] The Messiah was presumed to be male, and Orthodox Judaism, like Christianity and tsarist rule, was unequivocally patriarchal. Women could not study or teach the Torah or attend the *cheder* schools to which every Jewish boy aspired. From behind a screen in the synagogue, women watched men conduct the religious services. Married women covered their heads with wigs or kerchiefs, symbolic of their deference and modesty. It is no wonder that Orthodox men thanked God every day that they were not born female. "It was not much to be a girl," recalled Antin.[6] Within the Jewish community and the Jewish family, male authority was seldom challenged and, therefore, was exercised as arbitrarily as within the church or the palace.

Nevertheless, the rigid patriarchy of Orthodox Judaism could be life-sustaining. The rituals and rules that governed the minutest details of daily life provided emotional sustenance for Jews vulnerable to the capricious cruelty of imperial rulers and Gentile neighbors. Antin explained: "The religious integrity of the Jews [was] a fortress erected by the prisoners of the Pale, in defiance of their jailers; a stronghold built of the ruins of their pillaged homes, cemented with the blood of their murdered children. Harassed on every side, thwarted in every normal effort, pent up within narrow limits, all but dehumanized, the Russian Jew fell back upon the only thing that never failed him, his hereditary faith in God."[7]

The fortress that sustained the old, however, could be a prison for the young. So it was for Emma Goldman, a female Jew in Russia, hedged around by proscriptions of the tsar and the Torah.

In *Living My Life,* Goldman interpreted her childhood in simplistic psychological terms: she was the unloved child of a loveless, sexually incompatible marriage. Taube's first husband, the true love of her life according to Goldman, had died in 1864 or 1865, leaving Taube with two small daughters, Lena and Helene. The marriage of the young widow and Abraham had been arranged "in the traditional Jewish orthodox fashion, without love."[8] Abraham, Emma claimed, was driven by sexual passion for his wife, but Taube, fearing pregnancy, "fought back his insatiable hunger." Emma's father, bearded, handsome, and brutal, appeared as the villain in this story. Goldman's autobiography recalled physical and verbal abuse, lashings with a strap, and her father's threats: "'I'll kill her! I will kill that brat! I will teach her to obey!'" When Emma received a bad school report, she wrote, "He pounded me and pulled me about, ranting: 'You are my disgrace! You will always be so! You can't be my child; you don't look like me or like your mother; you don't act like us!'" Goldman decided not to bear children herself because, she said, "My ghastly childhood stood before me, my hunger for affection, which Mother was unable to satisfy. Father's harshness towards the children, his violent outbreaks, his beating my sisters and me."[9] Consequently the autobiography, as Alice Wexler and others have noted, portrays an abused and love-starved orphan, frozen by her parents' coldness toward each other and toward herself.[10]

This is a puzzling self-portrait by a woman then almost 60 years old and long since reconciled with her father and family. There is little point in challenging the legitimacy of her remembered emotions, but the portrayal is less surprising if readers recall that Goldman wrote her autobiography while she was politically homeless and in exile, cut off from family, friends, and allies. Perhaps she had been rejected in the past by her parents. Certainly she was rejected at that time by her two mother countries.

Moreover there are earlier, more positive interpretations of her childhood. In 1910, for example, when Goldman was at the height of her American popularity, a biographical sketch accompanying *Anarchism and Other Essays,* written by fellow anarchist Hippolyte Havel and based on information provided by Goldman herself, described her childhood as a "beautiful idyl." Any conflict with her parents stemmed from the natural antagonism between generations in a changing world.[11] Goldman also described her parents positively to Harris in 1924. "At the age of six," she remembered fondly, "my father carried me, comfortably seated astride his shoulders, to an election meeting." Her mother, she told Harris, was "a very beautiful woman, vivacious, and a born diplomat," often chosen to negotiate with the Russian soldiers for the release of a draftee.[12] In the autobiography, however, it is the stable boy Petrushka, not Abraham, who carries Emma on his shoulders. Petrushka is described as awakening her first erotic feelings, and Taube punishes her daughter for masturbating.[13]

Parental cruelty or love may have been in dispute, but Emma's birth order was not. She was the eldest child of Taube's second marriage, which also produced two living sons, Herman and Morris. Emma was thus doubly a "middle child," between her two step-sisters and the younger brothers. Her sisters were considerably older: Helene was born in 1860 and Lena in 1862. Helene became a much loved and admired older sister whom Emma tried hard to emulate. Emma also remembered and idealized a younger brother who had died as a child. The death of this boy, Abraham's first son, made Emma's two surviving brothers even more prized, as males traditionally are in Jewish culture. Goldman claimed—probably correctly—that her own birth was a disappointment to her father.

Emma thus lived her childhood lost in the family shuffle, in constant, anxious competition for parental attention with siblings who always won because they were older or because they were male. Her frequent temper tantrums and displays of disobedience were evidence of her lust for attention, but they provoked her already burdened parents to anger and blows.

Both Havel and Harris emphasize Goldman's Jewish background. And so did she, unintentionally. When Harris asked her in 1924 to describe the "formative influences" on her life, for example, Goldman mentioned two childhood incidents that explained why she became an anarchist. Significantly, both incidents revolved around her Jewishness. The first involved her father's defeat in a re-election for manager of the local stagecoach. "The town hall was thick and ill-smelling with smoke from bad tobacco," Goldman recalled. "The peasants were drunk. . . . It was a vile, brutal scene, the peasants gesticulating, screaming, and

5

swearing as only Russian peasants can. Presently the results of the votes were announced. My father was defeated. Hooting, yelling, and jeering followed him out of the hall. On the way out, I asked him why the other man had been chosen. 'Because we are Jews, dear child, and the other man gave more vodka.' I was puzzled. 'Jews'? and 'more vodka'?" The second anecdote was a testimony against "militarism in all its naked savagery." The drafting of the young peasants took place at her father's inn. "[T]he heartbroken mothers would tear their hair, beat their breasts, and fill the air with their plaints and lamentations." The brutality of one soldier so enraged sister Helene that she "threw herself on the officer and pounded his chest with her small fists. The affair came near landing our whole family in prison, and possibly causing a pogrom against the Jews."[14] As anarchist Havel noted, "Early she learned to know the beauty of the State: she saw her father harassed by the Christian *chinovniks* and doubly persecuted as petty official and hated Jew."[15]

Abraham Goldman was not successful in business. Having lost the money left to his wife by her first husband, he lost his bid for the stagecoach position because he did not ply the peasants with vodka. Later he had to borrow from Taube's family to invest in a St. Petersburg grocery store. Goldman acknowledged that "the failure of [Abraham's] life . . . had embittered him and made him ill-natured and hard towards his own." He was a Jewish patriarch, unable to control his own fate, who sought to control his family instead.[16] Nevertheless Emma's family, best described as *meshchane* or lower middle class, was better off than most Jews. Although neither wealthy nor financially secure, her father was never reduced to peddling or "living on thin air," like the Jewish *luft-mensch*. In Papilen, where the family had moved shortly after Emma's birth, he managed an inn as well as the stagecoach. The family's financial position may have been as much Taube's as Abraham's doing. She helped to run the inn, for example, which was no easy task when domestic chores, such as keeping a Kosher kitchen, were defined by Orthodox regulations. Managing a household on a tight budget was also burdensome. If she appeared uncaring to her middle daughter, it may well have been that Taube's responsibilities as financial manager, housekeeper, and mother of five did not allow her much time for any of her offspring.

Both Abraham and Taube were observant Jews, and Goldman claimed that she herself was devout until her adolescence. But her parents came from different religious backgrounds. Abraham's family was Orthodox, and Taube's Judaism reflected the Haskalah movement, which was influenced by the western European Enlightenment and especially German culture and thought. These *maskilim* (enlighteners), inspired by Moses Mendelssohn, hoped that a more secular and rational version of Judaism would ease Jewish assimilation into Russian culture. Encouraged by the early liberalism of Alexander II, the *maskilim* supported secular education and a benevolent monarchy. Taube admired German culture; her four brothers had converted to Christianity so that they could practice law.

Taube's ideas about Judaism may have been enlightened, but she did not question her husband's right to rule his family. It was Helene, not Taube, who stood up to Abraham when he beat Emma. When Abraham forbade Helene to marry her sweetheart, who was not Jewish, or when Abraham tried to arrange a marriage for Emma herself, Taube either could not or did not want to defy him.

Although they could not become scholars themselves, Jewish women, at least those of moderate means, were encouraged to get an education. The expectation was that they would marry but that often meant they also had to help support a scholarly husband and their children. Possibly at her mother's wish, therefore, Emma was sent to live with her maternal grandmother in Königsberg so that she could attend a private school there. Königsberg was the capital of East Prussia, near the German border, and a center of German culture. A lonely Emma missed the fields and hills of home and hated sharing the cramped quarters with her aunts and uncle. When her grandmother left Königsberg on business (she was a smuggler), her uncle pocketed the money for Emma's schooling and put her to work scrubbing floors and washing clothes. One day, in a rage, he pushed her down the stairs, causing Emma to sprain her ankle. Emma was rescued from the household by Abraham, his heart moved to see his daughter thin, pale, and unhappy.

Emma soon returned to school when her whole family moved to Königsberg. The autobiography again recounts cruelty and abuse: as, for example, in her description of the tyrannical instructor of religion who recognized her as the class mischief-maker and beat her for it. But far worse, she recalled, was the geography teacher who put his hands on the girls' breasts and terrified them into keeping silent. "I learned scarcely anything," she claimed.[17] In fact, however, she learned to dislike and reject Orthodox Judaism and to admire German literature and culture. Both Havel and Harris noted her self-proclaimed admiration of German culture; both, taking their cues from her, described her as a "German Gretchen."[18]

A lifelong love affair with the theater began for Emma when her favorite teacher, an admirer of Mendelssohn, took the young student to Verdi's romantic *Il Trovatore*. Years later she recalled the magic of the stage, the "fairyland more magnificent than any ever pictured in the stories I had read."[19] Goldman would later imitate the heroine, Leonora, who rescued her lover by selling her own body. She would fail in her role as a prostitute, but she would become an enormously successful actress on the political stage, where her talent for self-display and self-dramatization would be a professional asset.

As Abraham's economic situation worsened, he moved in 1880 to St. Petersburg. He apparently met the residency requirements and had been promised a job in a drygoods shop. Emma planned to stay in Königsberg to attend the *Gymnasium,* or high school, and perhaps to study medicine. She was denied admission, however, because her religion teacher refused her a letter of good character: "I was a terrible child and would grow into a worse woman," she was told, "[and] . . . I would surely end on the gallows as a public menace."[20] When Taube promised she could go to school there, Emma decided to accompany her mother to St. Petersburg. Although the drygoods shop closed before Abraham even got there, in 1881 his wife and children were smuggled across the border through deep snowdrifts and icy water to join him.

Cosmopolitan St. Petersburg was home to 20,000 Jews. A handful were wealthy, but most, like Abraham, lived close to poverty, working in small shops and in the clothing trade. Nevertheless the city that was built by Peter the Great at the beginning of the eighteenth century bore the cultural imprint of this reformer and westernizer. St. Petersburg had schools and universities, theater, opera, books, newspapers, and, most important for the adolescent Emma who sought to differentiate herself from her parents, revolutionaries.

Shortly before Emma arrived, Alexander II was assassinated. The assassins were members of the *Narodnaya Volya,* the People's Will, a Russian revolutionary group that had its roots in the first half of the century, and the best known of the first generation of Russian radicals—the so-called "fathers" of the 1840s—was Michael Bakunin. Bakunin was born into a noble family with liberal and radical leanings. Rejecting the military life that was traditional for the Russian aristocracy, the young Bakunin decided to study philosophy. He came to admire Western thought, especially the German romanticism of Hegel. But Bakunin soon tired of theorizing about change and became a practicing revolutionary. He was

8

imprisoned for complicity in the Prague and Dresden revolutions of 1848–49. After six years in the Peter and Paul Fortress, Bakunin was exiled in 1857 to Siberia. Four years later, he escaped to the United States where, on the eve of the Civil War, he became something of a celebrity. He then returned to Europe to continue his revolutionary adventures. In 1869 Bakunin joined the International Workingmen's Association (the First International), founded in 1864 by philosopher-revolutionary Karl Marx.

Bakunin and Marx agreed that private property should be replaced by public ownership of the means of production and distribution, but they disagreed over how to achieve this revolution and how to govern the resulting society. Marx argued that the proletariat should seize political control and that, at least initially, a strong state, a "dictatorship of the proletariat," would be necessary. Bakunin, fearing that any state would be a dictatorship, maintained that workers' collectives should govern. Marx believed that the revolution would come inevitably and gradually, led by the proletariat; Bakunin, that it would come immediately, spontaneously, and destructively, from peasants led by the intellectuals. "The urge to destroy," Bakunin argued, "is also a creative urge." In 1872 he was expelled from the International for advocating violence and terrorism as revolutionary strategies. His followers became known informally as "anarchists" although there was as yet no well-defined anarchist movement.

Russia's next generation of radicals, the "sons" of the 1860s, were inspired as much by Bakunin's actions as by his theories. These men and women thought of themselves as realists, not romantics, envisioning a new society based on reason. They called themselves nihilists because they rejected all existing values and customs. Nihilism, however, called for private gesture rather than political action, so in the 1870s, radicals developed another social and economic program called Populism. Like Bakunin, the Populists envisioned a peasant revolution. The young intellectuals, mostly students and former students, began the peaceful process of "going to the people," living in the country villages as teachers or doctors to prepare the peasants for the revolution. Their efforts failed. The peasants did not rebel and in fact turned some Populists over to the police. Widespread arrests and mass trials of the revolutionaries took place in 1877.

The radicals then turned to the alternative strategy of conspiracy and terrorism. In 1878 a young woman, Vera Zasulich, seriously wounded the military governor of St. Petersburg and escaped without punishment. A year later, the radicals split. One group, the Black Partition, endorsed gradual economic and political reform. The second, the People's Will, endorsed assassination, believing that the murder of one key official in a highly centralized government would destroy it. Members staged a series of abortive assassination attempts that killed several people, but not Tsar Alexander II.[21] In 1881, however, the terrorists succeeded. All involved were caught and hanged immediately, except one woman whose pregnancy gave her a brief respite from death.

Emma was 12 when she arrived in St. Petersburg. There Abraham's daughter would find a place for herself, at least in her imagination, among the revolutionaries. Her personal rebellion found reinforcement and direction in the political rebellion she saw around her.

Emma's German education had led her to expect the worst of the "barbarian" Russians, but she was enchanted by the color, the gaiety, and the vitality of St. Petersburg, and particularly by its revolutionary politics. "We arrived in the winter of 1881," she told Harris, "the historic year in Russian revolutionary life. Tsar Alexander had just fallen, and the blackest reaction followed. Every breath of life was suppressed, yet the passionate youthful desire for ideals could not be stifled. . . . My spirit caught the white flame of Russian idealism."[22] Havel also recalled the enthusiasm for "the heroic executors of the death sentence upon the tyrant. . . . The names of the Nihilist martyrs were on all lips, and thousands were enthusiastic to follow their example. The whole *intelligenzia* of Russia was filled with illegal spirit. . . . It was inevitable that the young dreamer [Emma] be drawn into the maelstrom. . . . Young enthusiasts were not then . . . a rare phenomenon in Russia."[23]

Most Jews, still hopeful about Alexander II's intentions, had remained loyal to him and were dismayed and fearful when he was assassinated. Yet a handful had joined the revolutionary movement during the 1870s, as they entered universities and came into contact with the Russian intelligentsia. Some may have found in radicalism a way of living out the messianic message of their Jewishness, the hope of freeing their people from the hated tsar. Most Jewish radicals, however, were assimilationists whose political activities identified them with Russia, not with Judaism. They believed that the problems of Jews would be solved when the problems of all the poor were solved. A few radical Jews even converted to Christianity, discovering that "going to the people" as Jews was futile since the peasants were anti-Semitic. The People's Will had again anticipated that the peasants would rise up and liberate themselves when

Alexander II was assassinated. The peasants did rise up, but they turned on the Jews, not on the tsars. Imperial officials looked the other way at the terrible pogroms of 1881. So did many Populists. As a result, many Jews became disenchanted with Russian radicalism.

But to Jews barely in their teens at the time, like Emma Goldman and her future companion Alexander Berkman, the glamor and excitement of Russian radicalism outweighed its anti-Semitism. In his *Prison Memoirs of an Anarchist*, Berkman recalled his own youthful enthusiasm: "I see myself back in the little Russian college town, amid the circle of Petersburg students . . . surrounded by the halo of that vague and wonderful something we called 'Nihilist.' . . . I sit among superior beings, reverently listening to the impassioned discussion of dimly understood high themes. . . . 'To the People! To the beautiful, simple People, so noble in spite of centuries of brutalizing suffering!' Like a clarion call the note rings in my ears, amidst the din of contending views and obscure phraseology."[24] Berkman had an uncle, Mark Natanson, who was a Populist leader and was executed for his political activities.

Emma, too, had a revolutionary in the family. Taube's younger brother Yegor had been imprisoned in the Peter and Paul Fortress for alleged complicity in an assassination attempt. Taube had begged successfully for his release with tears and bribes. The huge stone prison remained for Goldman a symbol of the consequences of political rebellion. Taube called the revolutionaries "cold-blooded murderers," but to Emma, chafing at parental restraint, they became heroic figures.[25]

Too young and too poor to attend a university, Emma was introduced by Helene to radical literature. Emma found particularly exciting N. G. Chernyshevsky's novel *What Is To Be Done: Tales about New People,* published in 1864. The author was in prison when he wrote the novel, a fact that may explain the colorlessness of its projected utopia: a small socialist cooperative owned and operated by young female textile workers. The novel's literary merits were minimal, but its critique of contemporary Russian manners and morals was scathing. *What Is To Be Done* inspired a whole generation of young Russian Jews, including Berkman and Abraham Cahan, later to become the Socialist editor of the New York *Jewish Daily Forward.* Emma admired the novel's liberated heroine, Vera Pavlovna. Vera successfully defied her materialistic parents' attempt to arrange a marriage for her by running off with an unsuitable young man, with whom she contracted an egalitarian and apparently chaste marriage. When she fell in love with his best friend, she rejected her first husband in favor of a second, although not without a struggle

of conscience. Vera decided to strike another blow for her own independence by becoming a doctor. Like Vera, Emma cherished dreams of medicine and financial independence; like Vera, she was susceptible to
romantic passions.

The People's Will provided glamorous and inspiring heroines as
well, women like Vera Zasulich who assaulted not only political tyranny
but also the conventions of Jewish womanhood. Sophia Perovskaya, who
died with her lover and coconspirator in the assassination of Alexander
II, became Emma's "ideal." Emma determined that she "would become
a Judith, and avenge the cruel wrongs of [her] race."[26]

Such heroic visions of self gave meaning and drama to Emma's adolescent life. They also worsened her problems with her parents, who
did not share her political enthusiasms or approve of her growing independence. Abraham's grocery shop did not do well enough for Emma to
continue her schooling, and both she and Helene had to go to work.
Emma first sewed shawls at home and then worked in a cousin's glove
factory, joining the growing Jewish proletariat. "There were six hundred
of us, of all ages, working on costly and beautiful gloves, day in, day out,
for very small pay. But we were allowed sufficient time for our noon meal
and twice a day for tea," she remembered.[27] She explained her paid em-
ployment to biographer Havel not as an economic necessity but as a
political gesture: she "resolved to achieve her independence. She saw
hundreds of men and women sacrificing brilliant careers to go *v narod*,
to the people. She followed their example. . . . She was now 17 years
of age and proud to earn her own living."[28]

Emma sought sexual independence as well. She often defied Abraham, for example, stealing out of the house to go to a dance and dragging
the reluctant Helene with her. Emma and the other girls flirted with the
young men who loitered outside the factory. When her father saw her
with a handsome young hotel clerk in the park, he beat her, "shouting
that he would not tolerate a loose daughter." Emma disobeyed him and
met her lover secretly. When the young man persuaded her to join him
in a hotel room, he plied her with wine and raped her. Emma afterwards felt "no shame—only a great shock at the discovery that the
contact between man and woman could be so brutal and so painful."[29]
She must also have thought bitterly that Abraham had been right after
all.

According to Jewish custom, Abraham attempted to arrange a marriage for his headstrong daughter. He was dissuaded, as she told the story,
only by her furious temper tantrum. The escalating conflict between or-

thodox patriarch and rebellious daughter was resolved only by her emigration to the United States. Lena had already left Russia and settled in Rochester, New York. When Helene decided to follow, Emma determined to go also. Again Abraham forbade her, and again Emma defied him, threatening to throw herself into the Neva River. Emma won, and in December 1885 she left Russia for "the promised land" with 25 rubles in her pocket.

As many Jews had feared, Alexander III was far worse than his predecessors. The new tsar's "counter-reforms," exemplified in the repressive "Temporary Regulations," were aimed initially at the People's Will, but they remained in force to stifle all political dissent from the press or the universities. Alexander III placed greater pressures on followers of all non–Russian Orthodox religions, including Roman Catholicism and Lutheranism. Again the chief targets were Jews. The tsar encouraged pogroms and reenacted harshly anti-Semitic laws, including quotas for Jewish students in the universities. Residence restrictions were tightened and enforced by police searches.

Russian Jews responded to this new wave of cruelty in a number of ways. Some joined a Lovers of Zion movement, which sent settlers to Palestine. Far more emigrated to the United States. Among those thousands were the Goldmans. No longer able to pay the bribes necessary to conduct his business, Abraham, with Taube and their two sons, followed the Goldman daughters to Rochester in 1886.

A family photograph taken in St. Petersburg in 1882 shows the Goldmans in a stiff and conventional pose, which nevertheless reveals a great deal about the family dynamics. Emma stands directly behind Helene, who is seated and holding the baby Morris. Emma's features are pretty but somewhat blurred, perhaps by her youth or perhaps by the photographer. Nevertheless, she stares unabashedly but soberly at the camera. Taube, Herman, and Abraham form a separate group. (Lena had already gone to the United States.) Abraham is seated, aloof, dignified, and as far from Emma as the camera will permit.

Emma eventually made her peace with her family. Taube came into her own after the family's emigration to Rochester, where she became prominent in Jewish relief work and philanthropy. Emma was proud of her mother's success, and Taube grew to admire her daughter in later years. Emma remained devoted to her sisters and to her nieces and nephews, particularly Lena's daughter, Stella Cominsky Ballantine. Her baby brother, Morris, became a successful doctor and sent Goldman much-needed money in her last years. She eventually sympathized even with her father, who became a fairly successful furniture store owner, but who never adjusted to the New World as his wife did.

Although she was finally comfortable with her family, Goldman was never quite at home with her Jewishness. The Judaism of tsarist Russia was confining and narrow at the same time that it made one vulnerable and invited persecution. Emma the adolescent raged at her father's injunction that Jewish girls needed to know only how to cook gefilte fish and chop noodles, even though as an adult she boasted about her cooking. She was sometimes urged, Goldman wrote, "that as a Jewish daughter I should devote myself to the cause of the Jews." She would respond "that at the age of eight I used to dream of becoming a Judith and visioned myself in the act of cutting off Holofernes' head to avenge the wrongs of my people. But since I had become aware that social injustice is not confined to my own race, I had decided that there were too many heads for one Judith to cut off."[30] Loyalty to Jews ran counter to the internationalism of her adult anarchism.

Dreams of Russian revolution, on the other hand, were liberating and exciting, transcended Jewishness and parents and conferred power and purpose. In St. Petersburg Emma was not yet an anarchist, but her later politics always bore the stamp of her youth in Russia. The political repression in Russia, especially of Jews, fostered her hatred of political rulers; the buying and selling of drunken votes in a tavern and the pogrom-crazed peasants fostered her sense of elitism.

When Goldman chose a career as an anarchist propagandist—front and center on the lecture platform—she had all eyes on her and was compensated at last for the neglect she had felt as a child. Moreover Goldman remained stagestruck all her life, often drawn more to dashing figures and dramatic poses than to political and economic arguments or principles. Although she never aspired to be a professional actress, she always wanted to be a dramatic presence on and off the lecture platform. She even received—and refused—two offers to perform on the vaudeville stage. Goldman loved to don disguises and assume false names. Sometimes she was truly undercover, hiding from police; sometimes the false identity simply dramatized her actions. When she later argued that art and politics both served the anarchist revolution, Goldman successfully combined her vocation as propagandist with her avocation as actress.[31]

But whether or not she acknowledged it, Goldman always owed something to her Jewish roots. Her first political comrades when she migrated to the United States were the Jews on New York's Lower East Side.

14

The Goldman family in St. Petersburg, 1882. Emma standing at far left; Taube, Herman, and Abraham; Helene seated with Morris.

Abraham Goldman. *Special Collections Library, the University of Michigan Library.*

Taube Goldman. *Special Collections Library, the University of Michigan Library.*

Emma Goldman, 1886. *Special Collections Library, the University of Michigan Library.*

2

A STRANGER IN THE LAND: THE IMMIGRANT LEFT, 1886–1901

On 4 May 1886, four months after Emma arrived in the United States, a bomb killed seven policemen in Chicago's Haymarket Square. Eight men were convicted of murder. All were anarchists, and all but one were immigrants. To Main Street America, the Haymarket bombing raised the terrifying specter of class warfare, ignited by unwanted "strangers in the land" like Emma.[1] For Emma and her community of immigrant radicals on New York's Lower East Side, however, Haymarket provided shared martyrs and a common link to their European past.

The Haymarket bombing that inspired Emma's politics also inspired Edward Bellamy's novel *Looking Backward,* published in 1887. This popular and influential book expressed the nation's profound ambivalence toward immigrants and radicals. Its hero, Julian West, waking from a hypnotic trance in the year 2000, recalls the public's fear "of a small band of men who called themselves anarchists and proposed to terrify the American people into adopting their ideas by threats of violence."[2] Yet Bellamy was no conservative; his novel was a powerful critique of the Gilded Age: the waste and inefficiency of free enterprise capitalism, the growth of giant monopolies and great fortunes, the exploitation of industrial workers, the ugliness of American cities, and the corruption of values. In the utopian twenty-first century of the novel, the state owned essential property and provided equally for the needs of all its citizens. Bellamy believed that a moral transformation would accompany these material changes; without greed and competition, innate human goodness would flower.

Bellamy's utopia derived not from Marx but from American communistic experiments of the antebellum period. Although his novel is often credited with making socialism respectable and palatable to Americans, Bellamy called his system "nationalism" because socialism sounded foreign. Nationalism would bring a humane and orderly society, he believed, but the price of order was uniformity. All Americans in the twenty-first century looked, talked, and dressed the same way; there was no room for ethnic, religious, class, or political diversity—no room, in short, for immigrants.

Americans were justifiably proud of their nation's ability to welcome the "poor, the tired, the huddled masses" of the Old World. Employers needed the newcomers to work in the multiplying mills and factories that were rapidly making the United States a great industrial power. Immigrants also bought the goods which poured out of those mills and factories.

At the same time, however, the disorder and chaos of society were made worse—or more visible—by the hundreds of thousands of immigrants who arrived in the last decades of the century. They settled in urban areas, where economic opportunities were greatest, and the foreign-born population of major cities grew rapidly, coinciding with and perhaps hastening the end of the "walking city" and the beginning of specialized uses of urban space. New arrivals lived together in the poorest city neighborhoods, while native-born Americans began their first significant exodus to the city outskirts. As Bellamy's hero Julian West explains, "each class or nation lived by itself, in quarters of its own. A rich man living among the poor, an educated man among the uneducated, was like one living in isolation among a jealous and alien race."[3] Many Americans, consequently, blamed immigrants for the problems accompanying the rapid and unplanned urban growth: crime, prostitution, drunkenness, and disorder in city streets; appalling poverty in slums and tenements; rising relief rolls; and corruption at the polling place and in public office.

They also blamed immigrants for worker unrest, which surfaced in the great waves of strikes that Julian West saw as the worst problem of his own time. In response to huge, powerful, and impersonal corporations, workers formed unions to offset their individual powerlessness.

16

The first important national labor organization was the Knights of Labor, formed in 1869 by skilled and unskilled workers. More successful was the American Federation of Labor, which included only craft unions of skilled workers. With or without union leadership, though, workers struck frequently and violently. In 1877 railroad workers struck over wage cuts, sparking riots from San Francisco to Baltimore. State militia and federal troops fired at strikers, and strikers fired back. Millions of dollars worth of property and dozens of lives were lost. The conflict was particularly frightening because it came only a dozen years after the end of the bloody Civil War.

Public opinion generally sided with employers and government, not the strikers. Workers' collective action, whether in strikes or unions seemed "foreign," like socialism—inimical to the tradition of American individualism and threatening to the status quo. The Knights opposed strikes in principle although in practice they sometimes became involved, especially as the numbers of strikes and participants rose through the 1880s. In 1886 more than 600,000 workers took part in at least 1,500 strikes. Labor protests culminated on 1 May 1886, when workers nationwide demanded an eight-hour day. The rally at Chicago's Haymarket Square was called to protest the killing by police of two strikers on 3 May at the McCormick Reaper Works. The bombing at the Haymarket rally offered business and government a pretext for a wave of labor repression in Chicago and elsewhere, and helped identify the labor movement with radical foreigners and anarchists with murderous bombthrowers.

Anxieties about alien radicalism were compounded by Anglo-Saxon ethnocentrism, then approaching its zenith. The great wave of immigration that began in the 1880s came from southeastern Europe—Italy, Hungary, the Russian empire, and what would become Czechoslovakia and Yugoslavia. Immigrants were often Catholic or Jewish. Their language, culture, religion, and appearance made them distinctive, feared, and often despised. Native-born Americans, persuaded of their own racial superiority, tried to "Americanize" the newcomers through the public schools, settlement houses, and churches and, at the same time, to segregate them in urban ghettos just as blacks were segregated in separate and unequal institutions and American Indians were placed on reservations.

Such was the "promised land" in January 1886 when Emma and Helene arrived at Castle Garden—a land in which Emma was at first no more at home than she had been in imperial Russia. The sisters made the trip in steerage, crowded below deck like cattle. As their ship came into the New York harbor, the new Statue of Liberty emerged out of the mist, a "symbol of hope, of freedom, of opportunity. . . . We too, Helene and I, would find a place in the generous heart of America," Emma believed.[4]

The two sisters disembarked amid the pushing, shoving crowd of strange faces and hostile officials. Like other immigrants, they sought shelter with a family member who had come before them: sister Lena, who was living in the Jewish section of Rochester. Although there were wealthy German Jews in the city, Lena's husband, Samuel Cominsky, was struggling to make a living as a tinsmith and a roofer. Lena had been in the United States for five years and had worked first as a domestic servant and then in a clothing factory until her marriage. Even with a husband and her own home, however, she had been lonely for her family, especially because she was pregnant with her first child. Lena welcomed the two newcomers. So did the other Russian Jews, refugees from the 1881 pogroms, who crowded into Lena's apartment to hear news from their homeland.

Whatever hopes Emma had about continuing her education were again sacrificed to family financial needs. Emma and Helene realized immediately that they must share the family expenses. Both found jobs typical for immigrant women: Helene retouching photograph negatives, and Emma working again in a textile factory. Her employer, Leopold Garson, was a German Jew and a noted philanthropist, but he was less generous to his employees. Emma worked ten and a half hours a day for two dollars and fifty cents a week. The workroom was spacious and well lighted, but she chafed at the iron discipline, the endless monotony, and the low wages. When Lena's baby was born, Emma felt she must contribute more than her one dollar and fifty cents a week to the family coffers. But when she boldly asked her employer for a raise, Garson, in the paternal manner that German Jews often took toward Russian Jews, accused her of having extravagant tastes. Emma quit. (Eighteen years later Goldman would have her revenge when she turned down his plea that she end a strike at his factory.) She quickly found another job at four dollars a week in a smaller shop, but it, too, was hard and exploitative work.

By this time Abraham, Taube, and Emma's two younger brothers, Herman and Morris, had also arrived in Rochester. The whole family moved into the small apartment that Emma and Helene had prepared.

The family's financial problems continued. Abraham, then in his early forties, found a poorly paying job in a shop where he was the only Jew and the target of anti-Semitic remarks.

As did many immigrant families who were trying to make ends meet, the Goldmans took in a boarder, Jacob Kersner. Emma had met Kersner at her shop and at first had found him attractive. He was Russian and better educated than she. Despite his intellectual pretensions, however, he could find work in the United States only as a tailor. Emma was vivacious and pretty, 17 years old, and anxious to have some fun. Kersner asked her to her first dance in America, and "he was the only human being I had met since my arrival."[5] To a young woman trapped and stifled on the job and at home, Kersner was certainly better than no beau at all and perhaps better than living in the cramped apartment with her parents and siblings. Emma and Kersner were married by a rabbi in February 1887.

On her wedding night Emma discovered that her husband was impotent. Her version of her husband's sexual inadequacy appears in the earliest pages of her autobiography and establishes, consciously or not, an often-repeated pattern of close connections between sexual and political passions. In this instance, for example, the autobiography suggests that the sexual drive that might have found expression in her marriage was diverted into politics. At Emma's urging Kersner consulted a doctor, but to no avail. Emma had stopped work when she married, so the couple was strapped for money, and Kersner began to gamble away what little they had playing cards. "Life became insupportable," she recalled. "I was saved from utter despair by my interest in the Haymarket events."[6]

Like Goldman's re-creation of her childhood, her intimate identification of politics and sexuality should be read with caution. She often found sexual partners within her radical circles—where else?—but in this interpretation of political activity as an outgrowth of sexual frustration, she characteristically underestimated the shaping influence of her own cultural past and present. As she herself often suggested, the Haymarket martyrs seemed familiar figures to this newcomer to American politics— they were "like our Russian heroes," political dissenters executed by a repressive government. Emma had been interested in anarchism for some time prior to her marriage. During their first months in Rochester, Emma and Helene had attended some meetings of a German Socialist Club. They were "uninteresting but an escape from the grey dullness of my Rochester existence," Goldman wrote later. One evening, however, she became enthralled by a speaker's "passionate indictment" of the Haymarket trials, which she had read about in the newspapers: What was this anarchism of which the accused men were guilty? She started to follow the trials more closely in *Freiheit,* a New York newspaper published by anarchist leader Johann Most. As she began to understand the American incident in European terms, her adolescent rebellion became a political mission: "A great ideal, a burning faith, a determination to dedicate myself to the memory of my martyred comrades, to make their cause my own, to make known to the world their beautiful lives and heroic deaths."[7] So Emma took her first steps toward anarchism.

"After the death of the Chicago anarchists I insisted on a separation" and then a divorce, she wrote.[8] She then fled from Kersner, her family, and Rochester. In New Haven, Connecticut, she found work in a corset factory and met a group of Russian students, including some socialists and anarchists. But the financial and physical strains apparently were too great. Emma returned to Rochester, hoping to board with Helene and her husband Jacob Hochstein, a scholar with little taste for making money at his printing trade. Helene had one child and was pregnant with her second. Nevertheless, she made room for her younger sister.

Emma went back to the factory, and her life, still confined to the Russian Jewish ghetto, made it inevitable that she meet Kersner again. He threatened suicide if she did not remarry him. In what must have been one of the lowest moments of her young life, Emma gave in. This time the marriage lasted only long enough for her to take a course in dressmaking so that she could earn her own living. After three months she left Kersner again.

Twice divorced at 20, Emma was ostracized by the Jewish community. She had one last bitter, violent quarrel with her father. As she scrubbed the floor of her mother's apartment, Abraham accused her of being a "loose character" and "a disgrace to the family." Pounding the scrub brush on the floor for emphasis, Emma in turn accused him of years of brutality and neglect. If she had not become a harlot, she shouted, it was not Abraham's fault.[9] This time she left Rochester for good.

In August 1889 Goldman arrived on New York's Lower East Side. There she would make her home until 1919, when she would be deported. This crowded, bustling neighborhood was also home to a vigorous community of radicals. Recently transplanted in the New World, they borrowed their intellectual and political leadership, their goals, strategies, and quarrels from the Old. Politics provided a familiar perspective, which gave order and meaning to their confusing and disorienting new life.

By the 1880s, the United States had a distinctively European left, which included both socialists and anarchists. Both groups dated back to the pre–Civil War period when German immigrants brought Marxist doctrine with them to the United States. By 1872 there were some 5,000 members in the American sections of the International Working Men's Association (later known as the First International). Despite ongoing debate over the strategy of political action through political parties versus direct action through union organizing, socialists formed a Working Men's party of the United States in 1876. A year later, after the federal and local governments had crushed the great railroad strikes, many workers became convinced that unions were not viable routes to power, and the Working Men's party became the Socialist Labor party (SLP). Building on some success at the polls and the prestige of the Social Democratic party of Germany, the SLP had an estimated 3,000 members in 1889. Its chief strongholds were eastern cities, especially New York, and its members were largely immigrants, most from Germany and a few from southeastern Europe.[10]

In the early 1880s, however, the division between Marxists and Bakunists in Europe played itself out within the SLP and led to the emergence of an anarchist movement in the United States. After Bakunin's expulsion from the First International in 1872, Marx had moved the organization's headquarters to New York to keep it safe from his rival's followers. There the First International remained until its demise four years later. But Bakunin's visit to the United States in 1861–62 had left its mark, and a number of American sections of the International had Bakuninist leanings, the best known of which was a section led by the notorious Victoria Woodhull and her sister Tennessee Claflin. Bakunin's work was translated into English by the American anarchist Benjamin Tucker, an admirer of Russian revolutionary thought, and published in German by Johann Most in 1884, and Bakunin continued to be influential in circles that considered Marx's reliance on political action too slow or too ineffectual.

Favorably impressed by the assassination of Alexander II, advocates of violence formed "social revolutionary" clubs within the SLP. This amorphous movement found a leader in Johann Most, who had arrived in New York in 1882. He had begun his political career as a socialist, a member of the First International, and an elected official in the German

Reichstag. When he abandoned political action for direct action, however, Most was expelled by the German Social Democratic party, and when his newspaper *Freiheit* praised the *attentat,* or propaganda by the deed that was the assassination of the Russian tsar, Most had been briefly imprisoned. Like other radicals, he had come to the United States seeking asylum and political freedom.

In 1883 a convention of assorted social revolutionaries met in Pittsburgh to create a national organization. Johann Most drafted the Pittsburgh Manifesto, which attacked the futility of political reform and endorsed the use of force to overthrow capitalism. The Manifesto became the basis for a new organization, modeled on Marx's First International and called the International Working People's Association (IWPA), a loose federation of anarchist propaganda groups. The IWPA expanded rapidly to an estimated 5,000 members by 1885. Its constituency, like that of the SLP, was mostly German and almost exclusively immigrant, and was strongest in Chicago and New York. There were a handful of English-speaking sections, including the one organized in Chicago by Albert Parsons (who would be one of the Haymarket martyrs). The IWPA was active in union organizing and, after initial reluctance, supported labor's fight for the eight-hour day. In several cities members of the IWPA armed themselves, ostensibly in self-defense against police and militiamen, who were often used to break strikes. Following Haymarket, Chicago police raided the *Arbeiter Zeitung,* the IWPA newspaper, and arrested its entire staff. After that the IWPA was finished as a national organization, although it did not officially die until World War I.[11]

On the Lower East Side in New York, radicals called themselves socialists *or* anarchists. The two political sects often quarreled bitterly, especially on the pages of their rival newspapers. Nevertheless they often worked for a common cause, as they organized unions and supported strikes, particularly among the garment workers. For both groups, the Haymarket executions symbolized economic and political injustice.

Anarchism attracted those men and women, especially among the Jewish immigrants, who were most radical and who, at the same time, retained the most tenacious intellectual and emotional ties to Europe. Author and editor Abraham Cahan, for example, fled Russia as an adolescent because of his association with the Populists. When he first arrived in New York, Cahan judged American socialism by European standards and found it tame stuff: "What kind of socialism could it be without conspiracy? What good was the fruit if it wasn't forbidden? The power of deeply rooted beliefs is greater than the power of logic and common sense. . . . If all is permissible and danger is absent, socialism becomes diluted and revolutionary heroism becomes impossible."[12] Cahan first called himself an anarchist, therefore, but he abandoned anarchism for the SLP after single-taxer Henry George, with labor and Socialist backing, made an almost successful run for the New York mayor's office in 1886, receiving more votes than mayoral candidate and future United States president Theodore Roosevelt. Cahan became convinced that in the United States political action was a more useful strategy than revolutionary heroism. Those who remained anarchists, of course, disagreed.

For Jewish anarchists, their rebellion was religious and cultural as well as political: they cast off the restraints of Orthodox Judaism just as they renounced government. The East Side anarchists held their annual ball on Yom Kippur, the most sacred Jewish holiday. Like the Nihilists and Populists, they thought of themselves as Russians, not Jews, and often spoke Russian rather than Yiddish.

This context affirmed Goldman's initial attraction to anarchism. She truly began "living her life" with her arrival in New York: "I was twenty years old. All that had happened in my life until that time was now left behind me, cast off like a worn-out garment."[13] Goldman did start a new life as a political activist, but there was actually much about the East Side that was familiar, especially its Russian Jews and their politics.

Leaving her sewing machine at the railroad station, Goldman trudged miles through the vast, confusing city, hoping to stay with an aunt. The woman had not been expecting Goldman, and seeing her dismay, Goldman changed her plans and sought out an acquaintance from New Haven, A. Solotaroff, a Jewish anarchist. Solotaroff welcomed her to his family's apartment, promising to find her a permanent place to live. He then took the new arrival to Sach's café on Suffolk Street, a meeting place for Jewish intellectuals and radicals.

It was there that Goldman met the most important man in her life, Alexander Berkman, or Sasha. She recalled hearing "a powerful voice call: 'Extra-large steak! Extra cup of coffee!'" and wondering who the glutton might be.[14] Berkman also remembered that first meeting: "The door opens, and a young woman enters. Well-knit, with the ruddy vigor of youth, she diffuses an atmosphere of strength and vitality." He arranged to meet Goldman, and "without constraint, we soon converse[d] like old acquaintances."[15] Berkman came from a more prosperous background than Goldman's. His father had been a successful wholesaler, and the family had lived in style in St. Petersburg until the father's death forced them to move to Kovno. But Goldman and Berkman had much in common: both had come from Lithuania, both admired the Nihilists, both had read Chernyshevsky, both admired Most. Both, in short, regarded themselves as anarchists, drawn to the movement because the dramatic martyrdom of the Haymarket radicals reminded them of adolescent Nihilist heroes and because anarchist doctrines resonated with their own need for personal freedom.

Berkman, who had been in New York for two years, took Goldman under his wing. "With great pride I introduce my new friend to the *intelligentzia* of the Ghetto, among the exiles of the colony. . . . The whole history of revolutionary Russia is mirrored in our circles; every shade of temperamental Nihilism and political view is harbored there."[16] Their first pilgrimage together was to hear Most, the preacher of revolutionary violence whose fiery editorials Goldman had begun to read.

The anarchist leader was immediately taken by Goldman's blue eyes and blond hair, by her obvious admiration for him, and by her potential as a public speaker. Most became Goldman's first formal instructor in anarchism. He discussed with her the great European radical thinkers and the conflict between Marx and Bakunin, and he lent her anarchist books and pamphlets.

Under Most's tutelage, Goldman launched her lifelong career as an anarchist propagandist and a star on the political stage. She knew little of anarchist theory and nothing of public speaking. Most's positions on many issues, including his distaste for the working class and his preference for an elitist revolutionary vanguard, were in sympathy with Goldman's own adolescent Nihilism. She easily and instinctively imitated his blunt, sarcastic platform style. Goldman did not yet speak English well, but she did speak German, the language of her immigrant audiences, and within six months Most arranged a speaking tour for her in Rochester, Buffalo, and Cleveland. He instructed her to speak against the eight-hour day, which was still a major goal of organized labor but, in Most's opinion, only a distraction from the struggle for revolution. On this first tour, Goldman was challenged by an elderly worker in Cleveland, who pointed out that he would enjoy the eight-hour day in his lifetime but might not be around for the revolution-to-come. Goldman had her first doubts about her teacher, she recalled, although not about anarchism. More important, she learned that her dramatic and impassioned rhetoric could move crowds.

Despite her marriages, Goldman was a novice at romance, and her account of her first months in New York read like pages from Chernyshevsky. Most was a political celebrity, having been imprisoned in this country as well as in Europe, and he was the acknowledged leader of the anarchist movement to which Goldman wished very much to belong. His appearance was unprepossessing: he was of medium height with a full head of gray hair, and the left side of his face, partly covered by a beard, was twisted and disfigured by a childhood operation. The disfigurement, he said, had kept him from his dearest ambition, to be an actor—an ambition that Goldman probably shared, although she never articulated it. Most was, in short, a dashing, romantic, and tragic figure. Moreover, he had enough money to buy Goldman dinners with wine and to indulge her passion for the opera. Goldman could not resist him. "He was hungry for affection, for understanding," she later wrote. "I would give him both."[17]

She and Berkman, political comrades, had also become lovers. According to *Living My Life,* they first slept together after their passions, political and sexual, had been aroused by Most's speech on the Haymarket martyrs. The two set up a cooperative household with Berkman's good friend "Fedya" (the name Goldman used in *Living My Life* for Modest Stein). Goldman's passion for Berkman was partly physical: at 19 he was a handsome, if rather solemn, young man who wore the steel-rimmed spectacles of the Russian intellectual. Moreover, Berkman was completely dedicated to the anarchist revolution. "A true revolutionist," he wrote in his memoirs, is "a being who has neither personal interests nor desires above the necessities of the Cause . . . [a] revolutionist first, human afterwards."[18] Goldman admired his single-minded commitment, but it didn't make him easy to live with. The two quarreled over her extravagant expenditures on flowers and pretty clothes. Her tastes were much more like those of the artist Fedya. And indeed Emma and Fedya enjoyed a brief love affair while all three shared an apartment. Berkman, always the good anarchist, could not object.

Goldman, however, soon had to make a choice between Berkman and Most. Most, she said, wanted her to become a German housewife and mother. Recalling her own unhappy childhood, Goldman did not want to become a mother. She had earlier decided not to have an operation to correct what doctors described as an inverted womb. The operation would have alleviated painful menstrual cramps and allowed her to become pregnant. Now her work as a political agitator was an added argument against motherhood. "To fulfill [my] mission I must remain unhampered and untied. Years of pain and of suppressed longing for a child—what were they compared with the price many martyrs had already paid? I too would pay the price."[19] Goldman would always describe herself as having a frustrated passion for children, but she would never undergo the necessary operation to make biological motherhood possible. Unlike Most, Berkman was a "revolutionist first, human afterwards." He would not ask Goldman to give up her work for the revolution. Most ceased to be a suitor, and the end to their romance was hastened when Goldman became friendly with Most's bitter rival in the anarchist movement, Joseph Peukert.

Living My Life contains a vignette from this period that, even if spurious, illustrates Berkman's crucial role as her conscience and her model of the true revolutionary. Berkman's cousin, dismayed by the headlong abandon with which Goldman was dancing at a party, chided her for being undignified (she was 22, and the cousin even younger): "[Her] frivolity would only hurt the Cause," he told her. Furious, Goldman shouted at him to mind his own business. "I was tired of having the Cause constantly thrown into my face." Besides, the dance, for Goldman, was an expression of what anarchism meant for her: "'freedom, the right to self-expression, everybody's right to beautiful, radiant things.'" The real target of this tirade was Berkman himself, who stood nearby, his face averted, "his eyes full of reproach. . . . I danced no more that evening."[20] Goldman would spend much of her life trying to live up to Berkman's ideals.

Despite her frequent protests against being regarded as "simply a female," Goldman actually cooked and cleaned for the cooperative household, which now included Helen Minkin, another Jewish anarchist. Goldman was the best cook in the group, and she preferred sewing silk shirtwaists at home to working in a factory.

Goldman and her friends became immersed in the vital and exciting social life of the East Side ghetto, which in many ways replicated that of their homeland. Their comrades were other anarchists and socialists, usually Jewish and often Russian. They met in immigrant cafes like Sach's, where they read the poems of the Yiddish anarchist David Edelstadt and argued over the columns in Most's *Freiheit* or *Freie Arbeiter Shtime*, the oldest Yiddish newspaper in the United States. Berkman joined the Pioneers of Liberty, which had been organized in 1886 in the wake of Haymarket to raise funds for the Chicago anarchists' legal defense.

With Berkman, Goldman became active in the East Side labor movement, especially among the needle trades. Some labor activities were primarily symbolic. For example, with other anarchists, socialists, and Yiddish unions, Goldman and Berkman planned a commemoration of the Haymarket martyrdom and a celebration of an international May Day. Goldman also threw herself into a cloakmakers' strike led by anarchist-socialist Joseph Barondess in 1890. Enthusiastically she organized dances and meetings to persuade women workers to join the strike. This was her only organizing effort, however. Berkman remained committed to unions, but Goldman did not, either because her version of anarchism was too individualistic or because, like Most, she secretly regarded unions, even anarchist unions, as pale substitutes for the revolution.

Also in 1890, Goldman and Berkman, energized by a wave of political persecution in Russia, briefly discussed a return to rescue their homeland from tsarist oppression. "We belonged to Russia," they felt.[21] To raise the necessary travel funds, Goldman, Berkman, and Fedya embarked on a series of money-making ventures. A cooperative dressmaking operation in New Haven failed. So did their attempts to sell Fedya's crayon portraits as the three traveled in a horse and buggy like Jewish peddlers through the countryside that surrounded Worcester, Massachusetts. Then, swallowing their aversion to capitalism, they invested their savings of $50 in an ice cream parlor, where Goldman's cooking skills brought them perilously close to economic success.

On the verge of making a profit in May 1892, however, they heard the news of the great strike at Homestead, outside of Pittsburgh. The strike was directed at the Carnegie Steel Company and led by a craft union, the Amalgamated Association of Iron and Steel Workers. The issue was union recognition, which plant president Henry Frick refused to grant. Frick locked the workers out and brought in strikebreakers, guarded by Pinkerton detectives. The drama of this conflict changed the two immigrants' plans to return to Russia. As Goldman recalled, "It was Homestead, not Russia; I knew it now. We belonged in Homestead."[22] Immediately abandoning the ice cream parlor, Goldman and Berkman decided to strike a blow for the revolution in Pittsburgh.

That blow, however, was conceived as though the young revolutionaries were still in tsarist Russia and the year was 1881. Goldman and

Berkman first composed a manifesto urging the workers to "throw off the yoke of capitalism . . . and to continue toward social revolution and anarchism."[23] But the manifesto was in German, which most of the union members probably could not read. As the conflict at Homestead escalated and shots were exchanged between the strikers and strikebreakers, Goldman and Berkman escalated their tactics as well. The drama of an *attentat*, a propaganda by deed, they decided, "would call the attention of the whole world to the real cause behind the Homestead struggle [and] would also strike terror in the enemy's ranks and make them realize that the proletariat of America had its avengers."[24] The target was to be Frick, not the owner of the company, Andrew Carnegie. Carnegie, the personification of American Gilded Age capitalism, would have been more appropriate, but he was inconveniently out of the country. Using Most's *Science of Revolutionary Warfare* as a textbook, the conspirators attempted to construct a dynamite bomb. When the bomb did not go off, they decided to use a gun. There was only enough money for Berkman's train fare to Pittsburgh, and it fell to Goldman to somehow raise the money for the weapon. Characteristically she assumed a dramatic pose borrowed from her cultural past. Like the heroine in Dostoyevski's *Crime and Punishment*, or perhaps Leonora from *Il Trovatore*, Goldman decided to impersonate a streetwalker. Disguised in borrowed lingerie, a corset, and ill-fitting high-heeled shoes, she tried to sell her body. She was rescued from the street by a gentleman who gave her ten dollars but did not demand her services. Goldman had to borrow the money for the gun from her sister Helene.

Thus armed, Berkman went to Pittsburgh and forced his way into Frick's office. Firing three shots, he wounded but did not kill the plant president. As Berkman tried to stab Frick with a knife, carpenters working nearby wrestled the assailant to the floor. Taken immediately to jail, Berkman attempted to kill himself by swallowing nitroglycerin, as Haymarket martyr Albert Lingg had done, but he was foiled by prison guards.[25] The *attentat* did not inspire the American workers to rise up and overthrow their oppressor. As Berkman soon learned in the Western Penitentiary, they were mystified by his behavior and his political ideas. The strike was lost.

Through her association with Berkman, Goldman instantly became notorious, harassed by the New York press and police. Evicted from a friend's home, she stayed first with her paternal grandmother and then in a brothel, where she found the prostitutes to be friendly patrons of her dressmaking skills.

Berkman's *attentat* divided the East Side left. Some anarchists and unions rallied to Berkman's support as he awaited trial. Just out of jail himself, however, Most ridiculed Berkman publicly, suggesting that he had not used a real pistol. The incident led to Goldman's final break with her first mentor. Hounded by the police and by her own remorse, Goldman demanded that Most retract his statement about Berkman. When he did not, she leapt onto the stage where he was speaking and dramatically horsewhipped him.

Berkman, kept in ignorance of the date of his trial until the last moment, refused a lawyer and attempted to defend himself in German before an English-speaking jury. On 19 September 1892, he was found guilty on six counts stemming from his single act and was sentenced to 22 years in the Western Penitentiary. The sentence was later commuted to 14 years.

The *attentat*, designed and executed while Goldman and Berkman were barely out of adolescence, unalterably changed their relationship and their lives. His memoirs suggest that he no longer thought of her as a lover. She became instead his tie to life outside the prison: "I clutch desperately at the thread that still binds me to the living—it seems to unravel in my hands. . . . But the Sonya thread [Goldman was referred to as Sonya, the Sailor, and Sister] I know, will remain taut and strong. I have always called you the Immutable." And he paid her the ultimate compliment: "She is the real Russian woman revolutionist."[26] He held similar importance for Goldman: "he brought home to me the realization that there was something greater than personal ties or even love: an all-embracing devotion that understands all and gives all to the last breath."[27] For both, the Homestead affair also represented personal failure: Berkman had failed to kill Frick, and Goldman had failed to go with him. Moreover, Berkman alone paid the price for the act that they had planned together. Goldman did not even admit her complicity until the publication of her autobiography in 1931. Both spent much of the rest of their lives trying to compensate for this personal and public disaster. Both would be suspects in most incidents of political violence in the United States until their deportation.

In addition, as Most had immediately realized, the act of these two individuals had a destructive impact on the immigrant left. Like the Haymarket bombing, Berkman's propaganda by deed persuaded many Americans that all political radicals were terrorists. The left would pay a heavy price for at least the next decade for Goldman and Berkman's misconceived adventure.

In October 1893, slightly more than a year after Berkman's imprisonment began, Goldman too went to jail, charged with inciting to riot. In a speech at Union Square to a throng of the unemployed she urged them to take the bread that was theirs. Although the message was no more inflammatory than others from the platform, Goldman, at 24, was already the best known speaker, thanks in part to her connection with Berkman. With him in mind, she rejected the temptation to appeal her case: "I must go the way many had gone before me. I would get a year or two; what was that compared with Berkman's fate. I would go the way."[28]

Unlike Berkman, however, Goldman was defended by a prominent attorney and former mayor of New York, A. Oakley Hall, who was perhaps attracted to the case by her notoriety. She was already something of a media personality, and the *New York World* offered to publish her courtroom statement. Also unlike Berkman, who did 3 years in solitary confinement for various acts of insubordination and 14 years in all, Goldman did 1 year of easy time in the city jail, Blackwell's Island. Put in charge of the prison sewing shop, Goldman won the friendship of the other inmates when she refused to enforce a speed-up order from prison officials. She received frequent visitors, including her grandmother, who arrived with Kosher food for the Jewish holidays, and she used her leisure time to read English and American literature. Most important, the prison doctor befriended Goldman and placed her in charge of the hospital ward, thus starting her career in medicine. Looking back at her year in Blackwell's Island, Goldman thought it had matured her and taught her to "see life through my own eyes and not through those of Berkman [or] Most."[29] She emerged from jail with her celebrity status enhanced, and promptly sold the *World* an exposé on prison conditions.

Berkman remained the moral but not the romantic center of Goldman's life. Her next lover was Ed Brady, whom she met in 1893: "tall and broad, well built, with soft blond hair and blue eyes," and politically acceptable. Brady was an Austrian immigrant who had spent ten years in prison himself for distributing anarchist literature. There he had taught himself English and French. He was older and far better educated than Goldman, and like Most, he became her teacher and mentor, introducing her to the classics of English and French literature. Brady was patient enough to wait out the year Goldman spent in jail, visiting her often, and he was good-natured enough to allow Goldman's younger brother Morris to move in with them at one point. Yet like her other relationships with men, her relationship with Brady proved tempestuous. As Most had, Brady wanted Goldman to give up her career to marry him and bear his child. Once again Goldman chose her work over motherhood. They quarreled and reconciled several times. Their romance ended in 1897. He married someone else and became a father, but Brady and Goldman continued to be good friends until his death in 1903.

Goldman spent the eight years after her release from Blackwell's Island trying to combine medicine, her early career choice, with her new work as an anarchist propagandist. Both occupations reinforced her intellectual and political ties to Europe. After her release from Blackwell's Island, Goldman quickly got work as a practical nurse, but because nursing was becoming professionalized, she realized that she needed more training. In 1895, therefore, traveling as Mrs. E. G. Brady, Goldman headed for Vienna to study nursing and midwifery. En route, she stopped in London, where she spoke at Hyde Park and sparred with the hecklers, admired the lush green parks, and was appalled by the poverty of the slums. Because London was also a center for political exiles, she met there for the first time many prominent anarchists, including the Italian Enrico Malatesta and the heroine of the Paris Commune, Louise Michel.

Goldman also met Prince Peter Kropotkin, who became her much-loved teacher. Like Bakunin, Kropotkin came from the Russian nobility and after military service in Siberia, where his interests in science and political reform both were stimulated, he resigned to study geography. Initially attracted to socialism, Kropotkin found himself believing more strongly in anarchism and began to write anarchist literature. In 1874 he was imprisoned in the Peter and Paul Fortress, but he made a sensational escape two years later. After Bakunin's death in 1876, Kropotkin became the most prominent European anarchist thinker and publicist although he was not a practicing revolutionary, as Bakunin had been. His vision of a stateless society rested upon his scientific evidence that both animals and humans were naturally cooperative. In his version of the anarchist utopia, therefore, "mutual aid" replaced private property and competition—he was an anarchist communist—just as voluntary associations replaced the state. Kropotkin endorsed acts of revolutionary violence, as had Bakunin. To show his sympathy for Berkman, for example, Kropotkin had tried to visit him in prison in 1897. Kropotkin, however, emphasized the gradual creation of the new society, not the immediate destruction of the old. For most of his followers, the sweetness of Kropotkin's personality and the gentleness and egalitarianism of his philosophy outweighed his support of the *attentat*. When the aristocratic and scholarly Kropotkin visited the United States in 1897–98, he was already well known and admired by American liberals as well as European radicals. Although they sometimes disagreed, Goldman admired Kropotkin all her life.

Goldman probably chose to study at the hospital in Vienna because the lectures were in German, easier for her than English. There were no courses in midwifery in the United States, where obstetrics was becoming a male medical specialty. She shared her rooms in Vienna with some Russian Jewish girls and threw herself enthusiastically into the rich cultural life of the European capital. Goldman read Nietzsche and satisfied her passion for the theater by listening to Wagner's operas and watching Eleanora Duse perform. She also heard Freud lecture, and she later wrote, "For the first time I grasped the full significance of sex repression and its effect on human thought and action. He helped me to understand myself, my own needs." Certainly Freud's influence is all too apparent in *Living My Life*.[30]

Returning to the United States in November 1896, Goldman resumed her life with Ed Brady and started working as a nurse-midwife, a career that would support her intermittently over the next few years. Midwifery on the Lower East Side was exhausting, and it paid badly. American women still delivered their children at home but were attended by male doctors, so Goldman's only patients were poor immigrants. Often they had submitted helplessly to unwanted pregnancies that they attempted to abort by swallowing home remedies or jumping off tables. Goldman had been taught in Vienna that abortions were medically dangerous. They were also by this time illegal under most circumstances in the United States. She therefore refused to perform abortions, and at this point she knew of no way to prevent conception. Her experience as a ghetto midwife taught her the need for legal birth control, which would become one of her most famous crusades.

Goldman pursued her real vocation on the lecture platform. Still speaking most often in German, she made two cross-country tours in 1897–98 and in 1899, promoting anarchism and selling Brady's photograph albums. Her sponsors were primarily immigrant and labor organizations, groups who were also likely to provide funds for Berkman's continuing legal battles. She spoke to Italian anarchists in Barre, Vermont, and, "in true anarchist fashion," baptized with beer the babies of Belgian and Italian miners. Her forceful platform style and her notoriety attracted good audiences of nonanarchists as well as anarchists. Perhaps to offset the nickname "Red Emma," she dressed demurely in black— "almost like a nun," one of her admirers joked.[31] Her lecture repertoire included "The New Woman," "Free Love," and, in response to the Spanish-American War, an attack on militarism entitled "Patriotism and War." While in Chicago, she visited Waldheim Cemetery and laid a wreath at the resting place of the Haymarket martyrs who had been her political inspiration.[32]

In 1899, two wealthy Germans, Herman Miller and Carl Schmidt (referred to as Carl Stone in *Living My Life*), offered to sponsor Goldman's further study of medicine in Switzerland. Although anxious about Berkman's pending scheme to escape from the penitentiary, she seized the opportunity. In London, she immediately plunged again into political activities, visiting with Kropotkin and other prominent Russian anarchists. Goldman herself had become a well-known figure in international anarchist circles, and she lectured to Jewish and German anarchists as well as to lively crowds of English and Scottish workingmen.

Goldman had made a final break with Brady and fell in love again, this time with Czech anarchist Hippolyte Havel, who would later become her biographer. He, too, had been imprisoned, and after wandering through most of western Europe, he had arrived penniless in London. Together they went to Paris to organize an international anarchist convention, where Goldman quickly expanded her circle of political acquaintances. Police surveillance in Paris forced the anarchists to meet secretly. Goldman also attended a Neo-Malthusian conference, where she received literature on birth control and contraceptives to take back to the United States.

Goldman's American backers, in the meantime, had second thoughts about funding her "old propaganda and . . . a new lover." Schmidt wrote: "'I am interested only in E.G. the woman—her ideas have no meaning whatever to me. Please choose.'" With characteristic bravado, Goldman fired back: "'E.G. the woman and her ideas are inseparable. . . . Keep your money.'"[33]

Goldman's idyll with Havel was cut short by the news that Berkman's plan to tunnel his way out of the Western Penitentiary had failed. The message was followed by the arrival of a conspirator in the escape attempt, Eric B. Morton. Their funds exhausted, all three returned to the United States in December 1900.

After another brief stint at nursing, Goldman again hit the lecture trail, probably informing her audiences of the latest events in European anarchism. On 5 May 1901, she spoke in Cleveland. At one of her talks she saw for the first time Leon Czolgosz. She was struck, she remembered, by his handsome, sensitive face. Czolgosz was an unemployed steel worker who apparently became interested in anarchism after taking part in an unsuccessful strike. Because they thought he was moody and possibly unbalanced, local anarchist groups did not trust him, although they did not turn him away either.[34] Czolgosz arranged to meet Goldman again some weeks later in Chicago, introducing himself as "Nieman." Chicago anarchists also distrusted "Nieman," and A. Isaak, editor of *Free Society*, warned in the columns of his newspaper that Nieman might be an agent provocateur.

The distrust was well placed. On 6 September 1901, at the Pan American Exposition in Buffalo, New York, Czolgosz shot President William McKinley. The president died eight days later.

Goldman may already have begun to have second thoughts about the European tactic of *attentat* in the American context. A month before Czolgosz shot McKinley, she had visited Berkman in the penitentiary. He had spent nine years in prison and had just finished a year in solitary confinement. She had seen him only once before, at the beginning of his sentence, but they had remained in almost constant touch through letters. Now she found him much changed: thin, gray, and mute after months without human contact. The personal price of the *attentat* was high indeed. Furthermore, it had accomplished nothing except to make anarchists more hated and to divide the movement's ranks. Yet she could not renounce the use of violence without renouncing Berkman as well, a dilemma she would not resolve for two more decades.

On tour in St. Louis, Goldman learned of the shooting and Czolgosz's arrest. The headlines screamed: "ASSASSIN OF PRESIDENT MCKINLEY AN ANARCHIST. CONFESSES TO HAVING BEEN INCITED BY EMMA GOLDMAN." The Cleveland *Plain Dealer* did even better: "'Emma Goldman Set Me On Fire,' Young Czolgosz Says. Her Lecture in This City First Started What He Calls 'The Craze to Kill,'" quoting Czolgosz's alleged statement to the Buffalo police.[35] Goldman was immediately the subject of a nation-wide manhunt. She decided to surrender to authorities in Chicago, where a dozen anarchists, including Havel and Isaak, were already being held without bail until she was located. Before she could give herself up, however, police discovered her at a friend's apartment, where she had disguised herself as the maid, and hurried her off to jail.

Whipped into a frenzy by the assassination, much of the American public screamed for vengeance. In the Chicago jail, Goldman cast herself in the role of the Haymarket martyrs she had revered as a new immigrant: "It was a repetition of the dark Chicago days. Fourteen years, years of painful growth. And now the end! The end? I was only thirty-two and there was yet so much, so very much, undone."[36]

An unwelcome immigrant in Edward Bellamy's nativist United States, Goldman nevertheless had found her place within the immigrant left. Her attacks on the state, on religion, on conventional morality were derived from her European teachers and mentors: Bakunin, Kropotkin, Nietzsche, Freud, Most, Brady, and Berkman. Anarchism was an international movement, and even in these early years, she was an international figure. Her most significant excursion into American politics—at Homestead—had failed.

Goldman would never lose touch with her immigrant past, any more than she would with her Jewish roots, but she had also begun to meet some native-born American radicals, including former abolitionist and journalist John Swinton and his wife, anarchist Voltairine de Cleyre, and Moses Harman, champion of women's emancipation from marriage and motherhood. Goldman had also begun to give halting lectures in English. In the next decade, responding to the shifting political climate, Goldman developed ties to an emerging American left.

3

EXILE AMONG THE IMMIGRANTS: RADICALIZING AMERICANS, 1901–1912

Leon Czolgosz's murder of President McKinley made the immigrant left the target of local and federal government persecution. When other anarchists—even Berkman—repudiated Czolgosz, Goldman, who sympathized with him, became estranged from her former comrades. As an indigenous American left developed, however, Goldman found a role for herself and redefined her anarchism within it.

Anxious to make the parallels between Haymarket in 1886 and McKinley's assassination in 1901, Goldman may untypically have understated the hysteria that followed Czolgosz's act. Killing Chicago policemen was a serious crime, but killing a president was far worse. McKinley had been a popular leader; he was credited with ending the hard times of the 1890s and had just begun a second term, which he had won easily. This second presidential assassination in 20 years, and the third since Abraham Lincoln's in 1865, shocked and frightened the American public. The two earlier assassinations could be understood as the acts of demented men with personal grievances, but McKinley's apparently was a political act with far wider implications—especially because this was the act of a professed anarchist. Anarchists had assassinated President Sadi Carnot of France, Prime Minister Cánovas del Castillo of Spain, Empress Elizabeth of Austria, and King Humbert of

Italy. Closer to home, Americans remembered not only the anarchists at Haymarket but also Alexander Berkman at Homestead.

Although Czolgosz always claimed that he had acted alone, the public, encouraged by local and federal officials, believed that he had been part of an anarchist conspiracy. All across the country, law officials and citizens sought revenge. Vigilantes attacked anarchists in Guffey Hollow, Pennsylvania, and threatened the newspaper office of the Italian anarchist publication *L'Aurora* in Spring Valley, Illinois. Even on New York's Lower East Side, neighbors assaulted the longtime anarchist editor of the *Freie Arbeiter Shtime,* Saul Yanovsky. Voltairine de Cleyre described the frenzy in Philadelphia: "The whole general atmosphere is so surcharged with brutality . . . that one feels oneself in a den of wild beasts."[1]

Local police broke up anarchist gatherings, raided clubrooms and offices, and made arrests. The Cleveland *Plain Dealer* reported that a crowd of delegates from the Grand Army of the Republic cheered as the venerable Civil War General O. O. Howard announced: "Anarchists Should Be Driven From [the] Country."[2] Meetings of the Liberty Club, where Czolgosz had first heard Goldman speak, were forbidden. Mayors of towns like Rochester, New York, and Paterson, New Jersey, which had small anarchist communities, prepared to take heroic measures against them. Johann Most, his repudiation of Berkman forgotten, was sentenced to a year on Blackwell's Island for reproducing a decades-old article on political violence. Berkman himself was briefly recommitted to solitary confinement in the Western Penitentiary.

New York, New Jersey, and Wisconsin passed laws against "criminal anarchism." Most ominous, federal officials also took dramatic action. Senator Joseph R. Hawley offered a thousand dollars for the opportunity to take a shot at an anarchist but turned down de Cleyre when she offered to be his target, free of charge. In a speech to Congress in December 1901, President Theodore Roosevelt, McKinley's successor, denounced all anarchists as accessories to McKinley's murder. Like other Americans, the members of Congress believed that most anarchists were foreigners. Because the American-born Czolgosz was an awkward exception, Congress discussed the desirability of banishing all anarchists, both aliens and citizens.

Goldman, the most visible and best known anarchist in the United States, was immediately suspected of complicity in the assassination. After police arrested and jailed her in Chicago on 10 September, they bullied and threatened her until she was taken under the protection of the chief of police. The chief—fortunately, and for reasons of his own—resisted the demands of Buffalo police that she be extradited. Goldman became very much of a celebrity in prison. "I began at once to lead the life of a society lady, receiving callers all day long, mostly newspaper people who came not so much for interviews as to talk, smoke, and relate funny stories." She turned down an offer of $20,000 from the Hearst newspapers for an exclusive interview.[3] Czolgosz admitted having heard Goldman speak yet, despite the headlines, never said that she had conspired with him. Police could not shake Czolgosz from his claim that he had acted alone, and when Buffalo officials could produce no concrete evidence linking her to the assassination, Goldman was released from jail. The Chicago chief of police—and her own fame—had saved Goldman this time.

The chief of police, however, could not protect her from the hate mail she received during her month in jail. "'You damn bitch of an anarchist . . . I wish I could get at you. I would tear your heart out and feed it to my dog,'" threatened one of her milder letters. "The description by some of the anonymous writers of what they would do to me sexually offered studies in perversion that would have astounded authorities on the subject," Goldman wrote.[4] So vicious was the public temper that de Cleyre, fearing for Goldman's life, came to her defense: "I have never liked Emma Goldman or her speeches; I don't like fishwifery or billingsgate; but I never heard her say, nor anyone of all I ever knew that heard her, that anyone could do any good by killing."[5] Goldman had offered to nurse McKinley in the week before his death, but this had not saved her from assault by a police officer while she was being transferred from the city to the county jail, or from attacks by the press. Her family in Rochester suffered as well. Her father was expelled from his synagogue, and her niece Stella Cominsky was detained by police and harassed by schoolmates. One of her nephews, a staunch Republican admirer of McKinley, was doubly wounded by the death of his hero and the alleged involvement of his aunt.

The Socialist left scrambled to distance itself from Czolgosz and from anarchists, realizing that Americans did not make fine distinctions between radicals, as is revealed in this headline from the Cleveland *Plain Dealer*: "Crime Done By Cleveland 'Red' Leon Czolgosz of This City."[6] The Cleveland *Citizen*, published by Socialist trade unionist Max Hayes, had carried an announcement of Goldman's fateful lectures of 5 May, describing her then as a "fearless lady orator and champion of free speech." The *Citizen* reporter who had covered the lecture, which was attended also by three Cleveland police officers, had described it in the paper's next issue as "nothing particularly new," adding that "her solutions for present problems are ridiculous." After the assassination, however, the *Citizen* described anarchists as "unbalanced people." The "idiot" Czolgosz had accomplished nothing, "except to inspire with new life the forces of reaction," the *Citizen* complained. In fact, the Socialist newspaper claimed, "Leon Czolgosz Is a Republican In Politics. . . . He was never a member or identified with the Socialist Party."[7]

Anarchists themselves wanted to wash their hands of Czolgosz. In 1892 some had supported Berkman, who had after all "paid his dues" in the movement. Czolgosz, however, was an anarchist only by his own declaration, distrusted by political regulars like A. Isaak. But the condemnation of Czolgosz's deed was more than ad hominem. By 1901 most anarchists had rejected Bakunin's glorification of the individual deed of violence in favor of Kropotkin's belief in collective and nonviolent resistance to the state. There were practical objections to the *attentat* as well. The waves of repression in the United States and Europe following each *attentat*, successful or not, had devastated the anarchist movement. Furthermore, other routes to revolution seemed more attractive. Radicals could take heart at the emergence in the West of militant unions, and at the founding of the Socialist Party of America, dedicated to revolutionary change.

Goldman disagreed with her fellow anarchists. In what appears to have been a willful act of political self-destruction, she continued to defend Czolgosz publicly and ardently. But there was a logic to her defense: she may have felt responsible for Czolgosz's behavior. Although she might have changed her own mind about the efficacy of propaganda by deed, she still could not repudiate those who committed it. She had publicly defended Berkman's failed *attentat* and Gaetano Bresci's 1901 assassination of King Humbert of Italy. It could be that Czolgosz had confused her defense of the assassin with a defense of assassination. It was a distinction that escaped most of her audiences.

The anarchist paper *Free Society* printed her plea for Czolgosz: "Leon Czolgosz and other men of his type, far from being depraved creatures of low instincts, are in reality supersensitive beings unable to bear up under too great social stress. They are driven to some violent expression even at the sacrifice of their own lives, because they cannot supinely witness the misery and suffering of their fellows. . . . My heart goes out to [Czolgosz] in deep sympathy, as it goes out to all the victims of oppression and misery, to the martyrs past and future."[8] The publication of that article, however, was as far as most anarchists would go in supporting Czolgosz. Goldman failed to raise funds for his legal defense within the anarchist community or to rally opinion behind him. Only de Cleyre was sympathetic.

Czolgosz was defended by reluctant court-appointed lawyers who overlooked their client's probable insanity. The jury deliberated only 34 minutes before handing down a guilty verdict. Czolgosz was executed on 29 October 1901, scarcely seven weeks after he had shot McKinley.

Not only had the immigrant left failed to support Czolgosz, but some, including East Side editor Yanovsky, had called Goldman's own actions irresponsible. Smarting from the criticism and from her failure to save Czolgosz, Goldman became embittered with her political comrades: "Our movement . . . lost its appeal for me; many of its adherents filled me with loathing. They had been flaunting anarchism like a red cloth before a bull, but they ran for cover at his first charge. I could no longer work with them."[9]

Goldman, therefore, entered a brief period of self-imposed political exile not only from the American public but from the left. She donned a disguise and a new (non-European) name, Miss E. G. Smith, symbolic of her new identity. She had little luck getting work as a nurse, for doctors who had employed her in the past now treated her as a pariah, and she was reduced to sewing piecework again. After one evening when someone shouted out that she was a murderess, she became afraid to attend public lectures. She became so paranoid that she turned down an invitation to speak at a strike rally, when a nightmare about Czolgosz gave her a premonition of disaster.

But the worst blow came in a letter from Berkman, written in December 1901. Berkman commended Goldman for courage in the face of the lynch mob outside the Chicago jail and for generosity in offering to care for the wounded McKinley. That gesture, he continued, marked "the great change wrought in us by the ripening years. . . . How impossible such a thought would have been to us in the days of a decade ago! . . . [I]t would have outraged all our traditions even to admit the humanity of an official representative of capitalism." Berkman continued, however, that although he and Goldman had matured together, they had also grown apart. Czolgosz may have been a sensitive soul whose act had personal significance, but in Berkman's view, the assassination had no "social necessity." In the United States—in contrast to tsarist Russia—the president was only a figurehead; the real oppressor was capitalism.[10] Goldman was stunned at the cruel irony of Berkman's words: "Sasha is using the same arguments against Leon [Czolgosz] that Johann Most had urged against Sasha."[11] Her trust in Berkman, her political and moral arbiter, like her earlier trust in Most, was shaken. As Berkman remarked in his memoirs, the disagreement over Czolgosz accentuated "the divergence of our views, painfully discovering the fundamental difference of attitude underlying even common conclusions."[12] For a time they stopped writing altogether. Berkman and Goldman would remain comrades to the end, but she would never again follow him unquestioningly.

Goldman's withdrawal from politics lasted only months. She soon rejoined her old friends on the East Side, roused to speeches and fundraising by the persecution of student radicals in Russia, by the great coal miners' strike of 1902, and especially by the threatened deportation of John Turner. In 1903 Congress passed a law that prohibited the entry into the United States of any "person who is opposed to all organized governments, or who is a member of or affiliated with any organization entertaining or teaching such disbelief in or opposition to all governments." Turner, a British anarchist and trade unionist, was the law's first target. He had just embarked on a second lecture tour of the United States when immigration officials arrested him and charged him with illegal entry. He was detained at Ellis Island for several months while his lawyer, Hugh O. Pentecost, staved off deportation.

Alarmed by the legislation's threat to the First Amendment, liberals joined radicals to form the Free Speech League, which raised funds so that Clarence Darrow and Edgar Lee Masters could take Turner's case to the Supreme Court. The two lawyers argued that Turner's philosophical anarchism did not represent a threat to the United States government and that the federal law violated freedom of speech. Turner, however, decided to return to England before the Court handed down its decision. That decision in 1904, not surprisingly, upheld the antianarchist law, and it remained on the books as an ominous reminder not only of the American fear of anarchism but also of the power of the federal government to curtail freedom of speech.

Goldman quickly became active in the Free Speech League. She made new friends among the its members, the "native intelligentsia," who invited her to speak about the dangers of the antianarchist law at the Manhattan Liberal Club, the Brooklyn Philosophical Society, and similar organizations. These American liberals, such as Bolton Hall and Elizabeth and Alexis Ferm, were often single-taxers. Although no anarchist would condone a tax of any kind, single-taxers were also libertarians who believed in minimal government (only enough to collect the single tax), and Goldman, like others on the left, found them politically congenial.[13]

Ironically, the attempt to halt the deportation of a European anarchist provided Goldman with the new American-born audience and new connections to liberals that she had long wanted to cultivate. "Henceforth," she wrote, "I gave more time to English propaganda, not only because I wanted to bring anarchist thought to the American public, but also to call attention to certain great issues in Europe."[14] In the next decade, therefore, Goldman "helped to build a bridge from immigrant radicalism to the native radical and liberal traditions" and entered the most politically and intellectually productive years of her life.[15]

Her success was made possible by the growing appeal of liberal and left ideas during the Progressive period. Called progressive because of its optimistic faith that change brings progress and improvement, the first two decades of this century were characterized by a wide variety of enthusiastic efforts to reform the American economy, American politics, and American behavior and morals. Responding to the economic and political ills described by Edward Bellamy, the urban, white, middle-class reformers usually sought moderate and modest change, thus winning the support of some corporate interests. Based securely in private-sector institutions like settlements and such organizations as the National Child Labor Committee and the National Civic League, Progressives nevertheless advocated public and political strategies, since they were people who knew how to make the political system work. Local, state, and federal governments, partially rejecting the nineteenth-century tradition of laissez-faire, passed laws to regulate and presumably improve the work and private lives of individuals—including protective legislation for women in industry and zoning restrictions for urban dwellers—and the economic lives of corporations, including antitrust measures.

Progressives belonged to the two major parties. Theodore Roosevelt, the first Progressive president was a Republican, as were his handpicked successor William Howard Taft and the great Progressive senator from Wisconsin, Robert La Follette. President Woodrow Wilson and the reformist mayor of Cleveland Tom L. Johnson were Democrats. In 1912, reformers broke with the Republican party to form the Progressive party, whose unsuccessful presidential candidate, again Theodore Roosevelt, won votes from both Democrats and Republicans.

To the Progressives' left had emerged American socialism. The Socialist Labor Party (SLP), led by Daniel De Leon after 1890, had maintained an almost exclusively immigrant following. De Leon, born in Curaçao and educated in Germany, was formerly a professor at Columbia Law School. Attracted to socialism initially by Edward Bellamy, De Leon repudiated Bellamy's gradualism and became an increasingly orthodox Marxist after he assumed SLP leadership. De Leon maintained that trade unions would be the revolutionary vanguard but distrusted the existing unions, especially those affiliated with the American Federation of Labor. Accordingly, De Leon founded a dual labor federation, the Socialist Trade and Labor Alliance. The SLP endorsed political action but opposed any political alliance with non-Marxist reformist organizations, such as the Populist party. In 1899 a group that included trade unionists Morris Hillquit and Max Hayes split from the SLP. This faction hoped to make common political cause with native-born American radicals.

That common cause was made in 1900 by Eugene V. Debs, the man whose political career epitomized the evolution of indigenous radicalism in the United States. Debs was born in 1855 in Terre Haute, Indiana, the son of German immigrant parents. He began his career as a Democrat and a trade union official with the Brotherhood of Locomotive Firemen, but when he came to the conclusion that craft unions were too exclusive, he founded an industrial union, the American Railway Union. In 1894 his union was destroyed by federal intervention in a strike in Pullman, Illinois, and Debs was imprisoned. "I found myself in Cook County jail," he later wrote, "with the whole press screaming conspiracy, treason, and murder." His cell overlooked the spot where the Haymarket anarchists had been hanged. Refusing to defend Debs, one lawyer explained, "you will be tried upon the same theory as were the anarchists, with probably the same result." The lawyer was wrong. Times had changed, Debs was neither an immigrant nor an anarchist, and he was not hanged. But during his months in jail, Debs recalled, "Socialism gradually laid hold of me in its irresistible fashion."[16]

The broken strike and his imprisonment proved to Debs that neither Republicans nor Democrats served the American workers, and in 1896 he voted for William Jennings Bryan on the Populist ticket. (Bryan was also the Democratic nominee.) In 1897, with Wisconsin Socialist Victor Berger, Debs formed the Social Democratic Society, which endorsed both political action and the formation of socialist colonies like the antebellum utopian communities of Fourier. Goldman first met Debs at the 1898 convention of the Social Democratic Society. She later paid him the great compliment of declaring him to be an anarchist despite his belief in political action: "Debs was so genial and charming that one did not mind the lack of clarity which made him reach out at one and the same time for opposite poles."[17]

Local political victories for the Socialists soon convinced Debs and others that political action was a more viable route to revolution than communitarianism. In 1901 these political actionists joined with others from the SLP to form the most important Socialist organization in American history, the Socialist Party of America (SP). Debs's speeches hammered on the themes of popular muckraking journalists and novelists—exploitative child labor, widespread poverty, political corruption. But he condemned the whole system, not just its parts: "the sordid capitalism which preys upon the life-blood of labor, whose ethics are expressed in beastly gluttony and insatiable greed, and whose track of conquest is strewn with the bones of its countless victims." The Socialist solution was not reform, but "revolution . . . a new social order." When the workers vote for the Socialist party, Debs predicted, "the government will pass into their hands and capitalism will fall to rise no more; private ownership will give way to social ownership, and production for profit to production for use; the wage system will disappear, and with it the ignorance and poverty, misery and crime that wage-slavery breeds; the working class will stand forth triumphant and free, and a new era will dawn in human progress and in the civilization of mankind."[18]

The SP committed itself to the establishment of the "cooperative commonwealth" in the future, a Socialist state in which the means of production and distribution would be publicly owned. This was to be achieved primarily through political action, which would elect Socialists to office as well as educate the American public about Socialism. In the short run, however, Socialists supported reforms like child-labor legislation, a graduated income tax, government regulation of monopolies, and even women's suffrage, which were later endorsed and sometimes implemented by the two major parties.

The SP's gradualist, nondoctrinaire vision of an equitable and just society attracted a wide and various following. Some former Populists abandoned the party of rebellious farmers for the SP, which gave it strength in the South and the West. The SP developed support among working-class immigrants in the industrializing midwestern states, including Ohio, Indiana, and Michigan, and in some cities, especially New York, Chicago, and Milwaukee, where Victor Berger ran a successful political machine.[19] Both the nationalism of Edward Bellamy and the Christian Socialism of the Social Gospel had also paved the way for the new party among middle-class Americans. At the party's first national convention in 1904 the great majority of its delegates were American-born, and in 1908 a party official claimed that 70 percent of its membership had been born in the United States.[20]

Inspired rather than led by Debs, the SP grew rapidly. In 1901 it claimed 10,000 members; by 1912, 118,000. Socialists published 300 periodicals in English and in several foreign languages. When Debs ran as the SP presidential candidate in 1904 and again in 1912, his powerful rhetoric and gentle personality also won votes from many who were not Socialists. In 1912 Americans elected 1,200 Socialists to local offices, and Debs got 6 percent of the popular vote. It was the high tide of SP political strength.

Although fond of Debs, Goldman was not impressed by the SP nor by its growing appeal to native-born Americans. But she had learned in the fight for John Turner that while American liberals were reluctant to join up for the revolution, they were easily aroused by issues such as freedom of speech and civil liberties. Tsarist Russia, for example, seemed the embodiment of political oppression to members of the American Friends of Russia, who consequently applauded the 1905 Russian Revolution. Through her friend Alice Stone Blackwell, daughter of feminist Lucy Stone, Goldman (still disguised as E. G. Smith) rallied support from the American Friends for Catherine Breshkovskaya, who was known as the grandmother of the Revolution. "Babushka" spoke to a wide range of American reformers, including Ernest Crosby, Bolton Hall, Socialist millionaire William English Walling, and settlement-house worker Lillian D. Wald.

At the height of the 1905 Revolution, the Russian theatrical troupe of Pavel Nikolayevitch Orleneff arrived in New York, homeless and almost destitute. Sympathetic to the plight of her fellow Russians and performers, Goldman came to their rescue. Acting as their manager and interpreter to American audiences, E. G. Smith organized performances and fundraisers in New York, Boston, and Chicago, and again rallied celebrities and liberals, including actress Ethel Barrymore and settlement-house leader Jane Addams. (Goldman recounted with pleasure a meeting with Addams, who did not recognize "Red Emma" under her pseudonym.) Goldman simultaneously lectured at anarchist gatherings under her real name.[21] In contrast to liberal support for Orleneff, the East Side immigrant community, hearing rumors that he was somehow associated with a wave of Russian pogroms, refused to advertise or attend his performances.

Orleneff thanked Goldman with a testimonial performance, which raised funds for *Mother Earth*, the journal that became Goldman's chief vehicle for reaching Americans—or, as she called it, "educating the bourgeoisie."[22] With this new audience in mind, Goldman had first wanted to name the magazine "The Open Road," after a poem by the American Walt Whitman, but she was told that this would infringe on the copyrights of another magazine. Goldman published *Mother Earth* from March 1906 until the federal government shut it down in 1918. *Mother Earth* was in English instead of German, Goldman's first platform language and the language of Most's *Freiheit,* or Yiddish, like the East Side's *Freie Arbeiter Shtime,* although Goldman began to lecture in Yiddish in 1908.

Goldman intended *Mother Earth* to be in the cultural as well as the political vanguard, so it included articles on European literary figures such as Henrik Ibsen and translations of the works of Tolstoy and Dostoyevski. Of course art took a back seat to politics, always Goldman's first priority, and first-rate writers and artists could make more money by publishing in other small literary journals, and win more prestige by publishing in more reputable journals, like *The Masses.*

As its cultural focus indicated, the journal was intended to introduce international anarchism to Americans. For example, it reprinted articles by Kropotkin, Proudhon, and Malatesta and featured news items about anarchists in Japan, Spain, Italy, and other countries. European contributors included Hippolyte Havel, Goldman's former lover, and Max Baginski, whose articles were written in German and then translated into English by Goldman. *Mother Earth* also had important American contributors, including Leonard Abbott, who was converted to anarchism by Goldman and who joined her crusades for birth control and against the draft, and Harry Kelly, an admirer of Kropotkin and Goldman. (He later offered to marry her.) The magazine carried pieces on Goldman's new American heroes: revolutionary Thomas Paine, the transcendentalist Ralph Waldo Emerson, and abolitionist and labor agitator Wendell Phillips.

The magazine's emphasis on culture and its frequent references to these Americans prompted criticism from within the anarchist movement that *Mother Earth* was not revolutionary enough, perhaps not revolutionary at all. Responding to negative comments from de Cleyre in December 1910, Goldman defended her new thrust: "The men and women who first take up the banner of a new liberating idea generally emanate from the so-called respectable classes. . . . [To] limit oneself to propaganda exclusively among the oppressed does not always bring desired results."[23] Perhaps because its protest was muted or perhaps because of the popularity of "little magazines" at the time, *Mother Earth* did succeed in broadening the size and the influence of Goldman's following. Its readership, estimated anywhere from 3,500 to 10,000, obviously included liberals as well as radicals.[24]

On 18 May 1906, two months after the first issue of *Mother Earth*, Berkman was released from prison, having served 13 years in the Western Penitentiary and an additional ten months in the local workhouse. His return was traumatic. Both he and Goldman recorded moving recollections of their reunion in the Detroit train station. "With an effort," he wrote in 1912, "I descend to the platform, and sway from side to side, as I cross the station at Detroit. . . . [M]y gaze falls on a woman leaning against a pillar. She looks intently at me. The wave of her hair, the familiar eyes—why, it's the Girl! How little she has changed. . . . I walk slowly toward her, but she does not move. She seems rooted to the spot, her hand grasping the pillar, a look of awe and terror in her face. Her lips move, but no sound reaches my ear. We walk in silence."[25] Goldman's impressions, written much later, echo Berkman's: "That strange-looking man—was that Sasha, I wondered. His face deathly white, eyes covered with large, ungainly glasses; his hat too big for him, too deep over his head—he looked pathetic, forlorn. . . . I was seized with terror and pity."[26]

The political world of the two revolutionaries had been transformed in 14 years, and Goldman's search for an American following had been part of that transformation. Berkman, insulated from political change, disapproved of her new friends and new ideas: "The little Sailor, my companion of the days that thrilled with the approach of the Social Revolution, has become a woman of the world. Her mind has matured, but her wider interests antagonize my old revolutionary traditions. . . . I resent the situation [as] I become conscious of the chasm between the Girl and myself."[27] Haunted by nightmares of his old life in prison, Berkman could not find a place for himself outside. Accustomed to the confinement and routine, he had trouble adjusting to freedom; accustomed to solitude, he was irritable in the company of others.

After the death in 1906 of Johann Most, their mentor-turned-antagonist, Goldman, anarchism's premier publicist, and Berkman, its leading martyr, emerged as the leaders of the anarchist movement in the United States. Goldman, therefore, arranged a lecture tour for Berkman, hoping that enthusiastic audiences of fellow radicals would lift his spirits and give his life new direction and purpose. Although well-intentioned, it was a bad idea. Exhausted and disappointed by an unresponsive Cleveland audience, he bought a gun, abandoned the tour, and disappeared. Goldman was frantic with fear that Berkman planned to kill himself. He did indeed contemplate suicide, but Goldman remained the "thread" that tied him to life. Three days after his disappearance, Berkman turned up in New York and telegraphed her to rescue him. Shortly afterwards, when anarchist comrades were arrested and threatened with deportation, rescuing them became the work Berkman needed. He had survived and achieved, he said, his "resurrection," at least for the moment.[28]

In 1908 Goldman asked Berkman to serve as editor of *Mother Earth*. While in prison he had taught himself to speak and write excellent English, as evidenced in his 1912 *Prison Memoirs*. Always more at home on the platform than at a desk, Goldman wanted to go on lecture tours to raise funds for the new magazine.

The personal friction between the two political comrades did not disappear. "Often I wanted to run away," she remembered, "never to see him again, but I was held by something greater than the pain: the memory of his act, for which he alone had paid the price. More and more I realized that to my last breath it would remain the strongest link in the chain that bound me to him. The memory of our youth and of our love might fade, but his fourteen years' Calvary would never be eradicated from my heart."[29] Their sexual relationship had only briefly revived after his release from prison. Berkman, then 36, became attracted to a 15-year-old girl who was pretty, uncritically admiring, and quite different from Goldman.

After Berkman—Goldman's closest tie to her immigrant past—ceased to be a romantic interest, she met in 1908 Benjamin Lewis Reitman, the "Grand Great Passion" of her life and her sexual and business partner for the next ten years. At 29, Reitman was almost a decade younger than Goldman. He had been born in St. Paul and grew up on Chicago's South Side. His parents were Jewish immigrants, but he had become a Baptist convert in his adolescence. At 11, Reitman had run away from home, riding the rails across the United States and taking tramp steamers across the Atlantic. He managed to get enough education to receive a medical degree in 1904 from the College of Physicians and Surgeons of Chicago (later the University of Illinois College of Medicine), and he taught at some local medical colleges. Reitman remained interested in the wandering hobos he had met on his own travels, and because of his efforts to provide them with education and medical care, he was known as the King of the Hobos. In 1907 he gained notoriety in Chicago when he was arrested for leading a march of the unemployed.

Goldman's first meeting with Reitman was inauspicious. A police-inspired furor over anarchists in Chicago had made it difficult for Goldman to find a place to hold a lecture. Suddenly Reitman appeared, "an exotic, picturesque figure with a large black cowboy hat, flowing silk tie, and huge cane," and offered her the storefront where he held meetings for his hobos. Goldman found him enormously attractive: "a tall man with a finely shaped head, covered with a mass of black curly hair, which evidently had not been washed for some time. His eyes were brown, large, and dreamy. His lips, disclosing beautiful teeth when he smiled, were full and passionate."[30] Fire inspectors halted plans to use Reitman's storefront, but Goldman scheduled a secret meeting at another site. Reitman was the only outsider who was told. When the police raided the meeting, she suspected—correctly as it turned out later—that he had tipped them off. Her physical attraction to him, however, overcame her suspicions about his ideas and behavior in this instance and in countless others over the next decade.

Reitman became the manager of Goldman's annual fundraising lecture tours. He arranged for the halls and the advance publicity and sold anarchist literature, relieving Goldman of these tiresome details and keeping her company on the road. He occasionally contributed to *Mother Earth* and sometimes spoke at her public meetings. Reitman typically spent part of the year on tour with Goldman and part in Chicago with his mother, to whom he was extremely attached. His mother was only one of Goldman's rivals for his affection, however. A compulsive womanizer, he had abandoned his wife and daughter when he was 22, and he flirted with and pursued countless other women from the beginning to the end of his love affair with Goldman. Yet, flattered by the passionate attention of this public figure, Reitman claimed that he loved only his "Mommy," Goldman. Certainly there was much that was childlike, or childish, about his behavior, and much that was maternal about hers.

Goldman's friends, especially Berkman, detested Reitman. His appearance, his manners, his adventurism, his politics, were all abhorrent. Berkman, the unrelenting revolutionist, "said plenty of cutting things to me," Goldman wrote later. "He scoffed at the idea that I could love such a man. It was nothing but a temporary infatuation, he felt sure. Ben lacked social feeling, he had no rebel spirit, and he did not belong in our movement."[31] Reitman, for his part, made little effort to please her colleagues and remained intensely jealous of Berkman.

Quite possibly, as Candace Falk has suggested, Goldman fell in love with Reitman partly to spite these old friends, especially Berkman. Perhaps what was attractive about Reitman was his wrongness, his inappropriateness, his unconscionable behavior, which allowed Goldman to play the martyred lover. Perhaps she was in love with the *idea* of being in love with him.[32]

In many ways this long love affair, in which bitter quarrels alternated with passionate reconciliations, proved disastrous and self-destructive for Goldman, physically and emotionally exhausting, a distraction from her writing and lecturing. In keeping with her emphasis on sexuality, Goldman claimed in her autobiography that her sexual passion for Reitman outweighed her lover's faults and the irreconcilable differences between their temperaments and their ideas. She described that passion in Victorian hyperbole: "I was caught in the torrent of an elemental passion I had never dreamed any man could rouse in me. I responded shamelessly to its primitive call, its naked beauty, its ecstatic joy."[33] The personal correspondence between Goldman and Reitman corroborates the unrestrained sexuality of the relationship. Using an erotic code, Goldman described in steamy detail their sexual intimacy. "Come warm me darling . . . pour your precious life essence into mine and let me forget, that I have neither home nor country. If I have you, I have the World. What more do I want? . . . If only I can wrap around that body of yours, if only I can drink *from the fountain of life*. . . . Darling lover sweet heart, champion f----- just 4 days more and then and then! . . . I wait for you in love and passion. Come. Mommy."[34]

But in this case as in others, Goldman was not entirely at the mercy of her emotions, and her personal and sexual preference for Reitman was not really politically perverse. Her assessment of Reitman's usefulness to her was shrewd—and revealing. "Ben was typically American in his love of publicity and of show. . . . [He] had the American swagger."[35] She had met another consummate showman whose dramatic flair matched her own. Reitman also became another means to Goldman's chief end during this period: reaching an American public. As Alice Wexler has noted, this love affair with Reitman was Goldman's way of consummating her "love affair with America."[36]

Reitman periodically described in *Mother Earth* the challenges of managing Goldman's tours. She could draw a sizable crowd with only a small notice in the local newspaper, but he had to find a meeting place. Reitman found her theaters, lodgehalls—"the Eagles Hall, the Owls Hall, the Elks, Odd Fellows, Masons" (but not the Catholic Knights of Columbus), courthouses, barns, saloons, and private homes.[37] Goldman later paid tribute to his considerable skills as a manager: "For fifteen years before this [1910] my lectures had been made possible by my comrades, who had always given me their best assistance. But they had never been able to reach a large American public. Some of them had been too centred in their own language-group activities to trouble about interesting the native element. The results during those years were scant and unsatisfactory. Now with Ben as my manager my work was lifted out of its former narrow confines. On this tour I visited thirty-seven cities in twenty-five States, among them many places where anarchism had never been discussed before. I lectured one hundred and twenty times to vast audiences, of which twenty-five thousand paid admission, besides the great number of poor students or unemployed admitted without charge. . . . I had made anarchism more widely known than in the previous years. And it had been the skill and devotion of Ben that had brought it about."[38]

At Reitman's urging, Goldman also began to make the university lecture circuit. Anticipating apathy, she was surprised to find interested and enthusiastic professors and students at the University of Wisconsin, the site of much Progressive reform activity. The local newspapers, however, infuriated at her presence, called for the dismissal of sociologist E. A. Ross, who had supported her right to speak on campus. Male students at the University of Michigan were rowdy and disruptive until Goldman stared them down and then dressed them down for their bad manners.

Despite the Progressive period's reformism, anarchists remained unwelcome speakers in many places. Beginning with the 1893 speech for which she received a year on Blackwell's Island, Goldman could never be certain that her lectures would be uninterrupted by the local police. She always carried a book with her so that she would have something to read if she had to go to jail. In 1906 the newly formed New York Anarchist Squad had begun to arrest anarchist speakers, and *Mother Earth* carried notices about a Free Speech Defense Fund to cover their legal expenses. The fund's biggest contributor at that time was the Yiddish *Freie Arbeiter Shtime.*

A serious depression in 1907–1908 sparked anarchist-led strikes and demonstrations by the unemployed in Philadelphia and other cities, and police cracked down on anarchist speakers. Goldman's meetings in Columbus, Toledo, and Detroit were halted. She was particularly irked in Toledo, whose mayor, Brand Whitlock, was a single-taxer and self-proclaimed champion of free speech. In the fall of 1908 she and Reitman were arrested in Seattle. In January 1909, they spent four days in a San Francisco jail, released only after friends wired the $5,000 bail. In May 1909 police stopped 11 lectures. *Mother Earth* reported in February 1911 that Goldman spoke in Indianapolis only after she had been "gagged in the usual, senseless police manner," suffering "police arrogance and brutal intimidation."[39]

These frequent arrests gave Goldman much free publicity. They also inspired the free-speech crusade that she had begun in *Mother Earth,* carried on now with the support of some American liberals. When the New York Anarchist Squad broke up Goldman's Sunday morning lecture on Ibsen in 1909, the "blue-blooded Americans" in the audience were outraged. Goldman became the toast of these "*Mayflower* descendants." Standard Oil executive Alden Freeman invited Goldman to speak at his New Jersey mansion, and Freeman and other liberals formed a Free Speech Society. In Philadelphia, police officers prevented her from even entering the Odd Fellows' Hall, outraging the waiting audience of anarchists, socialists, single-taxers, and liberals.[40]

During these years Goldman also became involved with a radical American organization, the Industrial Workers of the World (IWW), or the Wobblies. The IWW was founded in 1905 in Chicago by various leftists, including Socialist Party of America and Socialist Labor party delegations and a large number of trade unionists, especially from the Western Federation of Miners. This assemblage shared a dissatisfaction with the growing political orientation of the SP and a fear that union organizing would be lost in the political shuffle. The IWW was the solution: an all-encompassing industrial union, organizing skilled and unskilled, female and male, black and white in the manner of the old Knights of Labor. Unlike the Knights, however, the IWW endorsed an overthrow of capitalism by direct action or a general strike. Workers would then govern through their unions, not by capturing the state as the SP predicted. Political strategies made little sense for the IWW's constituency, many of whom were voteless migrant workers.

The IWW belief in direct action and government by trade unions resembled European anarcho-syndicalism, but the IWW was indigenous. Its best-known leader, Big Bill Haywood, was the quintessential American: "celebrated by journalists, novelists and poets as a real son of the American West, the frontiersman as proletarian radical," according to his biographer Melvyn Dubofsky.[41]

The IWW's militant songs and slogans envisioned a workers' millenium, but Wobblies were also practical organizers who built unions among the migrant farmworkers, lumberjacks, and steel workers ignored by the craft unionism of the AFL. The IWW also supported strikes, winning a victory in 1909 at McKees Rocks, Pennsylvania, against a local steel company but losing others against the steel industry in Pennsylvania and the lumber industry in the South. In 1912, however, the IWW leadership, including Haywood, Carlo Tresca, and Elizabeth Gurley Flynn, took charge of a wildcat strike in Lawrence, Massachusetts, against the textile mills there. The Wobblies won the strike by unifying thousands of immigrant workers of 25 nationalities and by a dramatic evacuation of hungry and ragged workers' children to New York City, which evoked public sympathy for the strikers. The IWW would never be able to repeat this victory, but it won the Wobblies temporary fame from the left and long-lived hatred from employers and governments.

Goldman was seldom enthusiastic about trade unions, but the IWW was different: it advocated revolution, and it was antigovernment. Its anarcho-syndicalist philosophy was much like her own. Therefore Goldman joined with the IWW in several ventures. In 1906 when Haywood and another IWW official were falsely accused of murdering the governor of Colorado, Goldman defended Haywood and publicized his case in *Mother Earth*. In May 1912 the magazine carried strike news from Lawrence and pleas for funds from Haywood and Flynn. Although neither was an anarchist, Goldman found them politically compatible. Goldman raised funds for the Lawrence strike with two debates with Socialists in which she supported direct action versus political action.[42] Haywood had just been expelled from the National Executive Committee of the SP for publicly repudiating political strategies: the triumph of the Wobbly strategy at Lawrence vindicated Goldman's position. In 1913 Debs, who had been a founder of the IWW, turned against it because it was an "'anarchist organization.'"[43]

Local officials often arrested IWW organizers to try to prevent them from holding their open-air meetings, and between 1909 and 1912 Wobblies engaged in a number of free-speech fights in cities along the West

Coast, filling the jails to protest the organizers' arrests. In 1912 in San Diego, Goldman and Reitman joined an IWW free-speech fight in progress and suffered a humiliating defeat. IWW headquarters had been raided and the Wobblies beaten, forced to kiss the American flag, and driven out of town. One had been murdered. Hours after Goldman and Reitman arrived, local vigilantes kidnapped Reitman, and Goldman fled to Los Angeles with the mob in hot pursuit. When Reitman rejoined her, she found that he had been beaten, tarred and feathered, and branded on his buttocks with the letters "I. W. W." Goldman was horrified but continued on to Seattle, where she refused to cancel her scheduled lecture, despite an anonymous threat on her life. In 1913 Reitman, anxious to conquer his fears, insisted that they return to San Diego, but when faced with another howling mob, he became terrified and begged that they leave with a police escort. "No play was ever staged with greater melodrama than our rescue from the San Diego jail and our ride to the railroad station," Goldman recalled. Goldman's final break with Reitman did not take place until 1917, but his fear in the face of danger was a crucial revelation to her: "Ben was not of heroic stuff. He was not of the texture of Berkman, who had courage enough for a dozen men and extraordinary coolness and presence of mind in moments of danger."[44]

While Goldman could ally herself occasionally with the IWW, her disagreements with the Socialists became sharper and more contentious. The rivalry between socialists and anarchists, muted in the late nineteenth century when both movements were powerless, became overt as they both gathered steam and adherents in the first decade of the twentieth. Goldman ridiculed the Socialists, who were forbidden to debate her, and both she and Reitman accused them of sabotaging her meetings: "the good Socialists are like the Catholics; they only go to their own church. Often the Socialists deliberately boycott us. I hope none of our readers will ever take it for granted that a town with a large Socialist vote necessarily means a radical town," sniped Reitman in 1911.[45] Goldman complained that a Socialist newspaper accused her of being in the pay of the tsar.[46]

The rivalry, however, encouraged Goldman to redefine her own anarchism, especially since she had begun to commit her ideas to writing in *Mother Earth* and in *Anarchism and Other Essays*, published in 1910. That redefinition reflected her new interest in American thought and culture. She referred more frequently to Americans in her essays, using abolitionists and Revolutionaries as evidence for her attack on majoritarian politics: "Always, at every period, the few were the banner bearers of a great idea, of liberating effort." Those "few" included her favorite nineteenth-century liberals: William Lloyd Garrison, Wendell Phillips, Henry David Thoreau, Margaret Fuller, and John Brown. These nineteenth-century Romantics had believed that a heroic individual could single-handedly change the course of human events.[47] Thoreau tried to end slavery by going to jail and John Brown, by his ill-fated invasion at Harper's Ferry. The parallels between Brown's violent attempt to trigger a slave uprising and Berkman's *attentat* were obvious. So were the similarities between Garrison's inflammatory abolitionist rhetoric and Goldman's own platform style.

Goldman was one of the few immigrant anarchists to make contact with the American anarchist movement, which also may have shaped her thinking. American anarchists shared the European antipathy to government, but they placed much greater emphasis on individualism and condoned private property. Goldman always considered herself a communist anarchist and condemned private property of any kind, but the American stress on the individual was congenial to her own position.

The slender and varied tradition of American anarchism had emerged in the decades before the Civil War and claimed Thoreau and Emerson as its ancestors. The real father of American individualistic anarchism, however, was Josiah Warren, an inventor and musician and originally a member of Robert Dale Owen's communistic utopia, New Harmony. Warren believed that New Harmony had failed because it tried to impose uniformity on human diversity. "Society must be converted so as to preserve the SOVEREIGNTY OF EVERY INDIVIDUAL inviolate," Warren argued, and he founded three separate colonies in 1834, 1846, and 1850, in which individual sovereignty was the guiding principle. In each colony, members were allowed to keep as much private property as their own labor could justify.[48]

Not surprisingly, later American anarchists were a motley group. They included one-time abolitionist and later advocate of women's emancipation Stephen Pearl Andrews; William B. Greene, champion of free speech and labor reform; and free thinkers and free lovers Moses Harman and Victoria Woodhull. By the end of the nineteenth century the best-known American anarchist was Benjamin Tucker, publisher of *Liberty*. Tucker came from a respectable New England family but had been seduced by Woodhull, to whom, at least according to legend, he lost both his sexual and political virginity. Tucker had become disenchanted with Woodhull—although not with free love—and had been further persuaded to anarchism by the writings of Warren and Greene. Tucker was familiar with European anarchist thought, and he translated Chernyshevsky and Bakunin. But he parted company with the Europeans when he rejected propaganda by deed as well as any kind of collective action, including collective ownership of property.

Goldman revered Woodhull's memory and applauded Harman as the first defender of legal birth control. She did not like Tucker, however, because he disapproved of Berkman's *attentat*, even though Tucker had joined her in the Free Speech League. She had closer ties with de Cleyre, although they were not friends. De Cleyre was American-born and, like Goldman, claimed that her anarchism was inspired by the Haymarket martyrs. Unlike Goldman, de Cleyre lived among the immigrant poor, barely earning a livelihood by teaching English, and she was critical of Goldman's cultivation of "the bourgeoisie." De Cleyre had supported Berkman in 1892, corresponded with him in prison, and had even sympathized with Czolgosz. An excellent writer herself, she helped Berkman with his *Memoirs* and contributed often to *Mother Earth*.

As her own thinking developed, Goldman attempted to accommodate the European anarchist tradition of collective behavior to an individualism that she had first admired in Max Stirner and Nietzsche and that was now reinforced by American anarchism and liberalism. In 1907 Goldman attended an International Anarchist Congress in Amsterdam, the first since the suppressed Congress of 1900. She and colleague Max Baginski tried to persuade their listeners that anarchism embraced both the "individuality" of Ibsen and the "mutual cooperation" of Kropotkin. Anarchism, they argued, offered "the possibility of [social] organization without discipline, fear, or punishment and without the pressure of poverty. . . . In short, anarchism strives towards a social organization which will establish well-being for all."[49] Before this European audience, the emphasis was on the collective good.

For Goldman's American readers, however, the anarchist vision often celebrated the liberated individual. For example, in an essay entitled "What I Believe," first published in 1908 by the *New York World* and often reprinted as a pamphlet, Goldman described the anarchist society in standard terms: "voluntary co-operation of productive groups, communities and societies loosely federated together." But this society was only the means to the end. The end was the development of the individual's "latent qualities and innate disposition . . . his soul cravings."

In a 1911 essay, "Anarchism: What It Really Stands For," she once more dismissed the idea of conflict between "the individual" and "the social instinct." In this essay, which also referred to Emerson and Thoreau, she defined the goal of anarchism as being "the freest possible expression of all the latent powers of the individual. . . . A perfect personality . . . is only possible in a state of society where man is free to choose the model of work, the conditions of work, and the freedom to work." Anarchism achieves that freedom by removing the artificial constraints of private property, state, and church, she concluded.[50]

Her analysis of anarchist strategies, also adapted to her American audience, contained contradictions. Most Americans condemned political uses of violence, such as the *attentat*, even though violence was a fact of American political life. In any case, Goldman wished to disassociate anarchism—and herself—from the deeds of propaganda carried out by individuals like Berkman, Czolgosz, and the assassins of European monarchs. She continued to explain political violence as "the response of sensitive human beings to the wholesale violence of capital and government." Yet by the 1910s it was harder than ever to believe that the actions of these individuals could trigger the anarchist revolution. Certainly neither Berkman nor Czolgosz had. The anarchist revolution, therefore, would be achieved collectively by "direct action against the authority in the shop, direct action against the authority of the law, direct action against the invasive, meddlesome authority of our moral codes," she argued. The most forceful example of direct action was the general strike, advocated by the American IWW.[51]

Goldman never became a convert to American egalitarianism or democratic values. (She described the workers as "brainless, incompetent automatons.")[52] But after losing faith in the immigrant left, she had found a new audience, new ideas, new strategies—and a new lover— among American liberals and leftists.

But even as Goldman tried to locate herself somewhere within this left, federal officials were beginning their efforts to remove her from the United States. As early as 1901, the Commissioner of Immigration had expressed his desire to deport Goldman, but she was protected by her marriage to Kersner, whose American citizenship guaranteed her own, even after their divorce. While in Europe for the Amsterdam conference, Goldman had read newspaper reports that she would be denied re-entry into the United States, and she consequently returned through Canada. Once back in the United States, she reasoned, she would be safe. But a federal law passed in 1906 permitted cancellation of citizenship that was obtained fraudulently, and in 1908, federal officials began a successful attempt to denaturalize Kersner—and thereby Goldman as well. As a result, she and Reitman cancelled a trip to Australia, fearing that under these circumstances she would not be allowed to return to the United States.

The efforts by the federal government to remove her from the United States may have encouraged Goldman to identify herself more closely with American causes. Among these causes would be the movement to liberate American women.

4

"THE TRAGEDY OF WOMAN'S EMANCIPATION": RADICALIZING WOMEN, 1910–1916

During the Progressive period, middle-class white women enjoyed greater opportunities in public and political life than ever before in American history, opportunities that reached their culmination in 1920, when American women won the right to vote. Emma Goldman, however, denounced the mainstream suffrage movement: its defining of "woman's emancipation" only in narrow political and economic terms, she asserted, was a "tragedy."[1] Distanced from these women activists by her political and sexual radicalism, Goldman formulated her own position on women's issues, and in her farther ranging critiques of American life and thought, she had female company on the left.

Goldman liked to think that she had shocked Jane Addams, perhaps her prototype of the "emancipated" woman, by revealing that the theatrical manager E. G. Smith was really the anarchist Emma Goldman. But Addams, the founder of the American settlement-house movement, was a hard woman to shock. From her front door at Hull House in Chicago, Addams had observed, with compassion but equanimity, the same late nineteenth-century society that had inspired the reformism of Bellamy, Debs, and other Progressives. The settlement house had opened on Halsted Street, a neighborhood that was home to Irish, Italian, Polish, and Russian immigrants, only three years after the Haymarket riot.

"The streets," Addams wrote in 1910, "are inexpressibly dirty, the number of schools inadequate, sanitary legislation unenforced, the street lighting bad, the paving miserable . . . and the stables foul beyond description." Sweatshops flourished, and "an unscrupulous contractor regards no basement as too dark, no stable loft too foul, . . . no tenement room too small for his workroom."[2] Addams saw, in short, an ugly, disorderly, unlivable city—and society—made chaotic by labor unrest and fragmented by class and ethnic differences. Women, Addams decided, must change all this.

At Rockford College—originally a sectarian seminary that encouraged its female students to become missionaries—Addams had been taught that she must do great and noble deeds for humankind. But after her graduation in 1882, she had found none to do in a society that dictated marriage and domesticity for privileged women like herself. After a failed attempt at medical school, Addams had a nervous breakdown. But six years later, inspired by a visit to London's Toynbee Hall, she and her friend Ellen Starr opened Hull House, where Addams found the public solution to the private problem of finding her life's work.

Hull House and dozens of other settlements like it allowed Addams and hundreds of well-educated, middle-class women to live useful lives and still conform—almost—to social conventions. The settlements were homes for these women who, like traditional wives and mothers, cared first for the needs of other women and children. When Hull House residents discovered that mothers had to lock their infants in their tenements while they were at work, for example, the settlement house opened a day nursery and a kitchen that provided inexpensive and nutritious meals. When the residents saw adolescents adrift on the streets and the elderly isolated in their homes, the settlement started teaching classes, holding parties, and organizing clubs for them. Expanding the definition of womanhood to include a public dimension, women like Addams became "social housekeepers."[3]

Settlement-house work became one of several new professions open to women in the early twentieth century. Growing numbers of women were attending college and then graduate school to acquire professional expertise and degrees; settlement-house workers went to social-work schools, just as nurses attended nursing schools. Most women professionals, however, were still becoming teachers in secondary and elementary schools, as they had throughout much of the nineteenth century. The older and more prestigious professions of law and medicine remained almost exclusively male.

Settlements were actually a result of the movement of middle-class women into reform activities. Women had been active in the temperance movement since the first quarter of the nineteenth century and had formed in 1874 the huge Woman's Christian Temperance Union. By then the social-purity movement had engaged many women in a drive that focused on ending the sexual double standard and eliminating prostitution. They saw prostitution as just one form of economic exploitation, however; reformers also sought to improve the wages and working conditions of women in industry and commerce. Those were the goals, for example, of the National Consumers' League (1899) and the Women's Trade Union League (1903).

These social housekeepers came to believe, as other Progressives did, that government—in the right hands—could solve problems. Because the "right hands" were women's, women needed the right to vote, and so reformers often became suffragists too. In 1910 Addams herself was a vice president of the National American Women's Suffrage Organization, and in 1912 she seconded the presidential nomination of Theodore Roosevelt at the convention of reformers who abandoned the Republicans and Democrats to form the Progressive party. The new party endorsed women's suffrage, hoping to capture the votes of women already enfranchised in nine states. The Socialist and Prohibition parties endorsed women's suffrage too, as they had in earlier presidential elections.

Despite the 1912 endorsements, the Nineteenth Amendment did not pass for another eight years. Women had first asked for the vote in 1848 at a convention in Seneca Falls, New York, and decade after decade women had fought countless battles for the vote at the local, state, and federal levels. But powerful opposition had blocked their suffrage, opposition from distillers and brewers, the employers of women and children, and politicians, all of whom were fearful that enfranchised women would vote them out of business. More important opposition came from men and women who were genuinely afraid that the political change would bring a social revolution as well. Antisuffrage cartoons showed men tending babies and women wearing pants. Women's suffrage would destroy the home and family, bringing dramatic increases in divorce and illegitimacy—so went the antisuffrage argument.

Not so, countered the suffragists. Voting was nothing more than an extension of woman's maternal role. "If woman would fulfill her traditional responsibility to her own children," Addams argued, "if she would educate and protect from danger factory children who must find their recreation on the street; if she would bring the cultural forces to bear upon our materialistic civilization; and if she would do it with the dignity and directness fitting one who carries on her immemorial duties, then she must bring herself to the use of the ballot. . . . May we not fairly say that American women need this implement in order to preserve the home?"[4] Motherhood, in fact, particularly fitted women to vote, according to the suffrage argument. Painfully aware of the presumed links between the vote and unconventional sexual behavior, suffrage leaders were careful to stay clear of controversial issues such as the reform of divorce laws or the legalization of birth control.

For some suffragists, the vote was an end in itself, because it meant full citizenship and political equality with men. For others—perhaps most—the vote was a means to the end: a decent, humane society in which the values of home and motherhood would prevail. According to Nancy F. Cott, suffrage was "an equal rights goal that enabled women to make special contributions; it sought to give women the same capacity as men so that they could express their differences."[5]

Less cautious than suffragists' arguments were the movement's collective strategies. These derived their political strength from the great numbers of women involved, and in turn gave the participants personal strength and courage. Their strategies included the 1890 formation of the 2-million-member National American Woman Suffrage Association and innumerable grass-roots campaigns of doorbell ringing, lobbying at state and federal capitals, soapbox speeches, and theatrical parades. While the ultimate suffrage victory had as much to do with the Wilson administration's need for the wartime support of American women as with the suffragists' skills or the justice of their cause, the suffrage movement had politicized generations of American women.

Goldman's own background might have made her sympathetic to the reformism of Addams and other Progressive women, given her immigrant origins and her family's financial and social difficulties in the United States. And certainly she knew something of female powerlessness. She had been raised under Jewish patriarchy, pressured into marriage, and had struggled to make her own living. Despite her stature in the anarchist movement, she was subordinate to powerful male leaders. But instead, much of what Goldman wrote and said about women during these years was a hostile response to the personal and political challenges that women reformers and suffragists apparently posed to her.

Anarchism and Other Essays (1910) contained her slightly earlier essay "The Tragedy of Woman's Emancipation," an attack on women professionals and suffragists. Her ill-disguised contempt for professional women may have stemmed from their class advantages, which she did not have, as this passage suggests: ". . . the position of the working girl is far more natural and human than that of her seemingly more fortunate sister in the more cultured professional walks of life—teachers, physicians, lawyers, engineers . . . , who have to make a dignified, proper appearance, while the inner life is growing empty and dead." Women who had chosen professions over marriage had become "compulsory vestals" or "professional automatons," she sneered.[6] Her own attempt to professionalize her nursing skills, of course, had been sidetracked by her love affair with Hippolyte Havel. Goldman often heaped scorn upon the suffragists. They "strike us . . . as a loudly clucking, aimless, constipated type of barnyard fowl," she proclaimed and described a suffrage parade as "forty thousand or forty million who troop up Fifth Avenue like a huge flock of sheep after the banner of a dead idea."[7]

Goldman's personal hostility was fueled by her significant philosophical objections to the suffragists' goals and strategies. She recognized that economic need drove women into prostitution, and like the reformers, she railed against the sexual double standard.[8] But from the perspective of a revolutionary like herself, working for laws to protect working women or to end prostitution was an exercise in futility. And she also disliked settlement houses. Addams had supported Orlenoff's performances in Chicago, had invited Kropotkin to Hull House, and at considerable expense to her own public reputation, had visited A. Isaaks when he was imprisoned after McKinley's assassination. As Goldman knew, Lillian Wald, founder and director of Nurses' Settlement (later Henry Street Settlement) had arranged receptions for Catherine Breshkovskaya ("Babushka"). Yet Goldman maintained that settlements did more harm than good, encouraging immigrants to eat with forks but not providing them with food.[9]

As an anarchist, Goldman believed that all governments—whether by emperor or empress, whether monarchical or democratic, whether created by the votes of men or of women—either oppressed or corrupted, or both. After the Socialist victories in 1912, for example, Goldman lectured on "Socialism: Caught in the Political Trap." A Socialist running for office must abandon his revolutionary principles, she maintained, and a Socialist elected to office must capitulate to the status quo. "The political trap has transferred Socialism from the proud, uncompromising position of a revolutionary minority, fighting fundamentals and undermining the strongholds of wealth and power, to the camp of the scheming, compromising, inert political majority." In any case a Socialist state, its powers swollen by control over the economy, might be even more oppressive than a state under capitalism.[10]

Goldman had even less use for women's suffrage. Not inaccurately, she argued that the suffrage movement was elitist: "a parlor affair, absolutely detached from the economic needs of the people."[11] Less accurately, however, she praised the "direct action" strategies of Victoria Woodhull and her sister Tennessee Claflin, forgetting that Woodhull had run for president in 1872. "The modern busybodies of the suffrage and feminist movements are the veriest pigmies in comparison [to Woodhull]," she claimed.[12] In 1915 when several states had enfranchised women and a few had even elected women to office, *Mother Earth* carried antisuffrage articles by both Goldman and Berkman. "Woman suffrage," he wrote, "has proved a delusion and a snare. The woman politician is as big a corruptionist—and in some cases even a bigger one—as the male of the species. . . . Whatever of educational value there once was in the [suffrage] movement . . . has long since been swamped in the narrow, bigoted, reactionary spirit of the female politician." Six months later, Goldman renewed the attack: "To vote in an American election is to insult your own intelligence, to inoculate yourself with the poison of mediocrity. Therefore it is truly a bitter, tiresome farce to witness the foolish women of many States clamoring for the Vote as the key to freedom and political purity, as the safe and sane means of education, as— why enumerate all the benefits they are going to derive from the vote. . . . [T]he grafters and bosses . . . are aware that woman suffrage will mean the increase in power of the political machine, an increase in graft, a greater and more fertile field of exploitation, and a wider possibility of meddling and 'regulating' morals and customs."[13]

"I am not opposed to woman suffrage on the conventional ground that she is not equal to it," Goldman argued. "I see neither physical, psychological nor mental reasons why woman should not have the equal right to vote."[14] But she often suggested that women, at least in their present circumstances, were incapable of making political judgments: "woman's narrow and purist attitude toward life makes her a greater danger [than men] to liberty wherever she has political power. . . . Her life-long economic parasitism has utterly blurred her conception of the meaning of equality." Here Goldman suggested that women's incompetence could be charged to their environment, but elsewhere she argued that women were "naturally" inferior. For example: "woman, essentially a purist, is naturally bigoted and relentless in her effort to make others as good as she thinks they ought to be," referring to efforts to make prostitution illegal in states where women could vote. "Woman, even more than man, is a fetich worshipper," Goldman maintained, and the vote, like religion, war, and family, was simply the latest "idol" before which woman prostrated herself.[15] She told the Women's City Club of Los Angeles in 1915, "It is really woman's inhumanity to man that makes him what he is. . . . Woman is naturally perverse. . . . She idolizes in [man] the very traits that help to enslave her—his strength, his egotism, and his exaggerated vanity."[16] Such a woman—not better but worse than man—could hardly better the world. Goldman also attacked the idea that motherhood equipped women to vote: "Motherhood today is on the lips of every penny-a-liner, every social patch-worker and political climber. It is so much prated about that one is led to believe that motherhood, in its present condition, is a force for good."[17]

Since European anarchists generally had no interest in women's issues and did not discuss women as a group having either particular problems or particular virtues, Goldman's thinking on women during this period, like her thinking on anarchist goals and strategies, reflected her growing ties to American anarchism and its individualist thrust. True emancipation, she accordingly argued, did not mean political or economic opportunity for women but freedom, not only from the external restraints of state and church but also especially from internal restraints of social convention. Goldman sometimes argued that the anarchist revolution would liberate women just as it would liberate men: when the economic revolution brought "social reconstruction," the emancipation of women would follow. But more often (here in the same essay), she urged that "true emancipation . . . begins in woman's soul."[18] Her model was Nora in Henrik Ibsen's A Doll's House: slamming the door on her husband and marriage, she "opens wide that gate of life for woman, and proclaims the revolutionary message that only perfect freedom and communion make a true bond between man and woman, meeting in the open, without lies, without shame, free from the bondage of duty."[19]

Rejecting the collective strategies of European anarchism and the American suffrage movement, Goldman implied that both the problem and the solution were individual. Just as she glorified the "banner bearers," the Thoreaus and the John Browns, so she glorified those women "pathfinders" and "pioneers" like the feminist writer Mary Wollstonecraft, who defied convention and sought personal liberation. The price of such rebellion was steep. Striking the anarchist pose, Goldman concluded, "the pioneers can not take root in the old, and with the new still far off they become outcast roamers of the earth."[20] She thought herself such a pioneer. Believing that she had overcome whatever obstacles she had faced as a woman, Goldman believed that others could do the same. Twenty years years later she would think differently.

Goldman often defined womanhood in sexual, gender-specific terms. "Emancipation should make it possible for woman to be human in the truest sense," she believed. "Everything within her that craves assertion and activity should reach its fullest expression." For a man, this meant choosing his work, she had argued earlier. For a woman, however, being "human" meant expressing her "woman's nature, her love instinct, and her mother instinct."[21] Her definition of woman as mother was not unlike the suffragists' definition, and Goldman referred to herself frequently in maternal terms and of course had named her magazine "Mother Earth." But unlike the suffragists, Goldman believed that a woman's instincts for love and maternity should be expressed without the constraints of marriage.

Practically speaking, for Goldman, women's emancipation was defined as sexual liberation—the right to have sexual relationships with whomever one chose. Marriage was an economic arrangement, an insurance policy for women, which turned them into dependent parasites, less honest even than prostitutes. Worse, marriage stifled love. Love, Goldman declared, was "the freest, the most powerful moulder of human destiny; how can such an all-compelling force be synonymous with that poor little State- and Church-begotten weed, marriage? Free love? As if love is anything but free."[22]

In theory, all anarchists should have been free lovers. In practice, they were not. Both Most and Brady had wanted Goldman to marry them. Berkman's beliefs were an exception to the European anarchists' conventional ideas about marriage. Within American anarchism, however, there was a firmer tradition of free love. Among the antebellum utopian communities, the Mormons, the Shakers, and the Oneida community of John Humphrey Noyes, all had radically altered monogamous marriage. Free love was also indebted to the spiritualist movement and its belief that men and women could have natural affinities for each other that were more compelling than legal marriage. To its nineteenth-century American advocates, however, "free" had meant sex without coercion by the male partner, and free lovers had often been more interested in restraining men than in pursuing unrestrained sexual pleasure.[23]

Woodhull was the most notorious free lover of the post–Civil War period. She made her 1872 run for the presidency on a free-love ticket.

Less famous but probably more influential was Moses Harman, the editor of *Lucifer*. Despite his public endorsement of free love, Harman was married. His daughter Lillian, however, went to jail for her "autonomistic marriage" to *Lucifer* co-editor Edwin Walker. Voltairine de Cleyre married none of her lovers, and Benjamin Tucker did not marry the mother of his daughter.

Main Street Americans who believed that women's suffrage would undermine the family were deeply offended and shocked by free love, which they identified with sexual promiscuity. On a lecture tour Goldman was awakened in the middle of the night by a man pounding on her hotel room door, demanding admittance and sex. I thought you believed in free love, he said, puzzled when Goldman rejected him.

Goldman also rejected offers of marriage, and she pursued her own "love instinct" with ardor and enthusiasm into her sixties. She prided herself on her ability to attract men, and occasionally in her autobiography, in rare flashes of humor, she admits to her personal vanity. Formal portraits from this period show her conventionally dressed in shirtwaist and skirt, soberly bespectacled, sometimes reading, always the serious revolutionist. Although not conventionally beautiful, she had many lovers (she only included the important ones in her autobiography), drawn to her passionate and sensitive nature, to the drama of her life, and perhaps to her fame.

Her love affairs with Berkman, Brady, Reitman, and others were public knowledge, since she never made any secret of them and she was much in the public eye. Very possibly it was her practice of free love as much as her political theories that got her deported in 1919. Her behavior may have been promiscuous by early twentieth-century standards, but most of her sexual and romantic relationships were enduring, although never placid and sometimes inappropriate. She usually remained friends with her former lovers.

Goldman had less satisfactory friendships with women. Until well into middle age, she saw most women as potential political or sexual rivals—as she did the suffragists, for example. And she did not necessarily like the women in her own political camp any better. In 1912, after the death of de Cleyre—the other prominent female anarchist—Goldman paid glowing tribute to her as a speaker and a writer, "beautiful in her spiritual defiance and filled with the revolt of a flaming ideal."[24] In life, however, there had been no love lost between the two, de Cleyre finding Goldman loud and coarse and Goldman finding de Cleyre ungrateful and weak-willed. (Each found the other physically unattractive.)

When women in her audience at the Los Angeles City Club, angered by her attack on suffrage, called Goldman "'a man's woman,'" she was not displeased.[25]

Candace Falk speculates that Goldman had a lesbian relationship with political activist and former prostitute Almeda Sperry. Goldman had heard lectures on homosexuality in Vienna and despite the disapproval of more conventional anarchists, occasionally lectured on the subject. At these lectures Goldman met some "inverts," as she described them in the terminology of the day. She also knew and liked lesbian Margaret Anderson and her female companion. Freedom to choose one's sexual partner was a legitimate concern for an anarchist. Nevertheless, although Sperry wrote love letters to Goldman, the evidence that Goldman was physically involved with the younger woman is inconclusive. Goldman once reassured the jealous Reitman: "I love your damn sex."[26]

In *Living My Life* Goldman occasionally laments that she had so few close women friends. But she did have political comrades among the women on the left, with whom she fought battles and shared interests.

A long-time labor agitator and organizer, for example, was "Mother" (Mary) Jones, who began her career in the 1870s with the Knights of Labor and became a walking delegate for the United Mine Workers in the 1890s. Jones admired Eugene Debs and attended the 1905 convention that founded the Industrial Workers of the World, but she did not affiliate herself with either the IWW or the Socialist party. A grandmotherly, white-haired figure dressed in respectable black, Mother Jones had a flair for the dramatic. In 1903 to publicize the evils of child labor, she led a group of thin, hungry mill children on a march from Philadelphia to President Theodore Roosevelt's home in Oyster Bay. She was given to violent language, if not violent action. At age 87, she shouted to a group of strikers, "You goddamned cowards are losing this strike because you haven't got the guts to go out and fight and win it. Why the hell don't you take your high power rifles and blow the goddamned scabs out of the mines?"[27] Like Goldman, Mother Jones was often imprisoned or run out of town by hostile employers. When local officials, "in true tsarist manner," deported Jones from a strike at Trinidad, Colorado, Goldman was inspired to lecture on labor's right to self-defense. Mother Jones did not like suffragists any better than Goldman did, telling one of her large audiences of women, "You don't need a vote to raise hell!"[28]

Mother Jones was too freewheeling to join a political party, but both the SP and the IWW included prominent women activists. Although the first Socialist party platform of 1904 endorsed women's suffrage, the party leadership was almost exclusively male and not much interested in women's issues, believing that equality between the sexes would come with the Socialist revolution. Nevertheless, in 1912 an estimated 10 to 15 percent of the SP membership was female, and women served as secretaries to state and local party organizations.[29] Even without encouragement, immigrant and American women, some persuaded by the Christian Socialism of Frances Willard, charismatic president of the Woman's Christian Temperance Union, joined the rank and file, and women occasionally got a place in the political limelight.

Kansas-born Kate Richards O'Hare was converted to Socialism by Mother Jones and became co-editor with her husband of the Socialist journal, *The National Ripsaw,* in St. Louis. In 1910 she ran on the Socialist ticket in Kansas for the United States Senate, and in 1916, she unsuccessfully sought the Socialist vice-presidential nomination. She was appointed to the National Executive Committee of the SP in 1912. O'Hare was a popular speaker in the Socialist Chautauquas of the Midwest. She tackled such women's issues as suffrage, birth control, and prostitution, but she also described herself as a woman who had sacrificed domestic joys for her cause. O'Hare sometimes brought her children onto the platform as she lectured on motherhood.[30] Goldman would become close friends with O'Hare while both were imprisoned in Jefferson City, Missouri, for their vocal opposition to American preparations for and intervention in World War I. O'Hare would be identified with the left wing of the SP after the war, but she would remain within the party until 1934.

Rose Pastor Stokes was also indicted for antiwar activities. She was sentenced to ten years in prison, although the federal government dropped the case against her in 1921. Stokes was born in Russian Poland and immigrated to the United States as a child. Her first job was in a Cleveland cigar factory, but her writing talents got her a position on the *Jewish Daily News* on New York's Lower East Side. There she met and married millionaire and socialite J. G. Phelps Stokes, and both joined the Socialist party. She also joined the Women's Trade Union League and walked the picket lines in the great 1909 shirtwaist makers' strike. Stokes was a charismatic speaker on behalf of labor and women's issues, including suffrage and birth control. With other free-speech advocates, she protested Goldman's silencing by the Philadelphia police in 1909. After the war, Stokes became a convert to Communism.[31]

Elizabeth Gurley Flynn's free-speech fights won Goldman's admiration early. Flynn was descended from Irish rebels, her father a Socialist and her mother a suffragist. She herself embarked on a career as a Socialist orator while she was still in high school and always referred to herself as a socialist. She made her reputation and her living, however, working for the IWW as a strike coordinator—at the Lawrence strike, for example, and later as the organizer of the "labor defense" of Wobblies and other radicals on trial or in jail during World War I. IWW songwriter Joe Hill dedicated his "Rebel Girl" to her. Flynn had a long-time unmarried relationship with fellow organizer and anarchist Carlo Tresca. Goldman recalled Flynn's "black hair, large blue eyes, and lovely complexion" and complimented her as "one of the first American women revolutionists of proletarian background." Goldman and Flynn parted company, however, when Flynn joined the Communist party in the 1930s.[32]

There were also a handful of women in the anarchist ranks. The best-known and most closely associated with Goldman was de Cleyre. De Cleyre wrote on women's issues—"Sex Slavery" and "Love in Freedom"—as early as the 1890s, as well as on economic and political topics.[33] When she died in 1912, no American-born woman took her place, and Goldman became the undisputed leader of anarchist women—perhaps of all American anarchists. Few anarchist women followed in Goldman's footsteps, however.

An exception was Mollie Steimer, who followed Goldman into prisons at Blackwell's Island and Jefferson City and finally to Bolshevik Russia. Steimer, like Goldman, was a Jewish immigrant from Russia; she had arrived in the United States in 1912. Her own poverty and Kropotkin's *Conquest for Bread* converted her to anarchism in 1917, just in time for her to receive a prison sentence for her opposition to the war. She was harassed, arrested, and briefly put in jail, where she threatened a hunger strike. Her 20-year federal jail sentence was commuted, and instead she and her comrades were deported to Russia in 1921. Goldman had met Steimer in 1919, after serving her own jail sentence. The courageous and outspoken younger woman reminded Goldman of the Russian revolutionary heroines of her own adolescence, and Goldman paid her a half-humorous compliment: Steimer was "a sort of Alexander Berkman in skirts."[34] The two women kept in touch during the 1920s as both wandered from one European country to another.

Like Goldman herself, these women on the left were political radicals first and foremost, interested in women's rights and equality only peripherally. Although Goldman herself had spoken and written on women's issues since the 1890s, these problems did not receive her full attention until the 1910s. Even then, Goldman focused on women's questions only after a series of frustrating defeats in the political arena. In 1914 in Ludlow, Colorado, the local national guard gunned down coal miners on strike against John D. Rockefeller's corporation, and burned to death women and children who were huddled in a tent city. The news appalled liberals as well as radicals. When Goldman offered to raise relief funds, however, she was turned down by labor organizations that did not want their cause associated with hers. Marie Ganz, a young woman claiming to be Berkman's protégée threatened to assassinate Rockefeller, and with a gun in her hand and a crowd at her back, marched into his office. Rockefeller was out, and Ganz was put in jail for disorderly conduct. After her release, she publicly denounced anarchism. Worse, three men, unknown to Goldman but friendly with Berkman, blew themselves up in a tenement house with a bomb possibly intended for Rockefeller.

In *Living My Life*, Goldman claimed that she was aghast at the "irresponsibility" of manufacturing the deadly device amidst innocent people. But she and Berkman had done the same thing in 1892. "In the zeal of fanaticism I had believed that the end justifies the means. It took years of experience and suffering to emancipate myself from the mad idea." She realized at this point, she said, that she could never again participate in violence that endangered the innocent.[35] Berkman apparently experienced no such epiphany. Defying police orders, he staged a huge public funeral for the victims of the bombing. Then he deposited the ashes of the dead men in a specially designed urn in the *Mother Earth* office. The July issue of *Mother Earth* published the speeches made at the funeral. Goldman later claimed to be horrified to discover that, except for Berkman's and Flynn's, they were full of violent language and "prattle about force and dynamite."[36]

Returning from a lecture tour on the West Coast, Goldman found her magazine deep in debt because of Berkman's political activities. Stifling her irritation with him, Goldman moved *Mother Earth* into smaller quarters and began to struggle to pay its bills. She relieved Berkman of his duties as editor and supported his decision to move to the West Coast to publish a labor weekly, which he had wanted to do for several years.

Discouraged, then, with politics-as-usual, Goldman turned her energies to cultural and sexual issues. She discovered an enthusiastic audience among American feminists of the cultural or "lyrical left" for her ideas about "women's emancipation." These were American-born middle-class men and women who lived or gathered in Greenwich Village in the 1910s and whose common bond was an enthusiastic belief that a political and cultural revolution was in progress. Reformer Frederic C. Howe, briefly a member of this group, described them as "brilliant young people, full of vitality, ardent about saving the world. . . . They protested against industrial conditions, suffering vicariously with the poor, [and] hated injustice."[37]

Their enthusiasm reflected political realities: the 1912 presidential election in which Eugene V. Debs received 6 percent of the popular vote, and the IWW triumph in the Lawrence strike. Contemporary literature and art seemed vehicles for this imminent revolution: the new literature in magazines like *Mother Earth*, the muckraking novels of Upton Sinclair and David Graham Phillips, the paintings of Robert Henri and the Eight of the "ashcan school," and the iconoclastic works of the 1913 Armory Show. In 1912 the enthusiasts founded *The Masses*, a lively, funny, and irreverent journal of politics and the arts. Nominally Socialist, the magazine often sided with the IWW. Contributors included editor Max Eastman and his sister Crystal Eastman, novelist Floyd Dell, journalist Jack Reed, cartoonist Robert Minor, and painter John Sloan.

At least briefly, the cultural left also included Wobbly leader Bill Haywood, Berkman, and Goldman. These three represented what a later generation would have called "radical chic": revolutionaries who had actually gone to the barricades. Goldman's autobiography did not discuss her brief involvement with this circle, although she mentions some of the individuals. For example, she was charmed by Margaret Anderson, editor of the *Little Review*, and Robert Henri painted her portrait. In Provincetown, Massachusetts, summer headquarters for this group and for the famous Provincetown Players, Goldman met feminist authors Susan Glaspell and Neith Boyce. Glaspell wrote of rebellious heroines who either defied convention or died trying; Boyce's heroines suffered desperately in conventional marriages.

Goldman may have found these Bohemians attractive primarily as American "bourgeoisie" worth educating. But she did share their belief that art should serve the cause of political revolution, as dramatized, for example, by the pageant staged by John Reed in 1913 at Madison Square Garden to raise funds for an IWW strike in Paterson, New Jersey. The cast included 1,200 strikers as well as Haywood and Flynn. The pageant was an artistic success but a financial and political failure. The strike was lost.

Nevertheless, the pageant was Goldman's own theory of the drama put into practice. Goldman believed, as did Dostoyevski, Emerson, Whitman, and Ibsen, that the purpose of all art was to express "spiritual and social revolt." Because theater is enjoyed by the masses, Goldman argued, it "is the dynamite which undermines superstition, shakes the social pillars, and prepares men and women for the reconstruction." She had lectured on European drama for some years, and in 1914 the lectures were collected and published under the title *The Social Significance of the Modern Drama*. Like her magazine, *Mother Earth*, the lectures were intended to introduce Americans to European culture. Goldman praised Ibsen ("uncompromising demolisher of all false idols and dynamiter of all social shams and hypocrisy"), Shaw, Tolstoy, and other European playwrights, but she could find no American playwright to include in the book, nor any representative from the vigorous Yiddish theater.[38]

The lectures, her most successful series of this period, were wonderful vehicles for her ideas about the political purposes of art and the emancipation of women. More important perhaps, in the lectures she found an appropriate vehicle for her most compelling presentation of herself in and out of the lecture hall—that is, as an actress. The lectures were less literary criticisms than dramatic readings. Here—much abbreviated—is a monologue from her talk on Githa Sowerby's *Rutherford and Son*. The heroine, Janet, addresses her father, who has just thrown her out of the house for falling in love with the family servant: "Oh, you've no pity," Goldman (as Janet) declaimed. "I was thirty-six. Gone sour. Nobody's ever come after me. Not even when I was young. You took care o' that. Half of my life was gone, well-nigh all of it that mattered. . . . Martin loves me honest. Don't you come near! . . . You think that I'm sorry that you've found out—you think you've done for me when you use shameful words on me and turn me out of your house."[39] During the performances Goldman read all the parts, male and female, and it is likely that her audiences came just to hear her one-woman productions. Frederic Howe, for example, recognized and appreciated her dramatic presence: "She presented her ideas with a brutal frankness and disregard for conventions that suggested the advocacy of force. Had she been staged in some more conventional activity, she might easily have been recognized as a remarkable person. She was an excellent dramatic critic and gave lectures in up-town halls before sympathetic audiences. . . . Tolerant of people, but intolerant of institutions, she denounced the latter unsparingly, and dramatized her own radicalism."[40]

Goldman was a good enough performer that she was offered an engagement at a vaudeville house owned by Oscar Hammerstein. Thinking that she might reach a larger audience, she visited the theater. She turned Hammerstein down, however, when she discovered that she would only have ten minutes for her act, "before the high kicker or after the trained dogs."[41] So Goldman remained a one-woman show primarily for the American middle class, separated during this period from most of her fellow anarchists, and from the immigrant working class that had been her first audience, by her interest in culture and women's issues.

The Greenwich Village women proudly called themselves "feminists," a term popularized by Heterodoxy, a group organized in 1912 by Howe's wife, Marie Jenny Howe, that sponsored meetings and lectures on feminism by noted liberals and leftists. Some feminists were suffragists as well, but feminism meant more than the vote or equal economic opportunities. Like Goldman, the feminists defined emancipation as individual, and especially sexual, freedom.[42] They had read Freud on the dangers of repressing sexuality and Havelock Ellis and Edward Carpenter on the joys of expressing it. Some of the group were conventionally married. Others lived with men to whom they were not married. A few, like Neith Boyce, did not take their husband's name.

To these young women, Goldman *was* the political and cultural vanguard. She had heard Freud in Vienna before most Americans had heard of him. She had lectured on "the new woman" in the 1890s before most Americans knew there was one. She was herself the quintessential new woman: she drank, she smoked, she was single but not celibate. She lived her life, according to Margaret Anderson, in "the great style."[43] Feminists applauded as Nora slammed the door shut on her "doll's house," and cheered at Goldman's assessment of the liberated heroine of Stanley Houghton's play, *Hindle Wakes*: "Woman's virtue . . . is the last fetish which even so-called liberal-minded people refuse to destroy. . . . It is beginning to be felt in ever-growing circles that love is its own justification, requiring no sanction of either religion or law. The revolutionary idea, however, that woman may, even as man, follow the urge of her nature, has never before been so sincerely and radically expressed."[44]

Goldman sometimes referred to suffragists as "feminists" (as in "The Follies of Feminism," an attack on the suffrage movement),[45] but she appreciated the young women's version of rebellion, which was much like her own, and she was encouraged by their "reaction against conventions and narrow moral ties" and "the scores of women who wish to live their lives."[46]

Many feminists and leftists joined Goldman in her fight to legalize birth control. The sale, manufacture, and distribution of contraceptive devices, or the dissemination of information about those devices, were prohibited in 1873 by the Comstock Act. The law was named after Anthony Comstock, postmaster general and the law's chief enforcement agent. The law's definition of contraceptive materials as obscene, the last gasp of high Victorianism in sexual mores, was in part an attempt to reverse a declining birthrate among middle-class white Americans by ending the legal sale of douches, condoms, and sponges used for contraceptive purposes.

Most Americans still believed, or said they believed, that the sole purpose of sexual intercourse was propagation and that to separate the two was immoral. Although some clearly did use contraceptive devices, most probably limited family size by abstaining from sex or by relying on male continence. Feminists like Charlotte Perkins Gilman, who feared that legal contraceptives would simply make it easier for men to sexually exploit women, supported voluntary motherhood: a woman's right to control her own body and to refuse her husband, not the right to use birth control devices.

The first challenges to the Comstock Act came from American anarchists and free-lovers. First to go to prison for disseminating information about contraception was free-thinker Ezra Heywood. Although Heywood's preferred methods of contraception were male continence and the rhythm method, he did publish in his journal, *Cupid's Yokes*, information about "unnatural" means of birth control such as sponges and condoms. He was arrested in 1877 by Comstock himself and received a two-year jail sentence. Heywood was arrested four more times but not convicted again until 1890, this time for publishing an article about oral sex. Moses Harman served his first jail term in 1896 for having published a decade earlier a letter about spousal rape, and his second jail sentence in 1906, when he was elderly and in poor health. Neither of Harman's convictions directly involved the dissemination of information about birth control, but both were designed to stifle one of its foremost advocates.[47]

By the 1910s the cause of legal birth control gained momentum from two sources: growing public support from activists on the left and the realities of changing sexual behavior of the middle class. Although the twentieth century's first "sexual revolution" is generally dated from the 1920s, it was probably well under way in the previous decade. Both qualitative and quantitative evidence indicate that the sexual attitudes and behaviors of middle-class women became significantly more liberal during this period, making more desirable the availability of birth control devices. Goldman and the Greenwich Village feminists may have been in the sexual vanguard, but not by much. They were, however, in the vanguard of the battle for legal birth control. Goldman was only the best known in a group that included Flynn, Stokes, O'Hare, Eastman, Dell, Debs, Tresca, and Margaret Sanger, as well as countless other lesser known liberals and leftists.

Goldman found the legal prohibitions against the sale and manufacture of birth control extraordinarily offensive to her anarchist principles. The Comstock law, for example, violated freedom of speech, for which she and others had long fought. Comstock had held up the mailing of a 1909 issue of *Mother Earth* because it carried an article on prostitution. A lecture on birth control, therefore, was an effective use of the anarchist strategy of direct action—that is, deliberate violation of an unjust law. Goldman also found sound economic and social reasons for legal birth control. In her pamphlet, *Why and How the Poor Should Not Have So Many Children,* she argued that superfluous children created poverty for parents and wealth for exploitative capitalists. Her arguments along these lines occasionally smacked of elitism and eugenics: "Indiscriminate and incessant breeding" produces "defective, crippled, and unfortunate children," she wrote in *Mother Earth.*[48] "[M]otherhood is today a sickly tree setting forth diseased branches."[49]

Goldman's demands for free love, the key to women's emancipation, were meaningless if a woman was not free to use contraceptive devices to avoid pregnancy. Goldman had early decided against biological motherhood for herself, although her references to her adult male lovers as "boys" or to *Mother Earth* as her "child" suggest that the maternal role was a congenial one for her. Her drama lectures often underscored the point that motherhood must be freely chosen: "woman must be given means to prevent conception of undesired and unloved children. . . . [S]he must become free and strong to choose the father of her child and to decide the number of children she is to bring into the world, and under what conditions. That is the only kind of motherhood which can endure."[50]

Frequent pregnancies also endangered a woman's health. In addition, the distribution of birth control information would prevent the last and worst alternative to an unwanted child, abortion. Abortions were, of course, illegal, and in any case Goldman, like most other Americans, opposed them. "It is a public secret," she wrote in *Mother Earth*, "that thousands of such operations are performed every year and that many of them result in death for the woman."[51]

Last but by no means least, public advocacy of birth control was good box office. A lecture on birth control almost guaranteed a large audience, if only because there was the real possibility that the speaker might be arrested. On Goldman's 1915–16 tour, Reitman concluded that "the Birth Control meetings were the largest and provoked the greatest interest."[52] Large audiences also meant good sales of the anarchist literature Goldman peddled.

Goldman reluctantly shared the birth control spotlight with Margaret Sanger, who is usually given credit for getting birth control legalized in the United States. Like Goldman, Sanger endorsed birth control for both personal and political reasons. Her own mother had died young, ill and worn out by 11 pregnancies. Sanger worked as a public-health nurse for immigrant women, whose inability to control their own fertility created misery and, all too often, death by abortion. A member of the Greenwich Village circle, Sanger was first a Socialist and then an IWW organizer, partipating in the strikes at Lawrence and Paterson. Sanger learned about birth control techniques in France, and after her return to the United States in 1914, she began to publish her own magazine, *The Woman Rebel*, which supported socialism, feminism, and birth control. The U.S. Post Office promptly denied her a mailing permit, and Sanger was indicted for violating the Comstock Act. She fled the country, but her husband, William, was arrested in 1915 for giving an undercover policeman her pamphlet, *Family Limitation*, which detailed contraceptive methods. Hundreds of copies had also been distributed by the Wobblies and by Goldman.

Goldman dated her own interest in birth control from the Neo-Malthusian Conference in Paris in 1900, and she had added the subject to her lecture list soon after. Goldman did not discuss methods of family limitation, however. Given her celebrity and the problems she already had with law enforcement officials, she would surely been jailed—and for speaking on an issue that she did not consider of great importance. Only after Sanger's censorship did Goldman decide that "I must either stop lecturing on the subject or do it practical justice. I felt that I must share with [the Sangers] the consequences of the birth control issue."[53]

In *Living My Life*, Goldman gave credit to Harman and Heywood for their pioneering work in birth control and then credit to Sanger as "the only woman in America in recent years to give information to women on birth control."[54] But although the two women often presented a united front, there was friction and rivalry between them. In the April 1915 *Mother Earth*, for example, Sanger criticized Goldman for not supporting her quickly enough after *The Woman Rebel* was banned; Goldman responded that her magazine's issues had already been committed at the time, but that she herself had mentioned Sanger's legal battle to her lecture audiences. "Under the circumstances," Goldman condescended, "it seems very unfair on the part of our comrade to accuse MOTHER EARTH of indifference. But then it is human to feel neglected when one faces one's first great battle with the powers that be, in behalf of an unpopular cause."[55] Subsequent issues of *Mother Earth* did raise funds for the Sangers' legal defense. In Margaret Sanger's autobiography, written in 1938, after she and her cause had become respectable, she charged that Goldman had "belatedly advocated birth control, not to further it but strategically to utilize in [her] own program of anarchism the publicity value it had achieved." Goldman, for her part, claimed Sanger had begun her work at the *Mother Earth* offices.[56]

Remembering her experiences as a midwife, Goldman resolved early on to use her Yiddish meetings to get contraceptive information to her former patients on the Lower East Side. Birth control, however, turned out to have middle-class rather than working-class appeal, and her talks on birth control, like those on drama, attracted the liberal intelligentsia—at the New York Sunrise Club in 1915, for example, or at her own Sunday meetings, often attended by Columbia University students.

Because the Comstock Act was not uniformly enforced, Goldman spoke freely on birth control in most cities. In February 1916, however, she finally was arrested in New York City, generating a special issue of *Mother Earth* in April that dealt almost exclusively with birth control. The magazine carried an appeal from Goldman for funds for her own legal fees; in pointed contrast, the same issue carried a letter from Sanger, who had been arrested but whose case had been dismissed, in which she explained that her goal was to change the law, not go to jail.[57]

Supporters held two meetings to protest Goldman's arrest, one at Carnegie Hall and the second at the Brevoort Hotel. Present were some of her allies from the free-speech movement: some single taxers, some fellow leftists, including Stokes, and cultural radicals like Reed, Henri, and John Sloan. At Carnegie Hall, Stokes engaged in some direct action herself, passing out typewritten sheets of information on birth control.

Goldman's trial was a public spectacle, "'a play, with Emma Goldman in the leading role.'"[58] She spoke dramatically for an hour in her own defense but concluded, in conservative fashion, that legal birth control meant "healthy motherhood and happy childlife."[59] The judge was not persuaded. Since Goldman refused to pay the fine, she went to the Queens County jail for 15 days. She was arrested for another speech shortly after her release, but was acquitted.

Reitman was not so lucky. He got 60 days in the Queens County jail, and six months and a $1,000 fine in Cleveland for public lectures on birth control. The February 1917 issue of *Mother Earth* carried a list of the fines and jail sentences served by the movement's supporters, including single taxer Bolton Hall, Socialist and feminist Jessie Ashley, and both Sangers, as well as activists from Portland, Oregon, and San Francisco.[60]

By this time there was considerable grass-roots support for legalizing birth control, thanks in part to Goldman. But by this time too, Goldman had turned her interests to the imminent entrance of the United States into World War I. Sanger, however, remained committed to the birth control movement, and so the ultimate triumph of its legalization probably belongs more to her. She was arrested in 1916 for opening a birth control clinic and spent 30 days in jail. Sanger's politics and strategies became more conservative in the 1920s, however, and she accepted court rulings that birth control information could be dispensed only by doctors and only to married women. Her American Birth Control League was renamed the Planned Parenthood Federation of America in 1942.

In 1915 Jane Addams, believing that mothers had a special responsibility for peace, helped to found the Women's Peace Party. Other founding members included suffrage leader Carrie Chapman Catt, feminist theoretician Charlotte Perkins Gilman, and settlement worker Lillian Wald. When party delegates petitioned European statesmen to end the conflict, Goldman wrote: "They persist in a sentimental plea to the very forces that make for war in behalf of peace. . . . Why, it is like seeing the Devil at his grandmother's court."[61] This distrust of the political system distanced Goldman from Progressive reformism and even from many radical women—O'Hare, Flynn, and Stokes, for example—who were enthusiastic suffragists. Yet they, and many other women on the left, joined Goldman as she waged her own war for women's sexual and psychological liberation.

And despite her antipathy to suffrage, Goldman found herself sympathizing with the suffragists picketing the White House to dramatize the hypocrisy of a "war to make the world safe for democracy" when American women could not vote. In an August 1917 editorial in *Mother Earth*, Goldman wrote approvingly, "The direct action of the militant suffragists is sure to bring results more quickly for their cause, as it ever does. Their bravery and devotion to their ideal invests it with a dignity no amount of lady-like lobbying, political wire-pulling, or indirect methods could accomplish."[62]

Many of these militant suffragists would soon go to jail, victims of wartime hysteria. Goldman would follow.

5

ENEMY OF THE STATE: THE REPRESSION OF THE LEFT, 1916–1919

The United States' entrance into World War I created a climate in which the federal government finally got its wish—to get Goldman. She was first jailed for attacking conscription and then deported for being an anarchist. Hundreds of other political dissidents also felt the wrath of the Wilson administration. Goldman was only the most famous of those sent into exile.

Goldman probably met Frederic C. Howe during her Greenwich Village days. He remembered her in his autobiography although she did not mention him in hers. Both a scholar and practicing politician, the reformer Howe was then director of the People's Institute, which sponsored a wide variety of liberal educational programs. In 1914, however, Howe was appointed United States Commissioner of Immigration in New York by his former colleague at Johns Hopkins University, then-president of the United States Woodrow Wilson. Howe presided over Ellis Island for the next five years, watching the federal government deport aliens and persecute citizens who opposed Wilson's foreign policy. In the beginning, Howe wrote, "I refused to believe that we were a hysterical people; that civil liberties should be thrown to the winds. But in this struggle there was no one to lean on; there was no support from Washington, no interest on the part of the press. The whole country was swept by emotional excesses." Howe himself was accused of being "red" simply for trying to protect the alien deportees in his charge. He resigned his federal post in 1919, disillusioned, embittered, and physically ill. A long-time advocate of minimal government, Howe became more convinced than ever of the dangers of a powerful state: "The Department of Justice, the Department of Labor, and Congress not only failed to protest against hysteria, they encouraged these excesses; the state not only abandoned the liberty which it should have protected, it lent itself to the stamping out of individualism and freedom."[1] Howe later overcame his disillusionment and took a position in the U.S. Department of Agriculture during the New Deal, but the anguish of this once-optimistic Progressive was a telling comment on the growing repressiveness of the federal government.

Howe dated the hysteria from 1914 and the outbreak of war in Europe between the Allied powers—Great Britain, France, Russia—and the Central Powers—Germany and Austria. At first the United States remained neutral. Neutrality allowed the country to trade with belligerent nations without military or diplomatic commitments to either side. In addition, the administration feared that the millions of new immigrants, many from the belligerent nations, might replicate in urban neighborhoods—around Hull House or in New York's Lower East Side, for example—the military conflict abroad or might commit subversion and espionage against the United States. Wilson thus urged Americans to be neutral in thought as well as in deed.

There was also substantial opposition to war from the several peace organizations that had been formed in the aftermath of the Spanish-American War, and which grew in the years after 1914. Some of these respectable, even conservative, groups of lawyers, educators, and businesspeople hoped that international arbitration or world federation would make warfare unnecessary. The World Peace Foundation and the Carnegie Endowment for International Peace represented this thrust of the peace movement. The peace movement also drew strength from women's organizations. In 1914 suffragists, social workers, and others organized a Peace Parade in New York City that brought out 1,400 women dressed in mourning to protest the outbreak of the conflict in Europe. Jane Addams's Women's Peace Party built on this activism, and by 1916 its initial membership of 2,000 had grown to 25,000. Also in 1916, settlement house workers, including Lillian Wald, established the American Union Against Militarism. The Union was instrumental in halting American military intervention in Mexico, which had been prompted by a series of revolutions and political upheavals there.

Several churches, including Quakers, Mennonites, and Brethren, had historically taken pacifist positions, and from these churches came most of the 56,800 men who received conscientious objector status when Americans did enter the fighting, for religious scruples against war were the only legally acceptable grounds for refusing military service. In 1915 Protestant clergymen and laymen formed an American branch of the Fellowship of Reconciliation, which was first organized in England.

In fact, on the whole the American public did not support military intervention. The Wilson administration had launched a military preparedness campaign in 1915, and Congress voted to enlarge the armed forces. Nevertheless, Wilson's 1916 re-election campaign slogan, "He Kept Us Out of War," had great appeal to voters. On 2 April 1917, however, angered by repeated German submarine attacks on American ships and anxious to have a significant role in making the peace, Wilson asked Congress to declare war on Germany. Congress did so, but 6 senators and 50 members of the House voted no, including the first woman ever elected to Congress, Jeanette Rankin.

Unlike Howe, Goldman had had no illusions about government and had always distrusted the compelling appeal of the nation-state. She was not surprised that European Socialists sided with their countries rather than with the international working class when war broke out in 1914, but she was greatly disappointed when her mentor Kropotkin supported the Allies. In February and March of 1915, *Mother Earth* published his earlier essay, "Capitalism and War," which Goldman felt refuted Kropotkin's current position. At the other extreme from Kropotkin, a small group of anarchists led by Domela Nieuwenhuis of The Netherlands were absolute pacifists, opposed to this and all wars.

Most anarchists, however, probably supported the "International Anarchist Manifesto on the War," published in the May *Mother Earth*, which opposed this particular war. Wars are the inevitable products of the State, the manifesto argued, whether the State was the absolutism of Russia or the democratic constitutionalism of England. These anarchists, therefore, were opposed to wars fought by one nation against another, or "all wars between peoples." But they did support war as a revolutionary strategy, the "one war of liberation: that which in all countries is waged by the oppressed against the oppressors, by the exploited against the exploiters." The manifesto urged anarchists to "foment insurrection and organize the revolution [which will] put an end to all social wrongs."[2]

As the American military buildup continued, Goldman must have seen as prophetic an essay on "Patriotism," which she had published in 1910. Patriotism, she wrote, was simply an excuse for government to build huge armies and navies for which the workingman had to pay: "The contention that a standing army and navy is the best security of peace is about as logical as the claim that the most peaceful citizen is he who goes about heavily armed."[3] Wilson's preparedness campaign, therefore, was anathema to her. The December 1915 Mother Earth carried a scathing, sarcastic denunciation of federal policy, "Preparedness: The Road to Universal Slaughter." "Ammunition!" Goldman wrote, "Ammunition! O, Lord, thou who rulest heaven and earth, thou God of love, of mercy and of justice, provide us with enough ammunition to destroy our enemy." The essay did not condemn violence, since Goldman still accepted violence that accompanied a social revolution. But this capitalist war, she maintained, was being fought to enrich the "privileged few and help them to subdue, to enslave and crush labor." Preparedness would take the United States into war, not keep it out. And such a war, she warned, with her American audience in mind, would betray "the fundamental principles of real Americanism, of the kind of Americanism that Jefferson had in mind when he said that the best government is that which governs least; the kind of America that David Thoreau worked for when he proclaimed that the best government is the one that doesn't govern at all."[4] She gave this lecture on preparedness over and over in 1916.

With Berkman, Goldman also became involved in the most celebrated labor case of the decade, triggered inadvertently by the preparedness campaign: the case of Tom Mooney. On 22 July 1916, at a San Francisco "Preparedness Day" parade, a bomb exploded, killing several people. Mooney, a union organizer sometimes associated with the IWW, was charged with murder, as were his wife and three comrades in the labor movement. Goldman was in San Francisco that Saturday and fortunately for her, had just postponed her own antipreparedness lecture. The headlines screamed "Anarchist Bomb" anyway, and local police immediately suspected Goldman and Berkman, especially after finding a letter from Goldman among the possessions of one of the accused.

Union members had been warned not to march in the parade because it was sponsored by local supporters of the open shop, and unions were reluctant to come to Mooney's defense. Berkman was not. He knew

Mooney and the others and was convinced of their innocence. Predictably, he saw ominous parallels between Mooney's case and the Haymarket trials. Both, he thought, were attempts to destroy the labor movement. He and Goldman quickly organized a defense fund for the accused and used the columns of his new weekly, *The Blast,* for fundraising and publicity. Police immediately ransacked *The Blast*'s office and briefly took Berkman into custody. Throughout Mooney's trial, the prosecutor tried to connect Mooney with Berkman through news items planted in the papers and through cross-examinations of the defendants in the courtroom. After months of this harassment, Berkman had to move the magazine's office to New York in the spring of 1917.

Berkman's long-standing ties with labor stood him in good stead in the Mooney defense. Berkman helped to organize the International Workers' Defense League of San Francisco, he found the defendants a prominent and able lawyer, and he rallied support from the Jewish unions in New York. The case was such an obvious frame-up that even AFL-affiliated unions finally contributed money. Responding to what had become an international incident and to the discovery of irregularities by a federal investigation of the trial, President Wilson urged a new trial. This was denied by the California governor. Mooney was sentenced to be hanged, but his execution was delayed, and in 1918 his sentence was commuted to life imprisonment. (He was released in 1939.)

In March 1917, as the United States drew closer to intervention, Goldman argued that only direct action by the workers could end the war. "The workers, they alone, can avert the impending war; in fact, all wars, if they will refuse to be a party to them. The determined antimilitarist is the only pacifist. . . . [H]e refuses to be ordered to kill his brothers. His slogan is: 'I will not kill, nor will I lend myself to be killed.'"[5] Two months later she tried to put the principle of direct action into practice. As Congress debated the Conscription, or Selective Service Act, she and Berkman organized the No-Conscription League. The league held its first meeting at the Harlem River Casino on 18 May, the twelfth anniversary of Berkman's release from the Western Penitentiary. Speakers representing several left-wing perspectives denounced the conscription bill before a huge crowd of almost ten thousand—including a government stenographer, whose transcript of their speeches would send Goldman and Berkman to jail.

That evening the Selective Service Act passed, requiring that men between the ages of 20 and 30 register for military service on June 4. The black borders on the cover of the June 1917 *Mother Earth* framed this epitaph, "In Memoriam: American Democracy." The No-Conscription League's purpose was described inside: to encourage "conscientious objectors to affirm their liberty of conscience and to translate their objection to human slaughter by refusing to participate in the killing of their fellow men." The league was described as being opposed not to war but to militarization. Goldman later wrote, and would also contend in court, that the league did not advise men on whether or not to enlist, because that would be contrary to anarchist beliefs. "We will resist conscription [not war] by every means in our power," the article concluded, "and we will sustain those who . . . refuse to be conscripted."[6] It seems unlikely, however, that a committed conscientious objector would seek out this league for political advice or moral guidance, since Goldman and Berkman, who supported wars of revolution, were not pacifists themselves.

The great majority of American men who were required to register did so, but widespread opposition to conscription and the war persisted. Local newspapers reported that significant numbers of men simply did not turn up at registration centers; many filed exemption claims; in a few cities, draft lists were stolen. There were scattered incidents of armed resistance in Texas and Oklahoma, where tenant farmers mounted the short-lived Green Corn Rebellion against military service.[7]

In this context, the No-Conscription League struck a responsive chord, and the *Mother Earth* office was filled with men asking for advice about registration. Branches of the No-Conscription League were formed in other cities. As they distributed handbills announcing an antidraft meeting to be held 4 June, several young men, including some anarchists, were arrested and charged with conspiring to advise men not to register. Goldman and Berkman wrote to the New York district attorney, insisting that they take responsibility since they had written the handbill. The district attorney did not respond, and the boys received heavy fines and jail sentences, an ominous portent of things to come.

At the 4 June meeting at Hunt's Point Palace, as officials of the U.S. Department of Justice and the New York Anarchist Squad looked on, sailors and soldiers charged the platform where Berkman stood. As Berkman's supporters joined the battle, Goldman rushed to the stage, grabbed the microphone, and got control of the crowd, narrowly averting a riot. Ten days later at a meeting in the Jewish Forward Hall, police arrested every man in the audience who could not produce a draft card. Goldman and Berkman decided that anticonscription lectures had become too risky and that they should concentrate on the printed word.

The following day, however, 15 June, they were both arrested by a United States Marshal, taken to the Tombs prison, and charged with conspiracy to prevent draft registration. Bond was set at $25,000 each. The two were held incommunicado for several days while the offices of *Mother Earth* and *The Blast* were searched and their contents confiscated. A federal grand jury indicted them on 21 June. By 25 June their attorney, Harry Weinberger, and Berkman's comrade, Eleanor Fitzgerald, raised the huge cash bail of $50,000 for their release. Their trial was set for 27 June, Goldman's forty-eighth birthday. Although the two seasoned revolutionaries obviously were not responsible for the draft evasion and resistance that was occurring nationwide, they were as always visible, vulnerable, and early targets for the federal government.

Goldman and Berkman at first reasoned that, as anarchists, they should ignore the indictment. When the judge warned that they would be defended by a court-appointed lawyer, however, the two decided to argue their own cases, hoping to use their trial as publicity for their views. Both were able debaters, and Berkman knew about courtrooms and the law from his long stretch at the Western Penitentiary. John Reed and journalist-muckraker Lincoln Steffens testified in their defense, and Weinberger gave them legal advice.

The prosecution attempted to show first that the two had urged men not to register for the draft, pointing to the No-Conscription League statement. In their own defense Goldman and Berkman argued that the league did not advise men not to register. This was technically true, since presumably "conscientious objectors" were already determined not to fight: the league simply affirmed what the men had already decided for themselves. In any case, the two argued, the Selective Service Act was signed into law two hours after their meeting had begun.

Much of the trial, however, revolved around the prosecution's charge that the two had advocated violence at the May 18 meeting. The prosecution's evidence was an unreliable stenographic report transcribed by a government agent at the Harlem River Casino. Since Goldman and Berkman's stenographer had not been present, they could not present their own version of what had been said. The prosecution also introduced as evidence the July 1914 issue of *Mother Earth*, which contained the "prattle about force and dynamite." The charge was not relevant to the indictment, and witnesses for the defense argued that no violence was advocated at the meeting. The introduction of the issue, however, was a predictable and logical ploy for the prosecution. Nobody had forgotten Homestead in 1892, and Berkman had never repudiated violence as a political strategy. Nor did he now. Although he and Goldman had publicly criticized violence used by the state in this war or against labor on any number of occasions, Berkman still believed that violence used by the working class to bring about "a war of liberation" was justifiable. In his closing argument to the jury, Berkman tried to explain his position. "[E]ach and every one of you," he said, "is a law-abiding, peaceful citizen, yet you support a war which is violent. We all believe in violence, and we all disbelieve in violence; it all depends upon the circumstances. I do not support this war," he continued, but "I believe in war under certain circumstances."[8] The jury could imagine all too well what circumstances those might be.

Goldman's parting words "on the stage set for the last act of the tragicomedy" expressed both her alienation from and love for her adopted homeland.[9] There was the usual sarcasm: "The methods employed by [the] Marshall and his hosts of heroic warriors were sensational enough to satisfy the famous circus men, Barnum & Bailey." There was the usual biting criticism: "There is not one single point to sustain the indictment for conspiracy or to prove the overt acts we are supposed to have comitted. . . . [We] refuse to be tried on a trumped-up charge, or to be convicted by perjured testimony, merely because we are Anarchists and hated by the class whom we have openly fought for many years." Then, likening herself and Berkman to the revolutionaries of the United States, France, and Russia, she provided her own eloquent definition of patriotism: "Our patriotism is that of the man who loves a woman with open eyes. He is enchanted by her beauty, yet he sees her faults. So we, too, who know America, love her beauty, her richness, her great possibilities. . . . [A]bove all do we love the people that have produced her wealth, her artists who have created beauty, her great apostles who dream and work for liberty—but with the same passionate emotion we hate her superficiality, her cant, her corruption, her mad, unscrupulous worship at the altar of the Golden Calf." In conclusion, Goldman asked the impossible: that the jury forget the fact of their anarchism and declare them not guilty on the strength of the evidence presented.[10]

The jury needed only 39 minutes to find them guilty. Both got the maximum sentence: two years in prison and a $10,000 fine. Federal Judge Julius Mayer also requested that immigration authorities receive the record of the trial and his recommendation that Goldman and Berkman be deported. "We have no place in this country," the judge concluded, "for those who express the view that the law may be disobeyed in accordance with the choice of an individual."[11] Both were taken immediately to prison, Berkman to the federal penitentiary at Atlanta and Goldman to the Missouri State Prison in Jefferson City because there was no federal prison for women.

Goldman and Berkman were among the first victims of the wartime repression of the left; they were by no means the last. Most public opposition to American intervention had ended after Congress declared war on Germany in April 1917. Congressional opponents generally fell into line behind the Wilson administration. The Women's Peace party and the American Union Against Militarism split over the issue, and many members of both supported the war. (The Women's Peace party became the Women's International League for Peace and Freedom after the war, and one segment of the American Union Against Militarism was the forerunner of the American Civil Liberties Union.) Addams did not endorse the military effort but did not actively oppose it either. Continued resistance came almost exclusively from the hard-core pacifists of the peace churches and the Fellowship of Reconciliation and from the political left.

The war became a pretext for unofficial and official harassment of dissidents and deviants of all kinds. Aliens, especially German-Americans, were intimidated and beaten on the job and on the street. The armed services attempted to force conscientious objectors to bear arms; recalcitrant men who refused to obey orders in military camps were court-martialed and imprisoned, some for lengthy terms. The federal Creel Committee on Public Information, with the help of prominent historians, fed war propaganda to newspapers and movies. Colleges and universities fired faculty members who spoke against the war. Militant suffragists picketing the White House were thrown into prison.

The chief target of repression, however, was the left. The chief vehicle was the Espionage Act, passed 15 June 1917. The act made it illegal to make "false statements" in order to interfere with the military or to obstruct the draft or military service. The act was revised in 1918 as the Sedition Act, which stiffened the punishments for obstructing the military effort and prohibited "disloyal, scurrilous, or abusive language" about the government, the flag, or the Constitution of the United States.

Unlike their European counterparts, the great majority of American Socialists continued to oppose the war. At an emergency convention in St. Louis on 7 April 1917 the party drafted a manifesto that condemned the war because it enriched capitalists and slaughtered the working class. Kate Richards O'Hare expressed the prevalent sentiment: "I will give my life and the life of my mate, to serve my class, but never with my consent will they be given to add to the profits and protect the stolen wealth of the bankers, food speculators, and ammunition makers."[12] A handful of delegates to the St. Louis convention—including Upton Sinclair, John Spargo, J. G. Phelps Stokes (and briefly his wife Rose), and some trade unionists—disagreed with O'Hare, believing that it was imperative to defeat the German kaiser. But in the early months of the war, the Socialist party became an important center of antiwar activity, and antiwar Socialist candidates for office ran well. Morris Hillquit, running for mayor of New York City, polled three times more votes than he had four years earlier.

Encouraged by the Wilson administration's attitude and legislation, however, vigilantes broke up Socialist meetings and parades. Dozens of Socialist and other left-wing newspapers lost their mailing permits. Goldman's former colleagues from the cultural left, including Max and Crystal Eastman, John Reed, and Floyd Dell, were indicted under the Espionage Act; so were long-time Milwaukee congressman Victor Berger and Rose Pastor Stokes (who had changed her mind). The bookstore owned by SP general secretary Charles T. Schenck was raided, and he was sentenced to six months in jail for possessing an antiwar pamphlet. The resulting Supreme Court decision, *Schenck v. United States,* upheld the constitutionality of the Espionage Act on the grounds that in wartime, freedom of speech could be abridged if it presented a "clear and present danger" to society. Three Ohio SP leaders went to jail. So did O'Hare for giving a speech in North Dakota that denounced the war and the draft.

Although Eugene V. Debs had supported the St. Louis manifesto, he did not publicly criticize American intervention in the war until after O'Hare was arrested and the three Ohioans were jailed. When, in Canton, Ohio, he did condemn both the war and government suppression of free speech, Debs too was arrested. Still denouncing the Espionage Act as "a despotic enactment in flagrant conflict with democratic principles and with the spirit of free institutions," Debs was sentenced to ten years in federal prison.[13] He was sent to the Atlanta penitentiary in April 1919, while Berkman was still there.

The IWW, however, was the most devastated of the left-wing organizations. By 1917 it had gained both martyrs and members. Its most celebrated martyr, musician Joe Hill, was executed in 1915, having been found guilty (possibly rightly) of murder. According to legend his last words were, "Don't mourn for me, organize." Whether in response to this or not, the IWW leadership did decide in 1915 to focus on organizing unions rather than on the propagandizing of the free-speech fights. The IWW's bitter strikes had made it hated and feared by local employers and governments, and the Wobblies now began to interest the federal government. A strike at the Mesabi Range, not called by the IWW but led by Elizabeth Gurley Flynn and Carlo Tresca, was ended by federal mediation. IWW strikes against copper miners in Butte, Montana, and the lumber industry in Washington led governors of several western states to ask for federal assistance. In July 1917, federal troops were sent to Arizona, Montana, Washington, and Oregon, ostensibly to prevent strikes that would hamper the war effort. In August, Frank Little, Wobbly leader and veteran of the Mesabi Range strike, was lynched in Butte.

In September, Little, "now deceased," and 168 other Wobblies were charged under the Espionage Act with conspiring to obstruct the war effort, after the U.S. Department of Justice staged simultaneous raids on IWW headquarters in 45 cities. Prior to American involvement in Europe, the IWW had condemned all wars. After intervention, it did not support the war but it did not oppose conscription, and many Wobblies did register for the draft. Nevertheless, IWW unions posed not only a political but an economic threat, and the federal government set out to destroy the IWW. State governments followed suit with arrests of local Wobblies.

Bill Haywood, who was indicted in September, urged that the Wobblies turn themselves in so their mass trial could be used for propaganda purposes. Flynn and Tresca got their cases separated from the others, and charges against them were eventually dropped. A Chicago federal court, however, found 101 of the Wobblies guilty as charged. Haywood and 14 other leaders were given 20-year sentences and fines of $30,000. The fines handed down totaled $2,500,000, and sentences for some of the Wobbly rank and file ran as high as 10 years.

Despite Goldman's two-year sentence, her initial stay at the Missouri State Prison lasted only two weeks. Weinberger was able to persuade Supreme Court Justice Louis Brandeis to approve an application for an appeal of their case and to release both Goldman and Berkman on bail. Returning to New York on 10 July 1917, Goldman was held only briefly in the Tombs until she was bailed out by Weinberger, who had raised another $25,000 cash bond. Berkman, however, remained in the Tombs to avoid extradition to California, where local police were still trying to prosecute him in conjunction with Tom Mooney.

Goldman's first task, then, was to arouse public opinion against Berkman's extradition to California, where Berkman might well be railroaded into state prison. She called upon his old friends in the United Hebrew Trades and other trade unions. The Yiddish press, especially *Freie Arbeiter Shtime,* came to his defense, as did the Socialist daily, the *New York Call.* At a fund-raiser for Berkman sponsored by left-wing organizations at the Kessler Theater, Goldman, who had been forbidden to speak by the federal marshal, brought down the house when she appeared on stage with a handkerchief stuffed into her mouth. An unexpected but welcome ally was SP official Hillquit, then in the midst of his campaign for mayor. Hillquit went to the state capital with dozens of labor leaders to plead with the New York governor on Berkman's behalf. (Goldman was grateful but declined the invitation to join Hillquit's campaign.) Russian sailors at Kronstadt, informed of Berkman's plight by returning Russian emigrants, also protested against Berkman's extradition and the imprisonment of Mooney, threatening to take hostage the American ambassador to Russia. This threat compelled President Wilson to urge the New York governor to stave off extradition, and when the California officials could not produce sufficient evidence, Berkman was released from the Tombs on $25,000 bond, which was raised mostly by the Jewish unions.

Like other radical publications, *Mother Earth* had been suppressed, but with financial support from friends, Goldman's niece, Stella Cominsky Ballantine, and Eleanor Fitzgerald began publication of a smaller journal, *Mother Earth Bulletin,* in October 1917, just a month before the Bolshevik Revolution. In December Goldman used the *Bulletin's* pages to applaud the Revolution and the Bolsheviks' withdrawal of Russia from the war: "the Revolution swept Tsarism into the gutter, and dispelled the myth that the Russian people wanted the war, that they were eager to die in the trenches. . . . In one mighty voice the people thundered from every nook and corner of Russia for peace, for fraternization with the people of Germany, and with all their oppressed and disinherited brothers."[14]

Goldman's disagreement with Reitman over the *Bulletin's* contents precipitated the end of their long love affair. Their emotional and political differences had grown greater and greater in the last few years. Goldman had been distressed at Reitman's terror after his near-lynching at San Diego in 1912, but sympathetic. She was less sympathetic when he moved his mother into the best bedroom of their crowded New York apartment, only to move her out again when she complained that she was uncomfortable. Reitman had started a Sunday School class in the *Mother Earth* office, which amused Goldman's fellow atheists and anarchists. As Goldman struggled to rally support for Mooney in the immediate aftermath of the San Francisco explosion, Reitman had begun to complain that he was stifled as her manager, that he had always wanted to write, that Berkman was always more important, and that Goldman would not bear him the child he had always wanted. Reitman brushed aside Goldman's response that he had already deserted one child, declaring that he now had "'a conscious feeling for fatherhood.'"[15] He had continued as her manager, however, and both were soon arrested in the birth control fight. Now, however, Reitman urged that the *Bulletin* not take an antiwar position, fearing that this would endanger its survival and Goldman's tenuous legal position. As Goldman faced federal prison for expressing her opinions on the lecture platform, however, she refused to curtail her speech in the *Bulletin* as Reitman advised. He was correct. A police raid shut down the *Bulletin* in April 1918.

When Goldman and Reitman parted as lovers, he was no longer politically or personally sympathetic or useful to her. Nevertheless Goldman later paid him (and herself) a warm compliment: "His best years, his tremendous zest for work, he had devoted to me. It is not unusual for a woman to do as much for the man she loves. . . . But few men have done so for women."[16] The end of this decade-long relationship left Goldman without a sexual and romantic partner, but their parting also allowed her to draw closer to the political friends and allies, particularly Berkman, who had always found Reitman objectionable.

As they waited for the Supreme Court to hear their appeal, Goldman and Berkman continued their lectures: Berkman on the Mooney case, and Goldman, on the glories of the Bolshevik Revolution. She distributed hundreds of copies of her pamphlet, *The Boylsheviki* [sic] *Revolution: Its Promise and Fulfillment*. The prospect of their imminent imprisonment swelled the crowds at meetings in Chicago and Detroit, although the outraged Daughters of the American Revolution prevented Goldman from speaking in Ann Arbor.

Weinberger appealed their case before the Supreme Court on the grounds that Goldman and Berkman had not engaged in "conspiracy," since their speeches and the organization of the No-Conscription League were public. More significantly, he argued that the Selective Service Act was unconstitutional, a violation of the Thirteenth Amendment's prohibition against servitude, the First Amendment's protections of free speech, and the Fifth Amendment's due process clause. Neither argument succeeded, and the Court upheld the Act. The Court also declined to grant Goldman and Berkman a rehearing.

On 4 February 1918 the two surrendered to federal authorities and returned to prison to complete their sentences. Berkman was an old hand at prison, but although Goldman had often been arrested, she had been imprisoned only three times and for relatively short periods of time: a year at Blackwell's Island in 1893–94 for inciting to riot, 15 days in the Tombs for distributing birth control information, and the two weeks she had already served in Missouri.

The state prison at Jefferson City was more comfortable than the city jail at Blackwell's Island, and Goldman did not have to share a cell. But the prison garb was unattractive and uncomfortable, and the prison food, terrible. Unruly women were punished by flogging or confinement to the "blind cell." The chief hardship, however, was the prison workshop. There inmates hunched over their sewing machines, much as Goldman had in the factories of her adolescence, and stitched clothing that was sold to private corporations. Goldman's stay was made bearable by the friends she made within the prison and the support of friends on the outside. Complaining of excruciating pains in her neck and spine, Goldman was briefly relieved of shop duty and cared for by the prison doctor. It may be that his attentions were encouraged by the prison director, who had long been friends with William Marion Reedy, editor of the St. Louis Mirror and a fan of Goldman's. Goldman received a cell with a window and permission to take three baths a week.

Prison life brought out the best in Goldman. Better educated and better off than the vast majority of inmates, she became their confidante and emissary to prison officials as she tried to make their lives more pleasant. Inmates were not "criminals," she wrote, "but only unfortunates, broken, hapless, and hopeless human beings."[17] Learning that there was no library, she had friends send books and magazines. She shared her abundant food and gifts and "played Santa Claus" on Christmas Eve in 1918. The other women reciprocated, helping her make her quota in the workshop. On her birthday, her "coloured friends," probably the first Black Americans she had ever known well, finished her full complement of jackets so that she could take a holiday.

After the armistice of 11 November 1918, two other political prisoners joined Goldman. The first she identified in her autobiography only as "Ella." This was Ella Antolini, another anarchist sentenced for antiwar activity. Although much younger than Goldman, Antolini was congenial and sympathetic company. She was released after two years. Kate Richards O'Hare entered the Missouri State Prison in April 1919. O'Hare was tall, gray-haired, and, to Goldman, forbidding. "Had we met outside," Goldman admitted, "we should have probably argued furiously and have remained strangers for the rest of our lives." In prison, however, their political differences were much less important than their shared plight. Goldman found O'Hare warm and courageous, sustained by frequent visits from her husband Frank. The publicity his newspaper gave to prison problems brought improvements, including new shower baths and whitewashed walls. (O'Hare later made a career of prison reform.) O'Hare was a good typist and helped Goldman with her extensive correspondence. After her own release, Goldman spoke at a fund-raiser for the still-imprisoned O'Hare, poking good-natured fun at her friend's elaborate coiffure, whose arrangement kept her up late at night. O'Hare, in turn, recalled Goldman's tender and maternal presence. "Thwarted in physical motherhood," O'Hare believed, "she poured out her whole soul in vicarious motherhood of all the sad and sorrowful, the wronged and oppressed, the bitter and rebellious children of men. . . . [T]he women worshipped her with an idolatrous worship."[18] During their imprisonment, the three political exiles became comrades, sharing adjoining cells and their leisure time.

Goldman also had some visitors. Among them was Eleanor Fitzgerald, who had originally joined the *Mother Earth* staff, then gone to San Francisco with Berkman as his helper and companion, and later had briefly managed the *Mother Earth Bulletin*. She brought news of Berkman, whom she had just seen in Atlanta. After the *Mother Earth Bulletin* folded, Fitzgerald went to work for the Provincetown Players; she maintained Goldman's ties to the American avante garde through the 1920s. Agnes Inglis also visited. She had met Goldman in 1914 in Ann Arbor and had often made Goldman's lecture arrangements there and in Detroit. Her friendship with Goldman dismayed and amused her well-to-do, respectable Detroit family. Inglis provided Goldman with funds on several occasions, including bail money in 1917. Goldman paid tribute to Inglis's friendship in *Living My Life*, particularly for sending newspaper clippings and letters so that Goldman could write the autobiography.

Inglis later became the first curator of the Labadie Collection (named after anarchist Joe Labadie) at the University of Michigan, where many archival materials on Goldman are currently stored.

Although her mail was read and censored, comrades and newspapers kept Goldman fully informed of political events on the outside, as the Espionage and Sedition Acts sent Socialists, Wobblies, anarchists, and others to jail nationwide. In August 1918 a group of young Russian-born anarchists, including Jacob Abrams and Mollie Steimer, was arrested for distributing leaflets that called for a general strike and attacked President Wilson for sending American troops into Russia to topple the Bolsheviks. Five of the accused were found guilty of hampering the war effort. Abrams was given 20 years in prison, and Steimer 15. Harry Weinberger argued the Abrams case before a New York federal court, which upheld the conviction. Liberals and radicals supported the appeal to the Supreme Court, but in *Abrams v. United States,* the Court upheld the Sedition Act's restrictions on speech. Abrams and two of the others jumped bail and attempted to escape the country. When they were captured, the three were sent to the Atlanta penitentiary, from which Berkman had just been released. Steimer was sent to Jefferson City in April 1920. All four were deported to Russia in November 1921.

And there were others whose stalwart opposition to the war was reassuring and gratifying to Goldman: Randolph Bourne, whose antiwar essay had been reprinted in *Mother Earth*; the professors James M. Cattell and Henry W. L. Dana, who had been dismissed from Columbia University; and particularly Roger Baldwin. Goldman had been unimpressed at earlier meetings with Baldwin but now found him courageous as he stood trial for attacking the draft. Baldwin would later become the director of the American Civil Liberties Union and a valuable contact for Goldman and Berkman during their exile in the 1920s.

Goldman spent her fiftieth birthday, 27 June 1919, in jail. She was deluged with presents and cards from all across the country; one from New York City bore the signatures of 50 well-wishers. On 28 August 1919 she and Berkman had served out their sentences, four months having been commuted for good behavior. Because they were unable to pay the $20,000 fine, however, both were forced to serve an extra month. "Two months for twenty thousand dollars!" Goldman exclaimed. "When did Sasha and I ever expect to earn so much money in so short a time."[19]

On 28 September 1919, accompanied by her niece Stella, Goldman left Jefferson City—free from prison but with her future uncertain. The Immigration Bureau had required that she post a $15,000 bond while the federal government decided whether to deport her to her homeland Russia. To Stella's dismay, they stopped in Chicago to see Reitman and his new wife and infant. The former lovers were polite, and Reitman would later provide materials for Goldman's autobiography. Her visit with her family in Rochester was far more emotionally wrenching. Sister Helene's son, David Hochstein, had volunteered for the army and died in the line of battle. His death had left his mother physically and mentally destroyed. Goldman invited Helene to live with her in New York, hoping this would help her recovery. Goldman's 81-year-old mother, always shrewd and self-assertive, had become "a veritable autocrat," Goldman reported, as driving a force for Jewish charity perhaps as her daughter was on the Jewish left. Despite the inconvenience and pain that Goldman must have caused her family, Taube was proud of her famous daughter. Told to cut short a speech before a group of local women, Taube once declared, "'The whole United States Government could not stop my daughter Emma Goldman from speaking, and a fine chance you have to make her mother shut up!'"[20]

Berkman was released from the Atlanta prison on the first of October. Seven months in solitary and isolation for protesting prison brutalities had broken his health but not his spirit. He also had to post a $15,000 bond.

Their deportation hearings were scheduled for 27 October. The timing could hardly have been worse, as the country was in the grip of a "red scare." As the cost of living escalated, 4 million workers had taken part in 3,300 strikes from the West to the East coasts. In January 1919 there had been a general strike in Seattle, one of the few in the country's history. In September, 350,000 workers had struck the steel industry. This widespread labor unrest triggered fears that the Bolshevik Revolution had spread to the United States. "For two years," Howe recalled, "we were in a panic of fear over the Red revolutionists, anarchists, and enemies of the Republic who were said to be ready to overthrow the government."[21] In fact, the arrests and jailings of 1919–20 were simply a continuation of the political repression begun by the Espionage and Sedition Acts. When a Radical Division was set up in the Justice Department, its ambitious young director, J. Edgar Hoover, inherited 200,000 cards bearing the names of "ultraradicals." The United States Congress twice denied Socialist Victor Berger the seat to which he had been elected; the New York State legislature denied seats to five Socialist representatives. In Cleveland at a 1919 May Day parade of Socialists and trade unionists protesting Debs's imprisonment, marchers, onlookers, and mounted police battled until 2 people were killed and 40 were injured. On 7 November federal agents raided dozens of meetings where the second anniversary of the Russian Revolution was being celebrated and hauled participants off to jail. Specially targeted by the federal government was the Union of Russian Workers, whose members were mostly unskilled workers—Russian immigrants—anxious to return to their native land.[22] The union's organizer, Bill Shatoff, an anarchist and a Russian immigrant himself, had decided after the October Revolution to take some union members back to Russia to participate in the ongoing battle. While Goldman and Berkman had been out on bail in early 1918, they had been guests of honor at a union dinner.

The anti-Bolshevik frenzy in the United States established a disastrous climate for Goldman and Berkman's deportation hearings. They had both already been the subject of congressional scrutiny. In 1918, the two had been accused of being German spies because of alleged connections to an Indian nationalist, Hay Dayal. After the November Armistice, the Senate Committee investigating the spy charge switched its focus to Bolshevism and published the report *Bolshevik Propaganda* (1919), in which Goldman was prominently featured. After her release from prison, Goldman was the subject of another government publication, *Investigation Activities of the Department of Justice* (1919). Here Hoover had put together a dossier on Goldman that resurrected the old charge that she was responsible for McKinley's assassination. Hoover had been working since August to get Goldman deported under an Immigration Act, passed in October 1918, which provided for the deportation of alien anarchists or disbelievers in organized government "any time after entry."[23]

Berkman had never become an American citizen, so his deportation was a foregone conclusion. While still in prison, he had refused to answer the immigration officials' questions about his politics, instead issuing an eloquent defense of freedom of speech: "I deny the right of anyone—individually or collectively—to set up an inquisition of thought. Thought is, or should be, free. . . . Free thought, necessarily involving freedom of speech and press, I may tersely define thus: no opinion a law—no opinion a crime. For the government to attempt to control thought, to prescribe certain opinions or proscribe others, is the height of despotism."[24]

Goldman, on the other hand, was determined to expose the "shady methods" by which the federal government had revoked Kersner's citizenship and her own. She was also determined to have the last word.

This took the form of a written statement in which she quite accurately placed her own deportation in a broader context. The purpose of the deportation hearing, she argued, was to stifle "the voice of the people, to muzzle every aspiration of labor. . . . With all the power and intensity of my being I protest against the conspiracy of imperialist capitalism against the life and the liberty of the American people."[25]

As the Immigration Board pondered, Goldman and Berkman made one last tour to Chicago and Detroit. Thousands, including federal agents, crowded into halls to hear them defend the Bolshevik Revolution. Goldman's American middle-class friends did not desert her. Aline Barnsdale, already a financial contributor to Mooney's defense, gave her a check for $5,000. Goldman was overwhelmed with gratitude. "To be driven out of the land I had called my own, where I had toiled and suffered for years, was not a cheerful prospect. But to come to other shores penniless and without the hope of immediate adjustment was for me a calamity indeed," Goldman later wrote. Her greatest fear—that she would become dependent on others—was allayed.[26]

On 3 December a telegram from Weinberger warned that Goldman and Berkman must surrender to federal authorities in two days. Berkman having gone on ahead, Goldman took a fast train from Chicago to New York and, with Berkman, a taxi to Ellis Island. She was dismayed to discover that her deportation writ had been signed by a single-taxer and former comrade in the free-speech fight, Louis Post, then Assistant Secretary of Labor.

Weinberger was determined to fight the deportation. He advised Goldman not to accept an offer of marriage from fellow anarchist Harry Kelly, which would have given her citizenship and allowed her to escape deportation. Weinberger then argued—incorrectly and unsuccessfully—that the revocation of Kersner's citizenship was null and void because Kersner was already dead in 1908. When this tactic failed, Judge Mayer allowed Weinberger time to appeal to the Supreme Court for a writ of error.

Goldman and Berkman meanwhile collaborated on a pamphlet describing the deplorable conditions at Ellis Island, worsened by the arrival of hundreds of other deportees who were charged with being politically or otherwise undesirable. Howe, then on the verge of his resignation, described the scene: "Men and women were herded into Ellis Island. They were brought under guards and in special trains with instructions to get them away from the country with as little delay as possible. Most of the aliens had been picked up in raids on labor headquarters; they had been given a drumhead trial by an inspector, with no chance for defense; they were held incommunicado and often were not permitted to see either friends or attorneys."[27] Goldman's two young roommates on the Island, for example, had been in the United States for some years but were not American citizens. They were not charged with any crime and were being deported to Russia although they knew no one there.

Weinberger's motion for a writ of error was denied, as was his motion to have Berkman's deportation delayed. Perhaps chivalrous, perhaps desirous of finally setting out on his own, Berkman urged Goldman to stay in the United States to propagandize for the revolution in Russia. But she decided to go with him: "He had come into my life with my spiritual awakening, he had grown into my very being, and his long Golgotha would forever remain our common bond. He had been my comrade, friend, and co-worker through a period of thirty years; it was unthinkable that he should join the Revolution and I remain behind."[28]

Hastily the two tried to provide for the needs of other deportees, rallying friends to supply funds and clothing. Goldman tried to control her grief at being parted from many comrades and family members, especially Helene, whom she believed she would never see again. (Helene died in February 1920.) Goldman caustically told the ever-present reporters that once in Russia, she would organize a Society of Russian Friends of American Freedom.[29] The deportees were assured that they would be given time to have their cases reviewed. But early on the morning of 21 December 1919, Goldman and 249 others were awakened and marched onto the aging *Buford*, which was to take them to Russia.

City, state, and federal authorities had suspected, pursued, harassed, muzzled, arrested, and jailed Goldman ever since Homestead in 1892. Now the United States was finally rid of her. The hysterical fears of wartime America and the restrictions on political freedoms claimed many other victims on the left as well. And even as she sailed out of New York harbor, leaving the country she had learned to love, Goldman was not alone. On board the *Buford* were many members of the Union of Russian Workers and, of course, Berkman.

Only two days earlier, she and Berkman had composed a last letter to their friends. "Be of good cheer, beloved comrades. Our enemies are fighting a losing battle. They are of the dying past. We are of the glowing future. Fraternally and joyously. Emma Goldman. Alexander Berkman."[30] Their future, however, was to be less joyous than they hoped.

6

DISILLUSIONMENT WITH RUSSIA: RETHINKING THE REVOLUTION, 1917–1928

While most of the American left remained enamored of the "cult of Russia" in the early 1920s, Goldman's firsthand experience shattered her early illusions about the Bolshevik Revolution.[1] By mid-decade, however, others on the left came to share her disenchantment. Goldman began a spiritual and political odyssey during which she reexamined her own beliefs about revolution and about women.

Goldman and fellow radicals were thrilled by the Bolshevik Revolution. Russia had entered the first World War on the Allied side, but the regime of Nicholas II, partly liberalized by the Revolution of 1905, could not keep the Russian troops adequately supplied, nor rally the Russian people to defend their homeland. Invaded by the Kaiser's forces, Russia suffered huge losses of life and property. The civilian population was ravaged by inflation and food shortages as well as by German soldiers. In March 1917 food riots in Petrograd (formerly St. Petersburg) triggered a mutiny among the troops. Nicholas II fled, and the reign of the tsars was over.

A new provisional government was quickly recognized by western nations. It soon established some political freedoms but did not end Russian involvement in the war or redistribute land to the peasants as promised. Instead, Russian officials began an ill-fated military offensive against the Germans in June. Alexander Kerensky took over the provisional government after an abortive soldiers' mutiny, just in time to fend off an attempted right-wing coup. The resulting political disorder, the people's dissatisfaction with the war, and the return from exile of Bolshevik leader V. I. Lenin, all worked together to encourage the November Revolution. Red troops stormed the Winter Palace, the Kerensky regime fell, and the Bolsheviks came to power. Lenin made peace with Germany with the Treaty of Brest Litovsk, and Russia withdrew from the war.

John Reed was the American publicist of this Revolution. The passionately engaged prose of his book *Ten Days That Shook the World* created for the American left its vision of the Bolshevik triumph. Reed was by profession a journalist, a contributor to *The Masses*, as well as the organizer of the Paterson strike pageant. Goldman had met him in her Greenwich Village days. Reed claimed to be antiwar, but he had a passion for the front lines and in 1914 had ridden with the troops of Pancho Villa in the Mexican Revolution. After the United States entered World War I, he became a war correspondent to the Eastern front for *Metropolitan Magazine*. Reed first visited Russia on assignment in 1916 and then returned just in time to see the Bolsheviks seize power. Already a Socialist, he was a partisan witness to and participant in the Revolution. His enthusiasm was infectious and inspiring. "It is still fashionable," he wrote in 1918, "to speak of the Bolshevik insurrection as an 'adventure.' Adventure it was, and one of the most marvellous mankind ever embarked upon, sweeping into history at the head of the toiling masses, and staking everything on their vast and simple desires." Reed described the Kerensky regime as corrupt and its political changes as partial and halfhearted, because the economy remained essentially unchanged. The Bolsheviks, however, had a program, he wrote: "'All Power to the Soviets. All power to the direct representatives of millions on millions of common workers, soldiers, peasants. Land, bread, an end to the senseless war.'"[2]

Reed dashed through the streets of Petrograd, dodging gunfire and fraternizing with the Red army. Very likely taking poetic—or journalistic—license, he contrasted the ongoing revolution in Russia with the corruption of American politics in this report of a conversation with a Russian soldier: "'Was it true,' the soldier asked, 'that people in a free country sold their votes for money? . . . Was it true that in a free country, a little group of people could control a whole city and exploit it for their personal benefit? Why did the people stand for it. . . . Had the

people no revolutionary feeling?'" Reed staged the finale of *Ten Days That Shook the World* much as he had staged the Paterson pageant. He described a great parade of soldiers, singing the *Marseillaise* and carrying banners proclaiming "Long live the union of the revolutionary and toiling masses" being joined by a crowd of peasants: "Two old peasants, bowed with toil, were walking hand in hand, their faces illumined with child-like bliss. 'Well,' said one, 'I'd like to see them take away our land again, now!' . . . 'I am not tired, [said the other.] I walk on air all the way.'"[3]

Like Reed, most members of the American left were predisposed to believe that this was the workers' revolution they had long dreamed of and worked for. The Bolshevik Revolution seemed to be the real thing. Marx had been right—the workers could rise up and seize economic and political power. Further, the Treaty of Brest Litovsk was proof that a workers' government would not wage wars. Betrayed and beseiged by the reformer-president Wilson, the left now hoped that if reform had failed in the United States, revolution had triumphed in Russia.

Reed's enthusiasm was echoed in books and articles written by his wife, Louise Bryant, and by Lincoln Steffens, labor organizer William Z. Foster, and other American liberal and left-wing journalists. Thus began the love affair with the Bolsheviks that would first unite and then divide the American left.

Eugene Debs, spokesman for the Socialist left, immediately declared himself "heart and soul with the Russian Revolution" despite its violence and bloodshed.[4] But the Socialist party, badly split in 1917 over support of the war and weakened by government repression and the imprisonment of much of its leadership, including Debs, was torn asunder in 1919. The Third (Communist) International, or Comintern, which represented all Communist parties that supported the Bolsheviks, called for immediate revolutions in the West to bolster the Bolshevik regime. The waves of serious strikes in the United States after the war seemed proof to some of the SP's left wing that an American revolution was imminent. At the same time, the United States' support of the counterrevolutionary White Russians against the Bolsheviks reinforced Socialists' pessimism about the American political system. This left wing, composed of some American-born members, including Reed and Kate Richards O'Hare, and most of the foreign-language federations, argued that the SP should join the International. The SP right wing, now including Debs, clung to its gradualist faith in political action and labor organization.

Fearing a left-wing takeover, the party's National Executive Committee expelled seven foreign-language federations and then the Michigan, Ohio, and Massachusetts state organizations. Angered, the left wing called its own conference in June 1919, from which two new political organizations emerged. The Communist party drew most of its support from the federations, and its members were often recent immigrants with strong emotional and political ties to Europe, especially Bolshevik Russia. The Communist Labor party, by contrast, wished to stay within the SP but to move it to the left. Reed and other English-speaking Socialists allied with this group. When the SP National Executive Committee refused to seat Communist Labor party delegates at an August convention, the Communist Labor party left the SP altogether. These schisms had an immediate and dramatic impact on SP membership. The party claimed 109,000 members at the beginning of 1919; a year later 40,000 remained.[5]

Members of the Industrial Workers of the World also were enchanted and divided by the Bolshevik Revolution. Reed had friends and admirers among the Wobblies and had worked with them during the Paterson strike. Although the IWW was distrustful of political parties and political action, some leaders became enthusiastic supporters of the Bolsheviks, most notably IWW leader Bill Haywood. Haywood had urged his fellow Wobblies to stand trial for their opposition to World War I in 1917. But with two long jail sentences hanging over his head and being in poor health, Haywood himself jumped bail and escaped to Russia. The IWW then split over whether to join the Red International of Labor Unions, an organization created by the Bolsheviks to persuade anarcho-syndicalists to join the Third International. Some Wobblies, like Elizabeth Gurley Flynn, cooperated with Communists in the defense of political prisoners but did not join a Communist party. (Flynn did join the Communist Party of the United States in 1936.)[6]

Although the "red scare" gradually subsided in the United States when the dynamitings predicted for May Day 1920 by Attorney General A. Mitchell Palmer did not take place, the federal government continued to attack the Communist party and the Communist Labor party. The U.S. Secretary of Labor ruled that membership in a Communist party was sufficient grounds for deporting an alien under the 1918 Deportation Act, a ruling that obviously threatened the many foreign-born members of the two parties. In 1920 "virtually the entire leadership" of both parties was indicted for violating state antisyndicalism and antisedition laws.[7] This legal persecution drove the Communist parties underground.

A legal political organization, the Workers' party, became the above-ground Communist body in 1921. Following directives from Lenin, however, the Communist party and the Communist Labor party were soon united into the Communist Party of the United States of America (CPUSA), which in 1923 claimed 15,000 members, many of them recent immigrants.[8]

When the dust had settled, the cult of Russia had seduced away from the old American left some of its distinguished activists, including former IWW and AFL union organizer William Z. Foster, and former SP official Charles Ruthenberg. Also lost to Communism were some of Goldman's comrades: Haywood, Rose Pastor Stokes, Robert Minor, once the cartoonist for *Mother Earth* and *The Masses,* and of course, John Reed.

Goldman had read Reed's book while she was in the Jefferson City prison. *Ten Days That Shook the World,* she later wrote, was "engrossingly thrilling. . . . I ceased to be a captive in the Missouri penitentiary and I felt myself transferred to Russia, caught by her fierce storm, swept along by its momentum, and identified with the forces that had brought about the miraculous change."[9] She and Berkman had already praised the Revolution in the *Mother Earth Bulletin,* and Goldman had defended the Bolsheviks before and after her two years in prison. Goldman knew that the Revolution had enemies not only within the Wilson administration but also within the anarchist movement. Although all anarchists welcomed the overthrow of tsarism, many feared the powerful state with which the Bolsheviks had replaced it. Saul Yanofsky, Goldman's early ally, warned the readers of his *Freie Arbeiter Shtime* that Lenin was dangerous.[10] And by 1919, Goldman herself was uneasy about Lenin's "dictatorship of the proletariat." At the same time, however, fearing that the beleaguered Bolsheviks might be toppled and the hated tsars reinstated, she was dismayed when Catherine Breshkovskaya ("Babushka"), who had spent a lifetime in the Russian revolutionary struggle, publicly criticized the Bolshevik regime before American audiences.

On 21 December 1919, when she and Berkman were deported, whatever misgivings Goldman had were irrelevant. Their ship, the *Buford,* which had seen service in the Spanish-American War, was barely seaworthy, and conditions for the 250 deportees were not luxurious. Most were workingmen, torn from their factories or homes. None, except for Goldman and Berkman, was a public figure. Goldman had no quarrel with the cabin she shared with two young women, but armed guards kept the three under surveillance constantly, even accompanying them to the toilet. The men's sleeping quarters were cold and damp, and there were only two toilets for the 246 male passengers. The food was inedible. Berkman, the veteran organizer, threatened the ship's command with a strike unless improvements were made. According to Goldman's autobiography, conditions aboard were so bad and the ship's sailors so admired Berkman that some talked of his leading them in a mutiny.

After crossing the Atlantic and sailing through the mine-filled waters of the English Channel, the exiles landed finally in Finland. There they were locked into heavily guarded trains that carried them to the Russian border, where they awaited escorts into the country. "It was the twenty-eighth day of our journey, and at last we were on the threshold of Soviet Russia," Goldman wrote later. "My heart trembled with anticipation and fervent hope."[11]

In the next months, she would be bitterly disappointed. The Bolsheviks had been in power for slightly more than two years. The Treaty of Brest Litovsk had ended Russia's participation in the war, but its terms had cost Russia the 60 million people and 5,000 factories located in the Ukraine, Poland, Estonia, Lithuania, and Finland. The central government had taken over much of the country's industry in a frantic effort to speed up the production of manufactured goods. Because food was in short supply, even though the peasants had been given land, they were compelled to turn over to the authorities much of what they raised on it. The Cheka, or secret police, suppressed the remaining political opposition.

The government justified its growing powers by pointing to the extraordinarily difficult circumstances. Russia had lost more people during the war than the other belligerents had. In addition, the Bolsheviks had to fight off the White armies, which tried to regain political power until their final defeat in 1920. The Western powers, including the United States, aided the Whites by sending troops in 1918 into Archangel and Siberia and by blockading Russian ports, preventing food and medical supplies from reaching the country. In 1920 the Bolshevik government also had to withstand a Polish invasion.

Nevertheless, Goldman and Berkman got a warm welcome from officials in their old homeland, heartening after being rejected by their adopted United States. But when the two arrived in Petrograd, Goldman was stunned by the appearance of the city of her adolescence: "The houses looked like broken old tombs upon neglected and forgotten cemeteries. The streets were dirty and deserted; all life had gone from them. . . . The people walked about like living corpses; the shortage of food and fuel was slowly sapping the city; grim death was clutching at its heart."[12] By contrast, Goldman and Berkman were housed at the Astoria Hotel, once a luxury facility for the wealthy, now used by Communist party members and important visitors. Their English-speaking host and party official, S. Zorin, extolled the glories of the Revolution and repeated the official explanations for the country's visible problems.

Those explanations were echoed by their old friend and fellow anarchist Bill Shatoff, now an officer in the Red army, who also greeted them. Brushing aside questions about how an anarchist could willingly take orders from the state, Shatoff cheerfully assured Goldman and Berkman that the Bolsheviks had indeed brought the long-awaited anarchist Revolution. Of course, he admitted, there were strong political leaders like Lenin and Leon Trotsky, but the real power behind them was the masses. Shatoff was still an anarchist, he said, but anarchists were too romantic about revolution, and the powerful Bolshevik dictatorship was "an unavoidable evil" until the enemies of the Revolution were conquered.[13]

But at a secret conference, the anarchists of Petrograd told Goldman a far different story. Although major anarchist thinkers, most notably Bakunin and Kropotkin, were Russian and the antistatism of the People's Will resembled anarchism, no indigenous anarchist movement had emerged until the early twentieth century. After anarchists were jailed and executed for their participation in the Revolution of 1905, a few became terrorists, turning to robbery and even murder. Anarchists also joined the Bolsheviks in the overthrow of the Kerensky government, but afterwards some again turned to counterrevolutionary terrorism. A bombing in Moscow in September 1919 killed a dozen prominent Communist party members. In response, the Petrograd group told Goldman, the Cheka had gone after all anarchists. There had been armed raids on their headquarters, imprisonment, and wholesale executions. The embattled anarchists accused Goldman of being naive and uninformed and Shatoff of being a "'Sovietsky' anarchist" who tolerated the murder of his comrades. Anarchists in Moscow later repeated these charges to Goldman.

The next months were discouraging. The repression of her fellow anarchists and other political dissenters was bad enough, but worse, most of the Russian people—for whom the Revolution had ostensibly been fought—were still destitute. Even some party officials went without material comforts; Zorin's pregnant wife, for example, could make little provision for her baby. The citizens of Petrograd froze in the winter because the bureaucracy could not organize a workforce to cut firewood from nearby forests. Hospitals were appalling, controlled not by doctors but by party functionaries. Travel was impossible without a *proposk* or pass. When Goldman was finally permitted to visit a factory, she was astonished at the "militarization of labour" and the control of factories by party officials rather than by the workers. She was especially shocked at "the sight of pregnant women working in suffocating tobacco air and saturating themselves and their unborn with the poison." Legislation protecting working women, which Goldman had considered "a cheap palliative" in the United States, now seemed imperative.[14]

There were also grave social inequities. Goldman found 34 grades of rations. Luxuries were available for those with money or political power. The Soukharevka market in Moscow, theoretically illegal, flourished while the workers and peasants went hungry. Perhaps most upsetting was the fact that she and Berkman, celebrated American immigrants, also received preferential treatment. They had housing, although thousands of common people did not; they had brought provisions into the country that staved off hunger; and they could buy luxuries with their American money.

Unused to such privilege, Goldman was also lonely and depressed. Since her arrest in 1917, one traumatic change had followed another: the two-year imprisonment, the uncertainty about her deportation, the removal from family and friends, and finally the exile to a now-strange homeland.[15] When she joined Berkman, her only friend, in Moscow, they lived an hour's walk apart, and there were no streetcars.

Goldman, who had once known all the answers, took her questions to others. John Reed soon "burst into my room like a sudden ray of light, the old buoyant, adventurous Jack that I used to know in the States," she recalled.[16] The United States government had dropped charges against Reed as a contributor to the antiwar *The Masses*, but had accused him instead of conspiring to overthrow the government. Reed had smuggled himself out of the country to petition the Comintern to recognize his Communist Labor party as the sole legitimate Communist party in the United States. Goldman wrote two accounts of this interview, one in *My Disillusionment with Russia* and the other in her autobiography. The first, closer to the event, may be the more accurate, but both described Reed as still being an apologist for the Bolsheviks and even for the Cheka's execution of 500 political prisoners—"counterrevolutionaries"—even though capital punishment had officially been abolished. In *Living My Life,* the conversation is recounted in much greater detail and focuses on the question of violence. "'Since when do revolutionists see in wholesale execution the only solution of their difficulties?'" Goldman asked Reed. "'In time of active counter-revolution it is no doubt inevitable to give shot for shot,'" she continued. "'But cold-bloodedly and merely for opinion's sake, do you justify standing people against the wall?'" At the time, her ideas about revolution were just "a little confused," he reassured her.[17]

Goldman sought out novelist Maksim Gorky. Once the defender of the Russian common people, Gorky startled Goldman when he declared that the backward and savage masses were not the vanguard but the obstacle to the revolution. Only the genius of Lenin had brought the revolution this far and could sustain it, Gorky maintained.

Goldman and Berkman managed a meeting with Lenin himself. The two were rushed through the streets in a limousine and into the Kremlin, where they waited an hour for their audience with "the man most idolized in the world and equally hated and feared." Lenin praised the exiles' defiant farewell addresses to the court. Believing that worldwide revolution was necessary, Lenin asked searching questions about the revolutionary potential of the American working class, about the American Federation of Labor, and especially about the IWW. Lenin's answers to their questions about Russian anarchists, however, were vague. There were no anarchists in jail for their political opinions, he claimed, only "bandits." In any case, the economic necessities of the revolution far outweighed any rights to express opposition to the Bolsheviks. "Free speech is a *bourgeois* prejudice," Lenin declared, just as Goldman's unwillingness to work for a government that persecuted anarchists was "*bourgeois* sentimentality." Find something useful to do, Lenin urged them. When Goldman suggested that she and Berkman establish a propaganda agency on behalf of political prisoners in the United States, a Russian Friends of American Freedom, Lenin responded enthusiastically with offers of government support. Realizing that he had not understood their objections to his government or their desire to remain independent, Goldman and Berkman left the audience almost as bewildered as when they came.[18]

More understanding of Goldman was Angelica Balabanoff, a lifelong revolutionary, whose own criticisms of the Bolshevik dictatorship got her removed from her position as Secretary of the Third International. When Goldman went to see her, she found Balabanoff ill and living in poverty. But she was a willing and affectionate listener to whom Goldman poured out her doubts, many of which Balabanoff shared. Yet Balabanoff could not—or would not—criticize or work against the Communists, and Goldman left the interview saddened to see this old rebel silent and defeated.

Goldman had one last—and most important—person to question: her inspiration and mentor, Peter Kropotkin. Kropotkin's writings had shaped Goldman's own anarchism and had often been reprinted in *Mother Earth*. Her affection and admiration for him had survived his endorsement of Russia's entrance into World War I. Kropotkin had returned to Russia from exile in June 1917.

In March 1920, Goldman and Berkman found Kropotkin and his wife and daughter in Dmitrov, nearly destitute. When they expressed their outrage at this treatment of the renowned philosopher, his wife explained that the proud old anarchist refused to be supported by the Bolshevik government, although without his knowledge, she did accept enough money so that they did not starve. There are again two versions of this conversation with Kropotkin, and again the later account is more detailed, although in *My Disillusionment*, Goldman acknowledges that she had taken no notes. Both accounts describe Kropotkin as saddened and dismayed by the powerful dictatorship that he believed was a betrayal of the Revolution. "We have always pointed out the effects of Marxism in action," he reminded her. "Why be surprised now?" This was hardly comforting to the two newcomers. But more important than what Kropotkin said, than his own loss of illusions, was what he did—or did not do. Goldman asked why he stayed in Russia and why he did not protest the dictatorship. There were two reasons, he explained. "As long as Russia was being attacked by the combined Imperialists, and Russian women and children were dying from the effects of the blockade, he could not join in the shrieking chorus of the ex-revolutionists in the cry of 'Crucify.' He preferred silence," he said. "Secondly, there was no medium of expression in Russia itself" since the government did not permit dissent. Goldman feared that the great thinker would go to his grave without telling the truth about the Bolsheviks.[19]

Finding few satisfactory answers to their questions, Goldman and Berkman returned to Petrograd and tried throughout the spring to find work that would aid the Revolution but not be controlled by the government. Mindful of their own difficulties as immigrants, they decided to set up a clearinghouse to provide shelter and jobs for some expected American deportees. Suitable buildings were renovated, but the deportees turned out to be German prisoners of war under the jurisdiction of the War Commissariat, and Goldman and Berkman's efforts were for nothing. Undaunted by this failure or by their lack of expertise in construction, the two then decided to oversee the conversion of some former mansions of the rich into rest homes for workers. But their work crews became swollen with party appointees who were lazy and inefficient, and party officials withdrew their support when Goldman and Berkman refused to evict some retired teachers living nearby. When the rest homes did open, Goldman found them ugly and uninviting. Food for the workers became their next project when Berkman volunteered to organize the public cafeterias in an efficient manner. But the bureaucrats dragged their feet, and Berkman was reprimanded for even thinking that "feeding the masses was the first concern of the Revolution."[20] Goldman offered to use her skills as a trained nurse in the public hospitals, but she was turned down because her political beliefs were not those of the Communist Health Commissar.

After four frustrating months and "with every hope of useful work gone," the two former revolutionaries became historians. They agreed to join the staff of the Petrograd Museum of the Revolution, headquartered at the Winter Palace.[21] Berkman and Goldman were to travel throughout the country collecting written materials and artifacts for the museum's archives. They were in fact working for the government, but with comparative freedom. And the expeditions would allow them to see for themselves conditions in the countryside.

While Goldman and Berkman waited for their travel arrangements to be completed, they met with some of the many visitors to the country who were eager to see the wonders of the revolutionary regime. A distinguished British Labour Mission was escorted through points of interest, for example, and wined and dined at palaces of the former nobility. The delegates, with the exception of the skeptical philosopher Bertrand Russell, saw and believed only what the Communist party officials wished them to. Goldman and Berkman's own criticisms of the Communists to the mission were muted, especially since war between Russia and Poland had endangered the government. Other visitors included anarcho-syndicalists from many European countries, who came to attend the Second Congress of the Red International of Labor Unions. Goldman and Berkman confirmed for them the rumors about imprisoned anarchists. Goldman had, in fact, recently persuaded the Cheka to release two young anarchist women by threatening to publicize the conditions of Russian prisons. ("Getting people out of jail had been among our various activities in America," she later wrote. "But we had never dreamed that we should find the same necessity in revolutionary Russia.") But in the spring of 1920, Goldman sent through the Congress delegates only a guarded message to workers abroad: "May they emulate the spirit of their Russian brothers in the coming revolution, but not their naive faith in political leaders."[22]

At last in June an old Pullman car with six compartments was located and refurbished for the museum expedition. Berkman became general manager, and Goldman, as usual, chief cook and housekeeper for the six-member crew. With delight she outfitted the car with elegant linen and china from the tsars' Winter Palace.

As she told the story in My Disillusionment in Russia, the expedition became for Goldman less a search for the truth about the Revolution's past than a quest for the truth about its present. The first stop was Moscow to pick up the credentials that would allow the museum staff to have in their possession counterrevolutionary documents. There Goldman and Berkman met Maria Spiridonovna, a revolutionary heroine who, at 18, had assassinated a tsarist general. She had been sentenced to exile in Siberia but was allowed to return to Russia after the Revolution. She had sided with Lenin and the Bolsheviks during the Revolution but was later arrested and persecuted when she opposed the Treaty of Brest Litovsk. Now she was ill and living under virtual house arrest, still defiantly supporting the peasantry against the Communist regime. Some months later she was imprisoned.

In July when the Pullman car was attached to a passing train, the archivists left Moscow and headed for the Ukraine. The Ukraine's strong tradition of nationalism and important natural resources had made it a battleground between the White army, the Red army, and local armies led by Nestor Makhno. In Kharkov, Goldman and Berkman found American comrades: fellow anarchists, one of whom had even worked on Mother Earth. These immigrants had come to Russia, they said, inspired by Goldman's glowing description of the Revolution in 1917. They had fought beside the Bolsheviks but now realized that the Revolution had been betrayed. How could Goldman not protest? they asked. Why did she and Berkman not join the rebel Makhno? Makhno had led his peasant armies first against the invading Austrians and then, at the urging of the Bolsheviks, against the White army. Makhno, however, had nationalist political ambitions of his own, and some weeks later, Makhno's wife asked Goldman and Berkman to join her husband in a military coup against the Communist regime in the Ukraine. Goldman and Berkman refused. Goldman believed that continued warfare would be destructive, and in addition she could not bring herself yet to engage in open opposition to the Bolsheviks. It was a prudent decision. When Makhno had outlived his military usefulness, the Red army shot his commanders in November 1920, and Makhno himself fled the country, eventually living in exile in Paris.

The travelers were painfully reminded of their privileged position. When crowds of rag-clad Russian peasants, bearing all their earthly possessions, pushed and swarmed to get on their train, undeterred by soldiers' rifle butts, Goldman persuaded the crew to allow a few to ride on the train's platform. Swarms of beggars, destitute and starving, met them at every station.

The trip to the Ukraine also reminded Goldman and Berkman of their Jewish roots, for the region was home to many Jews. In Fastov, the visitors found a Jewish settlement in utter destitution, its women terrified at the very sight of strange men. Summoning up her Yiddish, Goldman discovered that the community was still in shock from frightful pogroms initiated by the White generals. One pogrom had killed 4,000 people outright, and thousands more died trying to escape. There had been wholesale rape of the Jewish women. "In spite of all certainty that there was no Jehovah to hear them, I was strangely stirred by the tragic scene in the poverty-stricken synagogue," Goldman admitted. The Jews of America might hear, though, and Berkman suggested that news of the Ukranian Jews be sent to the Yiddish press in the United States.[23] The Bolsheviks had halted the pogroms and, consequently, had defenders among the Jewish intelligentsia whom Goldman later met, but no one denied that anti-Semitism persisted.

The expedition's travel plans were complicated when the White army moved north and invading Poles threatened Kiev. Nevertheless the train reached the port of Odessa, which was under martial law. The local Cheka gave the visitors from the museum a cold reception. But in Odessa, too, they met a group of anarchists, a few of them American, who confirmed suspicions that the local bureaucrats were not only corrupt but inefficient—further proof for the anarchists of the evils of government.

After four months on the road, the expedition headed back to Petrograd. En route, Berkman's coat was stolen out of the train compartment. Berkman was amused to think that the thief would never discover the $1,600, the last of their American money, which he had sewn into the coat's lining. Goldman was not amused, however, for the theft had robbed them of their economic independence of the Bolshevik government.

In addition to their growing uneasiness about the Bolshevik government, two deaths—of Jack Reed and Peter Kropotkin—helped to further undermine Goldman and Berkman's ties to Russia. Reed's health, always precarious, had been seriously damaged by confinement in a Finnish jail, where, en route to the United States, he had been held captive as a Russian spy. Then a futile errand for the Communist party, to the Congress of Eastern Races at Baku, where he contracted typhus, had killed him. Reed had died disillusioned—if not with communism, then with the Communist leadership. In Petrograd, Goldman joined Reed's wife, Louise Bryant, who had smuggled herself into Russia only to arrive at his deathbed. Reed's funeral took place in Red Square on a gray, overcast day. "No beauty for the man who had loved it so, no colour for his artist-soul," Goldman mourned.[24] Reed became the first American to be buried in the Kremlin Wall.

Kropotkin died of pneumonia on 8 February 1921. On the eve of Goldman's departure to the Ukraine, Kropotkin had tried to shore up her crumbling hopes. She accepted the inevitability of some violence during a revolution, she told him, but the "callous indifference to human life, the terrorism, the waste and agony" in Russia had almost destroyed her faith in the Revolution. Kropotkin again tried to reassure her. It had been a great Revolution, he maintained, striking deep "into the hearts and mind of the Russian people." The Communist belief in a centralized state, however, meant that the Revolution had inevitably gone astray, he repeated. Perhaps anarchists themselves had not thought long and hard enough about how to achieve a revolution, especially about the need to organize the economy. The workers' collectives of anarcho-syndicalism, he concluded, might be the answer.[25]

Goldman had been notified of Kropotkin's illness but was unable to reach his side before his death. Persecuted, silenced, and forced into retirement by the leaders whom he had helped into power, the gentle Kropotkin died, as Goldman had feared, without having made public his sorrow and dismay over the Bolshevik dictatorship. Yet he had never despaired of anarchism and had continued to write about it until his last hours.

Kropotkin was a world-renowned figure, and his funeral was to be a significant public occasion attended by the European and American press. The Funeral Commission, which Berkman helped to organize, threatened authorities with an international scandal if imprisoned anarchists were not released for the ceremony. Only seven, however, were permitted to act as Kropotkin's pallbearers. Their presence symbolized another heartbreaking commentary on the failed ideals of the Revolution. Sophie Kropotkin asked Goldman and Berkman to stay in Moscow and establish a museum to commemorate her husband's life. They agreed; their work for the Museum of the Revolution was over. A second, brief expedition to the Archangel had been interesting and rewarding—Goldman even admired some nuns teaching in the schools there—but the Communist party had decided to take more direct control of the Museum of the Revolution, and the two anarchists refused to work under those conditions.

A month after Kropotkin's death came the Kronstadt rebellion. The Russian economy, in a shambles when the country pulled out of the war, had been further devastated by the civil war between the Bolsheviks and the Whites. Industrial and agricultural production had almost ceased, and a terrible famine hit in 1921. In Kronstadt, sailors struck in sympathy with Petrograd workers whose food and fuel rations had been cut and whose protests had been brutally put down. Kronstadt had long been a bastion of revolutionary activity, and the sailors had been brave and enthusiastic participants in the Revolutions of 1905 and 1917. (They had also staged effective demonstrations against Berkman's extradition to California.) Communist officials declared the Kronstadt strike a counterrevolutionary mutiny, and the Red army beseiged the shipyards. Goldman and Berkman decided that they could not remain silent. Their letter to the chairman of the Petrograd Soviet of Labor and Defense, however, was markedly cautious. Maintaining that as anarchists they would "fight with arms against any counter-revolutionary attempt," the two simply urged that force not be used against the sailors and workers and that a commission including two anarchists be sent to mediate between the strikers and the government.[26]

Their letter was to no avail. The strike at Petrograd was broken. The Kronstadt sailors fought back for ten days but ultimately capitulated to the government's greater firepower. Thousands died, most of them on the government's side. Until then Berkman had continued to believe that the economic revolution the Bolsheviks had achieved outweighed the loss of political freedoms. But as he listened to the artillery fire pounding at the Kronstadt garrison, he recorded in his diary, "Days of anguish and cannonading. My heart is numb with despair; something has died within me."[27]

Their emotional and political loyalties to the Bolshevik regime finally destroyed, Berkman and Goldman decided they must leave Russia. Yet they remained, paralyzed and unable to act on their decision, as one devastating blow followed another. In the wake of Kronstadt, there were more wholesale arrests of anarchists, and anarchist centers in Petrograd and Moscow were shut down. Goldman and Berkman, financially sustained by funds smuggled in from Goldman's mother, had moved out of their party-sponsored hotel in Petrograd to an apartment in Moscow. They found themselves under suspicion, their quarters ransacked and searched. Although Goldman and Berkman did not realize it, they had been under surveillance by both the Russian and the United States governments since their arrival in Russia. The American agent watching them was Marguerite Harrison, an Associated Press correspondent who had been their next-door neighbor and confidante. The Communist officials read and sometimes halted their correspondence to and from the United States.[28]

Lenin's New Economic Policy, a reversal of the movement toward economic equality, further dismayed Goldman and Berkman. The policy, an attempt to rescue the economy, brought a partial return to free enterprise. Economic recovery, however, was accompanied by more restrictions on political opposition.

In the summer of 1921, another Congress of the Red International of Labor Unions brought home to the two exiles their political isolation. From the United States came old allies who were now Communists: Mary Heaton Vorse, a friend from Greenwich Village days; Ella Reeves Bloor, a former Socialist who had visited Goldman at the Jefferson City prison; William Z. Foster; Robert Minor; and Bill Haywood. Haywood claimed that he had jumped bail and fled the United States not because he feared a long prison sentence but because he wished to see revolutionary Russia. Goldman and Berkman were not delegates to the Congress, but as leading figures in the international anarchist movement, they attended some sessions and socialized with participants. Goldman now did not keep her opinions of the Communist dictatorship a secret, and the American delegates soon kept their distance from her. Worse, still smitten with enthusiasm for the Revolution, the Americans did not vigorously protest the forced deportation of imprisoned anarchists. Goldman was infuriated at the cowardice of the Americans as well as at the deportations: "What a commentary on the Communist State outdoing Uncle Sam!" she remarked later.[29] The American delegates returned home to follow the Communist line, except for Haywood, who remained in Russia. Old friends on the left were friends no longer.

Goldman and Berkman finally applied for passports at the end of October or early November. Invitations to an anarchist conference in Berlin gave them a destination, and after anxious weeks and the intercession of Angelica Balabanoff, their passports arrived—even though Goldman, as an anarchist, refused to swear loyalty to the Soviet Union on her passport application. Along with Alexander Shapiro, a syndicalist, the two American deportees left Russia on December 1, 1921.

In *Living My Life* (1931) and in the narrative published as *My Disillusionment in Russia* (1923) and *My Further Disillusionment in Russia* (1924) Goldman explains why she left Russia, but she does not explain satisfactorily why she had stayed so long under a political regime that she describes as anathema to her almost from the beginning. It is possible, in fact, that Goldman became disenchanted later than these accounts suggest. Moreover, although both accounts emphasize for obvious reasons the economic failures and the political repressiveness of the regime, Goldman did acknowledge that the Bolsheviks had made some improvements, which may have encouraged her to remain hopeful. The hated tsars were gone, and there were schools for the peasants and workers. The Communist government in Archangel was efficient and compassionate. And the Bolsheviks had ended the vicious pogroms, which may have been more important to Goldman than she would admit.

Then there was Berkman. He had not given up hope until Kronstadt. Goldman had had misgivings earlier, although maybe not as early as she claimed. The two had disagreed often during their stay in Russia, but she had not been able to bring herself to quarrel seriously with him or to leave the country without him. She had, after all, followed Berkman into exile when there was a chance that she could have stayed in the United States. He was still her model of a revolutionist.

And there were the compelling examples of Balabanoff and especially Kropotkin, their teacher for three decades who had remained persuaded of the rightness of the Revolution despite the wrongness of the Bolsheviks. Goldman and Berkman had staked their long lives and careers on the viability of a revolution, a revolution that—until 1917—

they had never seen. And as Kropotkin admitted, anarchists knew little about how to bring about a revolution or what to do once it had arrived. More important, despite his despair, Kropotkin had stayed in Russia. But he had died without voicing his real beliefs, and Goldman did not want to do that.

Last but not least, if they left Russia, where could Goldman and Berkman go? Having offended the powerful governments of the United States and Soviet Russia, they could not count on a welcome anywhere in western Europe. Anarchists with loyalties to no state, they became politically homeless.

By the time Goldman published My *Disillusionment in Russia* and My *Further Disillusionment in Russia,* however, some of the American left had also become disillusioned with the Bolsheviks. The left's bellwether, Eugene Debs, backed off from his initial enthusiasm for the Revolution in 1924. Other prominent Socialists had already done so. As early as 1920, the SP's National Executive Committee refused to go along with the stringent conditions attached to membership in the Third International. The committee later changed its mind, but by then the International was not interested in the SP. Abraham Cahan, editor of the Socialist *Jewish Daily Forward,* began open opposition to American communism and Soviet Bolshevism in that journal's pages. On the Lower East Side, Socialists literally fought off a Communist takeover of the predominantly Jewish International Ladies Garment Workers Union in a drawn-out and demoralizing struggle in the mid-1920s. The exodus of youthful leftists into the two Communist parties turned the SP into a centrist body, its conservatism heightened by the political temper of the prosperous 1920s. As membership dwindled, the SP tried to save itself by allying with non-Marxist organizations such as the Conference on Progressive Political Action, formed by the railroad brotherhoods. In 1924 the SP actually endorsed the Progressive party's presidential candidate Robert La Follette. As the "red scare" had shown, the American public did not distinguish between varieties of leftism, and the SP could not afford to be identified in any way with communism. In 1925 the SP leadership openly and sharply opposed the Soviet Union.

There was disenchantment also on the cultural left. Max Eastman, John Reed's colleague and friend, editor of *The Masses* and then *The Liberator,* remained favorably impressed with the Communists for most of his stay in Moscow in 1923–24. However, the power struggle between Joseph Stalin and Leon Trotsky after Lenin's death in 1924 dismayed

Eastman enough that he wrote an exposé of the conflict and began his own move to the political right. By 1928, according to Daniel Aaron, "only a tiny percentage of American intellectuals looked to the U.S.S.R. for guidance and salvation."[30]

Like the SP, the IWW had lost members to the Communists in the enthusiastic aftermath of the November Revolution. Those who remained in the IWW became increasingly distrustful of Bolshevik centralization. Further, in *Left Wing Communism: An Infantile Disorder* (1920) Lenin had denounced dual unionism, the chief mission of the IWW since its founding in 1905. Communist sympathizers were forced out of the IWW at conventions in 1923 and 1924.[31] Haywood, still in Russia, became dispirited and homesick. When he died in 1928, half of his ashes were buried in the Kremlin Wall near Reed and half at Waldheim Cemetery in Chicago, near the Haymarket anarchists and Voltairine de Cleyre.

Anarchists had early criticized the Bolshevik Revolution and American Communists. When Mollie Steimer, Jacob Abrams, and others who had violated the Espionage Act were deported to Russia in 1921, the *Freie Arbeiter Shtime* warned them to expect not liberation but repression, for Communist jails were full of anarchists. (Steimer's efforts to free those prisoners got her expelled from the Soviet Union in 1923.) The *Freie Arbeiter Shtime* also carried anti-Communist articles by Goldman and Berkman, as well as Berkman's book *Now and After: The ABC of Communist Anarchism* (1929). New York anarchists rejoined their old allies, the Socialists, against the Communists in the battle over control of the garment workers' unions.[32]

There were even those within the fledgling American Communist movement who became dissatisfied with the Bolsheviks. Some viewed Lenin's *Infantile Disorder* as a betrayal of the Revolution, because it urged Communists to cooperate with trade unions and to form a legal political party. After Trotsky was driven out of the Soviet Union, he developed an American following, who were then expelled from the CPUSA in 1928 and later joined the Socialists. As CPUSA leadership became "Bolshevized" and took its orders from the Soviet Union, its membership dropped from about 16,000 in 1925 to about 9,500 at the end of the decade.[33]

Liberals, too, became disenchanted. The *Nation*, while remaining generally pro-Soviet, carried some critical articles: by foreign correspondent Henry Alsberg, for example, who had accompanied Goldman and Berkman on the museum expedition. Alsberg had also interested

Goldman's friend Roger Baldwin, then with the American Civil Liberties Union, in the plight of political prisoners in Russia. With substantial but unacknowledged assistance from Berkman, Baldwin published in 1925 *Letters from Russian Prisons*, which was critical of the Communists' denial of political freedoms. (Baldwin recanted his protest in *Liberty Under the Soviets*, published in 1928, but in 1940 changed his mind again and expelled Elizabeth Gurley Flynn from the board of the ACLU for her membership in the CPUSA.)

Goldman remained scornful of any qualified criticisms of the Bolsheviks. Having seen the power of the Communists within Soviet Russia, she overestimated the power of communism outside of it. Inside Russia Goldman had lost her illusions about the Bolshevik Revolution. Now outside, she did not change her perspective.

Berkman and Goldman, who was traveling now as Mrs. E. G. Kersner, had left Russia without visas for Germany, where the anarchist conference was scheduled for late December, or for the countries through which they would have to travel. As a result the two were detained briefly in a Latvian jail. Even the jail, she wrote later, felt like freedom after life under the Communists. (And even there, she managed to cook Christmas dinner for Berkman and their companion, Shapiro.) Goldman was sure that their detainment had been engineered by the Bolsheviks. She did not know that the U.S. State Department was also involved. The travelers' personal papers, including Berkman's diary, were seized, copied, and sent to the State Department, which informed western European countries of their travel plans.[34]

The two companions were able to get as far as Stockholm, where they spent more anxious days and where Goldman was besieged by American journalists eager to know the worst about the Bolsheviks. Goldman decided to write the story herself, even though she realized that the articles would provide the American and European political right with ammunition against the Bolsheviks. She wanted to reach a larger American audience than the anarchist press could provide; she wanted the liberal middle-class audience that she had assiduously cultivated before the war. But liberal journals like the *Nation* and the *New Republic* turned down her articles. Almost destitute, she sold the series to the *New York World*, which had earlier published her writing. Berkman, who had written for the Socialist *New York Call* and other left-wing papers, predictably disapproved, but other anarchists, including Enrico Malatesta and Rudolf Rocker, told her to go ahead. Her seven articles, which appeared from late March to early April 1922, predictably widened the breach between herself and the Communists, who accused her of amassing a fortune by pandering to the capitalist press. Goldman wished it were so, for she had received only $2,100. Rose Pastor Stokes, once an ally in the birth control fight and now a Communist, wanted Goldman hanged, "at least in effigy."[35]

The Swedish government came under fire from the political right for allowing the two revolutionaries even temporary asylum. At the same time, the publication of Goldman's critical articles ran the risk of offending the Soviet Union, even as the Swedish government considered granting the new Soviet government diplomatic recognition. Goldman and Berkman's stay in Sweden, therefore, ended almost before the two had visas to go elsewhere. Berkman, impatient with the delay, had already gotten into Germany by stowing away on a tramp steamer. Goldman followed with a visa that arrived only at the last minute.

The *New York World* series became the basis for *My Disillusionment in Russia*, which Goldman began when she reached Berlin in April 1922. Although her original visa was only for ten days, she stayed in Germany where there was an active and vigorously anti-Communist anarchist community, for 27 months. Goldman was encouraged to write *My Disillusionment* by an American publisher, Clinton P. Brainard, who argued that an exposé of the Bolsheviks would sell well, especially with an introduction by then-Secretary of Commerce Herbert Hoover. Dismissing his suggestion about Hoover, Goldman sold the rights to the book to Brainard for a desperately needed advance of $1,750 and started work. The manuscript was originally titled "My Two Years in Russia" and had 24 chapters. Somehow, Doubleday and Page, to whom Brainard had sold Goldman's work, received only the first 12, which it retitled *My Disillusionment in Russia* and published in 1923. Goldman was furious, because she felt that the title incorrectly suggested that she was disillusioned with the Revolution, not with the Bolsheviks. Moreover, the book did not include her important afterword. At the insistence of her former lawyer, Harry Weinberger, Doubleday published the remaining 12 chapters in 1924 as *My Further Disillusionment in Russia.*

The book was difficult for Goldman to write not only because it would have obvious political repercussions, but also because it involved a painful reexamination of some of Goldman's long-held beliefs. *My Disillusionment* was, first, an explicit admission that she had been wrong about the Bolsheviks in 1917. This error in judgment had had practical implications for others, for her early pamphlets and speeches had persuaded some anarchists to emigrate to Russia, where they were imprisoned or executed. The book contained another damaging admission: for almost two years Goldman, the life-long, outspoken critic of the status quo, had remained silent. She had acquiesced, if unwillingly, to economic injustice and political repression that she never would have tolerated in the United States. The book, then, was a way of atoning for past sins and a way too of assuring herself that, unlike Kropotkin, she would not die with her piece unspoken. In her preface to *My Disillusionment*, Goldman explained that she had left Russia expressly to tell the working classes of the world the truth about the Bolsheviks, which would have been an impossible task under their brutal regime.

All her life the polemicist, Goldman was uncomfortable in her unaccustomed role as objective narrator. Aware that her credibility was weakened by her politics, she defended herself and the politically engaged historian: ". . . real history is not a compilation of mere data. It is valueless without the human element. . . . It is the personal reactions of the participants and observers which lend vitality to all history and make it vivid and alive."[36]

Goldman borrowed much of her analysis of the Revolution from Kropotkin, or from what she had re-created as Kropotkin's. For example, she made repeated distinctions between the Revolution and the Bolsheviks. In her early support of the Bolsheviks, she wrote, she had assumed that although they were Marxists, they were fighting for the anarchist goal of a stateless society. "But after the high tide of revolutionary enthusiasm had carried them into power, the Bolsheviki discarded their false plumes. It was then that began the spiritual separation between the Bolsheviki and the Russian Revolution. With each succeeding day the gap grew wider, their interests more conflicting. Today it is no exaggeration to state that the Bolsheviki stand as the arch enemies of the Russian Revolution."[37] She had not been naive enough to suppose that the anarchist utopia would be accomplished by 1919, but in fact, she pointed out, the plight of the Russian peasants and workers had continued to deteriorate, not improve.

And as always, Goldman had to discuss the issue of revolutionary strategy. Although violence might accompany a revolution—she used the American Revolution as an example—the Bolsheviks had "institutionalized" the "principle of terrorism," she argued, continuing to use it as a matter of course long after the internal and external enemies of the regime had been defeated.[38] In view of these ugly realities, Goldman concluded that the anarchist revolution, a true revolution, could not be

accomplished through the violent overthrow and destruction of the economic and political order. An anarchist revolution whose goal was liberty must be accomplished through libertarian means, not through
coercion: the means must be morally congruent with the ends. Values,
not political leaders, must change, and the "real regeneration of society"
must be based on "the sense of justice and equality, the love of liberty
and of human brotherhood." Anarchists, who were after all better prop-
agandists than revolutionaries, must lead the way in the sweeping "trans-
valuation of values" that would prepare the people for the better world
to come. Libertarian organizations of workers would maintain this "better world," as seen in the anarcho-syndicalist vision of Kropotkin.[39]

As Goldman had anticipated, My Disillusionment was greeted with
hostility by Communists, and Haywood and Foster accused her of being
in the pay of the United States government. Even the Nation's reviewer
suggested mildly that Goldman's deep-seated distrust of Marxists and her
deeper-seated distrust of Russia had distorted her perspective.[40] The
mainstream press, however, which had carried hostile articles on Bolshevik Russia since 1917, praised the book.

In Berlin American friends and Goldman's niece Stella Cominsky
Ballantine and her young son, Ian, joined Goldman for her fifty-fourth
birthday. (Her happiness about the family reunion was lessened, however, by Taube Goldman's death a month later.) Goldman found companionship with Rudolph Rocker, the respected German anarchist and
author, and his wife Millie. Mollie Steimer and her companion Senya
Flechine also arrived in Berlin, which had become a center for Russian
émigrés. Nevertheless Goldman could not find a place for herself in Germany, despite her early love for German culture. Because English was
now the language that she spoke and wrote most easily, it was difficult
to earn a living. Furthermore, since she still had only a temporary visa,
her legal status in Germany was uncertain. On an excursion to Munich,
Goldman was visited by the local police. To her surprise they had a photograph of her taken in 1889 by her uncle, doubtless a gift to the Munich
police department from the American Federal Bureau of Investigation.
When her friend and biographer Frank Harris got her a visa to England,
Goldman left Berlin on 24 July 1924.

Goldman welcomed the opportunity to address English-speaking audiences again. Although she had found the English to be stuffy and unresponsive on earlier visits, London had historically been a refuge for
anarchists in exile, and it was there, years before, that she had met Kropotkin and other European comrades. There was still a small but divided

anarchist community in London—including old friend John Turner—that gave her staunch support. She met Havelock Ellis and Edward Carpenter, whose writings about sexuality had influenced her own thinking, and Paul Robeson, whose magnificent voice delighted her. Goldman also lectured to a group of American students at Oxford University; their professor, historian Samuel Eliot Morison, many years later described her as "about the finest woman orator I have ever heard."[41]

Goldman was initially cautious about publicly expressing her opposition to the Communist regime, but her views were already well known. She repeated them at a dinner arranged for her by novelist and journalist Rebecca West, to the dismay of the prominent leftists and intellectuals in the audience. Goldman organized a British Committee for the Defense of Political Prisoners in Russia, which gave her a platform for her attacks on the Soviet Union. She had little success, however, in rallying support either for the prisoners or for her own criticism of the Bolsheviks. Even Bertrand Russell, who had seen and disliked Lenin's government but feared that the alternatives would be worse, did not want to associate with her.

Goldman was angered and depressed by a report from the British Labour Mission, based on its six-week stay in Russia, that denied any political repression. Officials of the Independent Labour Party informed Goldman that any news of Bolshevik repression would damage their own political fortunes, and her criticisms of the Labour Mission's report made her more enemies on the left. Consequently, as too often had become the case since her departure from the Soviet Union, she found herself in odd and uncongenial political company. "My situation is really a desperate one," she wrote Berkman, who was then in France working on his own manuscript, *The Bolshevik Myth.* "The tories have taken a stand against the communists, in France they are being hounded, the Pope comes out against them. And here I am doing the same. It is no wonder that everybody refuses to join me. It really means working hand in glove with the reactionaries. On the other hand," she continued grimly, "I know I must go ahead and that our position is of a different nature."[42]

Frustrated and disappointed in her political activities, Goldman turned again to the theater. She spent happy hours doing research in the British Museum for another book on the drama and attended an exciting performance of George Bernard Shaw's *Caesar and Cleopatra.* The book's publication fell through, however, and despite her connections to American avante-garde theater through the Provincetown Players and one successful lecture on Russian drama for the British Drama League in London, two series of drama lectures, given in English and Yiddish, did not make money.

In this difficult period, Goldman also had to rethink her earlier ideas about women's "emancipation." This reevaluation was carried on in her personal correspondence with Berkman, not in her public writings. Soon after Goldman had arrived in Berlin, she had been joined by a young lover, a Swedish worker and former Wobbly whom she had met in Stockholm. Arthur Swenson was 29; Goldman was 53. The romance had been short-lived, and when Swenson's interest in her young secretary became obvious, Goldman had sent him away. Now she realized painfully that the independence she had always prized also meant loneliness. "We all need love and affection and understanding, and a woman needs a damn sight more of that when she grows older," she confessed to Berkman. "I am sure that is the main cause of my misery since I left America. For since then I have had no one, or met anyone who gave a fig for what I do and what becomes of me. . . . I am consumed by longing for love and affection [,] for some human being of my own."[43]

In 1906, at a relatively youthful 37, Goldman had believed that a woman could achieve her own emancipation by an act of will. Two decades later, she was willing to concede that social conventions were more powerful than she had imagined, particularly those governing a woman's sexual partner. Berkman had found a much younger companion, Emmy Eckstein. Goldman had found no one. She chafed at the injustice of a man being able to have a younger lover while an older woman with a younger man was ridiculed. Goldman also redefined the "tragedy of woman's emancipation." The "tragedy of all of us modern women," she mourned to Berkman, is "that we are removed only by a very short period from our traditions, the traditions of being loved, cared for, protected, secured, and above all, the time when women could look forward to an old age of children, a home and someone to brighten their lives. . . . [M]ost modern women, especially when they see age growing upon them, and if they have given out of themselves so abundantly, begin to feel the utter emptiness of their existence, the lack of the *man*, whom they love and who loves them, the comradeship and companionship that grows out of such a relation, the home, a child. And above all, the economic security."[44]

In October 1926 Goldman, the longtime champion of free love, got married—not for economic security or companionship but for citizenship, a custom common among political exiles. She became a British citizen through her marriage to Welsh coal miner James Colton, a widower and fellow anarchist. Harry Kelly had renewed his earlier offer to marry her, but the passage of the Cable Act in 1922 had meant that marriage would no longer automatically make Goldman an American citizen.

British citizenship allowed Goldman, now "masquerading under the name of Colton," to travel to Canada for a lecture tour in the fall of 1926.[45] There she hoped to make a new start. Montreal and Toronto had active and hospitable Jewish anarchist communities, and she would be close to the United States. Her sister Lena, her brother Morris, and even Ben Reitman visited her in Canada. Goldman's lectures on politics and the drama were successful enough that she could raise funds for herself and for the release of political prisoners in Russia. The Toronto anarchists, working-class and Yiddish-speaking, asked her to make her home with them permanently. But she found herself again caught in the political cross fire between local Communists, who sometimes picketed her lectures, and a conservative government whose anti-Communism she did not want to abet. As a brief love affair with Rochester anarchist Leon Malmed (referred to as Leon Bass in her autobiography) came to an end—he was a longtime admirer and financial supporter but a married man—she decided to leave Canada.

Goldman refused friends' offers to smuggle her back into the United States. Not realizing that the American government still kept her under surveillance, she had hoped that she might somehow be permitted to reenter the country legally. Her longing for her adopted homeland, however, did not blind her even now to its failings. In 1927 the state of Massachusetts executed the Italian anarchists Nicola Sacco and Bartolomeo Vanzetti, legally charged with murder but found guilty because of their political beliefs and their immigrant background in a mockery of a trial that became a cause célèbre among liberals and leftists. Their execution reminded Goldman of the country's long history of persecuting political dissidents: the Haymarket martyrs, Mooney, the Wobblies, Berkman, and herself. "How could I have believed that Sacco and Vanzetti, however innocent, would escape American 'justice,'?" she lamented. Like others on the left, she denounced their trial and then spoke at a memorial meeting for the two men.[46]

Assured by several writers, including Theodore Dreiser, that it would be a great literary success, Goldman decided to write her autobiography. American friends, including the editor of *Freie Arbeiter*

Shtime, raised enough money to give Goldman some financial security, and in 1928 she left Canada for a cottage in St. Tropez in the south of France, not far from Berkman, to begin writing *Living My Life.* She optimistically hoped to finish the book in a year, in time to mark her sixtieth birthday.

More than a decade after the Bolshevik Revolution, Goldman was less optimistic about the future of anarchism. She wrote friend and author Evelyn Scott: "I will have given forty years to my ideas. I realize that most of them were spent in chasing windmills, in trying to present to the world an ideal which to me contains all the beauty and wonder there is in life. . . . The world less than ever wants to know about [anarchism]. . . . [But] I would despair utterly if I did not believe in the ultimate triumph of my ideal."[47] In 1928 the *Little Review* asked her and a dozen other celebrities whether they considered their "worldviews" and themselves "reasonable": "No, I am not a reasonable being, nor do I consider our scheme reasonable. Who the hell wants to be reasonable?" Goldman responded.[48]

Berkman remained the touchstone of her political faith, and as she read the manuscript of his book, *What Is Communist Anarchism,* she was more candid and even more pessimistic. "The entire old school, Kropotkin, Bakunin, and the rest, had a childish faith in what Peter calls 'the creative spirit of the people.' I'll be damned if I can see it. If the people could really create out of themselves, could a thousand Lenins or the rest have put the noose back on the throat of the Russian masses?" she asked.[49] Her elitist distrust of the people was not new, only more emphatic.

The question of violence in a revolutionary situation continued to haunt both Goldman and Berkman, more than a quarter of a century after Homestead. Berkman was still the perpetrator of the *attentat,* and she was still his defender but no longer a defender of violence as a strategy. In 1926 Goldman wrote for *American Mercury* a graceful, posthumous tribute to Johann Most in which she tried again to explain both her horsewhipping of Most and the *attentat* itself: ". . . we were young and impatient. Youth is cruelly impatient and critical. . . . I became embittered against my former teacher, and I added my stone to the many that were hurled at him." But, she concluded, "one's own spiritual Calvary makes one understand things."[50] In *What Is Communist Anarchism,* Berkman carefully argued that most anarchists no longer believed in propaganda by deed, or terrorist acts, and that education must precede a successful revolution. Violence, however, remained an option for him, at least in defense of the revolution.[51] Not for Goldman. "You are loath to let go the thought of revolution in terms of destruction and terror. And I am done with that for all times."[52]

By the end of the decade, Goldman and Berkman were no longer the only "voices in the wilderness," proclaiming the evils of Communist Russia, for others on the left had now joined them. But as her political isolation ended, Goldman came to some new conclusions about the revolution she had long sought. Her dialogue with Berkman continued: "I insist if we can undergo changes in every other method of dealing with social issues, we will also learn to change in the methods of revolution. I think it can be done. If not, I shall relinquish my belief in revolution."[53]

The old radical did not relinquish her belief in revolution, although she would change her mind again about how to achieve it.

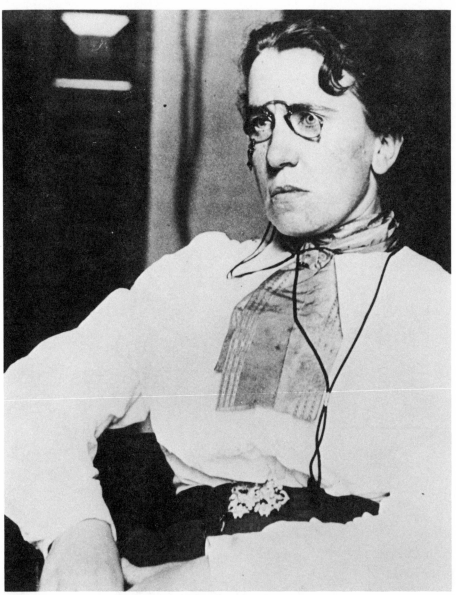

Goldman as a Russian revolutionary, ca. 1890s. *National Archives.*

Pen and ink drawing of Goldman at the outset of her career as a platform speaker. *UPI/Bettman Newsphotos.*

Alexander Berkman, ca. 1914. *Special Collections Library, the University of Michigan Library.*

Goldman speaking on birth control in Union Square, 1916. *UPI/Bettman Newsphotos.*

Ben Reitman, Goldman's long-time lover and campaign manager. *Cleveland Public Library.*

Goldman and Alexander Berkman, 1919. *UPI/Bettman Newsphotos.*

Goldman, Berkman, and friends in St. Tropez, ca. 1929. *Special Collections Library, the University of Michigan Library.*

Goldman with her lawyer Harry Weinberg arriving at Ellis Island for her deportation, 1919. *UPI/Bettman Newsphotos.*

Goldman speaking to reporters on her brief visit to the United States in 1934. *UPI/Bettman Newsphotos.*

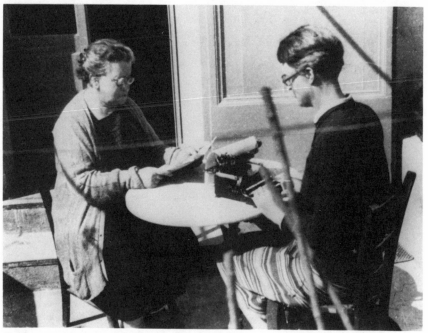

Goldman and her secretary working on her autobiography. *UPI/Bettman Newsphotos.*

Formal portrait of Goldman by Carl Van Vechten, 1934. *New York Public Library Special Collections. Reprinted by permission of the Estate of Carl Van Vechten, Joseph Solomon Executor.*

7

NOWHERE AT HOME: NOWHERE THE REVOLUTION, 1929–1940

As the political systems of western Europe and the United States moved toward collective solutions to the problems of the Great Depression, Goldman and her libertarian vision became politically homeless. The New Deal of liberal president Franklin Delano Roosevelt triumphed in the United States, and the armies of General Francisco Franco triumphed in Spain. Although Goldman and the American left made costly moral compromises, the possibility of a left-wing revolution anywhere became increasingly remote.

In 1912 Progressive muckraker and journalist Lincoln Steffens had contributed $200 toward the publication of Berkman's *Prison Memoirs*, and in 1917, at Goldman and Berkman's trial, Steffens had testified in their defense. Steffens was not an anarchist, but an eclectic liberal and sometime single-taxer, best known for his exposé of political corruption and malfeasance in local governments, *The Shame of the Cities* (1904). Steffens had become John Reed's mentor when Reed had come to New York, and like Reed, Steffens had reported on the Mexican Revolution. He had been in Russia in March 1917 and had seen the Kerensky regime come to power but had left before the Bolsheviks overthrew the provisional government. Thoroughly disillusioned with liberalism by Woodrow Wilson's unjust peace at Versailles, Steffens had later returned to

Russia to embrace the Bolsheviks: "I have seen the future, and it works," he wrote in his 1931 autobiography.

Steffens did not join an American Communist party, as Reed did, nor was he an uncritical admirer of Soviet Communism. But the Bolsheviks, he believed, represented a "future" in which the artificial distinctions between economic and political power that he had uncovered in *The Shame of the Cities* would be dissolved, and the "government of business and political government [would] be one." The Soviets had created an "all-comprehensive combination which should finally abolish the political state and be left standing as the government of Russia and of all the men and things Russian. There would be no privileged, no propertied persons," he explained. All men and women would work for the state, "disciplined hard" on the job "but outside of that—free, not governed at all."[1]

This future was most visible in Soviet Russia, Steffens believed, but he observed the trend toward collectivism elsewhere in Europe as well. For example, although he "balked" at the tyrannies of Benito Mussolini, Steffens explained that Mussolini was simply reestablishing the old sovereignty of the state under modern conditions. Steffens admired the German manufacturer Hugo Stinnes, who built an industrial monopoly and then moved to control the German government as well, even though Steffens recognized that Stinnes had laid the groundwork for Adolph Hitler's rise to power.[2]

Even as Steffens formulated his new political philosophy, the bottom fell out of the American economy. Many Americans had not shared in the celebrated prosperity of the 1920s, as Republican tax and tariff policies favored the rich at the expense of the poor. In some regions, the Depression had begun well before the stock market crash in fall 1929. Industries laid off workers, and laid-off workers stopped buying goods and services. As unemployment figures escalated, President Herbert Hoover sought solutions, guided by his personal and political distaste for government intervention. Hoping for their voluntary cooperation in rescuing the economy, Hoover called business leaders to the White House. Not knowing how futile those talks would be and how serious an economic debacle would follow, Steffens interpreted those meetings as the American version of his vision of the future: "an acknowledgement of the desirability of the union of business and politics, as in Russia."[3]

In some ways, Steffens's collectivist vision resembled Bellamy's in *Looking Backward.* Bellamy, however, thought anarchism was dangerous;

Steffens thought anarchism was a joke. He poked genial fun at his old friend Goldman for her attacks on Soviet Russia: "Emma Goldman declared [the Russian Revolution] was not an anarchist revolution. . . . As I told [her], to her indignation, she was a Methodist sent to a Presbyterian heaven, and naturally she thought it was hell."[4]

The apparent collapse of the free enterprise system, long foretold by orthodox Marxists, gave the American left an opportunity to capitalize on the correctness of that prediction. Only the Communist Party of the United States of America, however, effectively did so. The Socialist party, left temporarily leaderless by Deb's death in 1926, had lost momentum, its membership hitting a new low in 1927. But in 1928 its presidential nominee, Norman Thomas, a former Presbyterian minister trained at Union Theological Seminary, provided the party with new energy. Thomas appealed particularly to middle-class intellectuals, and in 1932, running on a reformist rather than a Socialist platform, Thomas won three times as many votes as he had four years earlier.

After Franklin Roosevelt's election in 1932 and the relief and recovery acts of the first hundred days of his administration, the SP found it more difficult to define itself to the left of the Democratic party, and some Socialists didn't bother. Upton Sinclair, who had rejoined the SP after the first World War, had run for the California governorship as a Socialist in 1930; in 1934, however, he ran as a Democrat. His platform was a variation on the Socialist cooperative commonwealth that he called EPIC, or End Poverty in California, based on production for use, not profit, and on partial public ownership. Some California Socialists, including Kate Richards O'Hare, left the party to support Sinclair. He lost a close election to his Republican challenger and was read out of the SP.

Norman Thomas continued to criticize some New Deal measures: the Agricultural Adjustment Act, which forced tenant farmers and sharecroppers off the land, and the National Industrial Recovery Act, which favored business over labor and the consumer. Nevertheless, those criticisms were muted. Compared to Hitler, who came to power in Germany in January 1933, Roosevelt appeared benevolent and democratic.

At the same time, the SP had to differentiate itself from the Communist party on the left. This too became harder as the SP's left-wing faction, the Militants, gained numbers and influence. In 1934 the Militants forced passage of a statement that pledged support to the Soviet Union. The SP's Old Guard, fearful (again) of a takeover, moved left in response, but energies that might have gone into creating socialist alternatives to the New Deal were directed instead into internecine party warfare.

Like the SP, the Industrial Workers of the World faced extinction in the late 1920s. Its leadership also badly split, IWW membership declined rapidly, and in 1928 it fell below 10,000. Unlike the SP, however, the IWW did not revive itself, even temporarily. It fought its last independent strike in the coal mines of Harlan County, Kentucky, where organizers for the CPUSA and the Congress of Industrial Organization would follow in the 1930s.[5]

Membership of the CPUSA had also declined in the late 1920s. In 1929, on orders from Stalin, international Communism turned "ultra-left" and moved into its "Third Period." As recounted in *Toward Soviet America* by William Z. Foster, then general secretary of the CPUSA, the party envisioned the overthrow of capitalism through "open struggle by the toiling masses." The resulting "civil war" would be led by the CPUSA, "the party of the toilers." The gradualism and political action preached by the Socialists were the chief obstacles to revolution, Foster claimed, and he denounced Socialists as "Social Fascists."[6] Political collaboration, such as the CPUSA had briefly attempted in 1924, was forbidden. Dual unionism, condemned by Lenin in 1921, was now encouraged, led by the Communist Trade Union Unity League.

In the early 1930s, however, the party gained new members as the Depression deepened in America. The stability of the Soviet Union's planned economy looked attractive to many liberals. In addition, Soviet Communism seemed the only bulwark against the rising tide of fascism in Italy and Germany. The CPUSA dramatized its revolutionary militance by organizing hunger marches, rent strikes, and unemployment demonstrations. Communists were actively involved in, although they did not control, the Bonus Expeditionary Force march on Washington in summer 1932, and they planned the hunger march of 2,500 people on the capital in December.[7] American Socialism seemed like timid reformism compared to the energy and bravado of the CPUSA.

In contrast, the anarchist movement was in retreat before the rise of powerful governments in western Europe and the United States. The freedom of the individual and the voluntarism that anarchism prized seemed no answer to worldwide economic depression or the rise of totalitarian dictatorships. The early measures of the New Deal, which seemed like hopeful reforms to the Socialists and duplicitous palliatives to the Communists, represented to anarchists the dangerous and intrusive growth of government. Taking their cue from exiled leaders Goldman and Berkman, American anarchists remained critical of Soviet Russia. Yet anarchists had no viable solutions or programs of their own to offer. Anarchist publications simply reprinted articles by the great European thinkers, for anarchism had nothing new to say.[8] The anarchist movement in the United States, moreover, had become again an immigrant phenomenon, kept alive by Spanish, Italian, and Russian Jewish newcomers.

In this discouraging political context, Goldman—her chances of returning to the United States remote and the future of anarchism dim—wrote the autobiography in which she played her most compelling role, the radical who was "nowhere at home." Goldman could not recover the private and public papers which had been seized from the *Mother Earth* office by federal agents when she was arrested in 1917, but she did recover over a thousand letters from countless friends, as well as materials collected by Agnes Inglis. Goldman could also rely on back issues of *Mother Earth* and on her two books about her experience in Russia. Benefactor Peggy Guggenheim had bought her the cottage at St. Tropez, and friends and political comrades had raised $2,500 for her to live on. She also acquired a secretary, Emily Holmes Coleman, a writer herself, who typed and edited Goldman's work. Her financial needs taken care of, Goldman sat down 27 June 1928, her fifty-ninth birthday, to the painful task of writing her autobiography: "It meant reliving my long-forgotten past, the resurrection of memories I did not wish to dig out from the deeps of my consciousness. It meant doubts in my creative ability, depression, and disheartenings."[9] She completed the 1,000-page manuscript in February 1931, and it was published in October of that year.

Her political exile at the time she wrote her autobiography left its mark on this version of her life. Throughout the book, Goldman plays the lonely individual, the "banner bearer" or the "pathfinder," battling against powerful governments and social conventions, alienated from friends and foes alike. Consequently, she emerges as "a symbol of the twentieth-century refugee . . . persecuted, imprisoned, repudiated and shunned . . . driven underground or into a crushing spiritual loneliness."[10]

The loneliness of her self-portrait was enhanced by occasionally insensitive and ungenerous portraits of others: her brutal, uncaring parents, the promiscuous Ben Reitman, the impotent Kersner, the inconsistent Johann Most, the ungrateful Voltairine de Cleyre, and the pushy Margaret Sanger, among others. Goldman had a long memory for slights and injuries. After the book's publication, some friends—Agnes Inglis, for example—complained, with justification, about unflattering descriptions of themselves or others, or too-flattering portraits of Goldman. Her only steadfast companion throughout this story was Berkman, and even her descriptions of his youthful zealousness and his deep depressions were sometimes uncomplimentary. Berkman, living nearby in St. Cloud and then in Nice, was her consultant and editor. (She had helped him with his *What Is Communist Anarchism,* published in 1929.)

As always, Goldman sought Berkman's approval and judged herself by what she imagined were his standards. Although there can be no dispute about his centrality in her life, his presence may have encouraged her to exaggerate his importance in the autobiography. For example, in *My Disillusionment* he was barely mentioned in her description of the museum expedition, but in *Living My Life,* he clearly directed it. In addition, the autobiography was yet another round in their never-ending competition. For example, here for the first time she admitted—or claimed—her complicity in his failed *attentat* at Homestead. Perhaps it is true that she had planned to go with him to Homestead, and perhaps she did trick herself out as a prostitute to raise the money to buy a revolver. It is possible, however, that she exaggerated her own role in order to share Berkman's glory—or disgrace.

The language of the autobiography helped to create an ambivalent literary persona for Goldman.[11] Sometimes her writing reflected her years on the platform, where she was self-assured: direct, blunt, and factual in discussions of political events. For example, her description of the 1896 presidential campaign: "The free silver campaign was at its height. The proposition of the free coinage of silver at the ratio with gold of sixteen to one had become a national issue almost over night," and she went on to explain perceptively why the eloquent William Jennings Bryan appealed to liberals and even to some anarchists. In contrast, her language was circuitous, coy, and abstract when discussing her personal and especially sexual relationships, where she perhaps felt disadvantaged by her age and, as she had already lamented, by her gender. "In the arms of Ed [Brady]," she wrote, "I learned for the first time the meaning of the great life-giving force. I understood its full beauty, and I eagerly drank its intoxicating joy and bliss."[12]

But even disguised in Victorian hyperbole, the descriptions of her several love affairs were highly unusual for a woman to write, and reviewers naturally remarked on them. When Goldman complained to

Berkman that the reviewer for the anarchist *Freie Arbeiter Shtime* had overemphasized her sex life, he reminded her, "in your life your love life was of an emphatic nature, and it is also emphasized in the book. . . . Sex has played a very great role in your life and your book would have been lacking if that role had not been mirrored in it." To Goldman, however, her love affairs were not just about sex, for she always saw connections and conflicts between her personal and her political lives. She had earlier explained to Berkman, "I do mean to cut out [of the autobiography] only casual love affairs, although all my experiences were so wrapped up with my work that it is difficult to separate them."[13]

Goldman and the book got good reviews. In a full-page lead article, the *New York Times*, for example, concluded that Goldman was "in her own right something which is rarely found, in palaces or hovels, in factories or offices, or on the barricades—an original and picturesque personality. Her autobiography is one of the great books of its kind."[14] At the same time that they praised Goldman, however, reviewers diminished anarchism. This was partly Goldman's fault, for throughout the autobiography, she described her anarchism as an emotional rather than an intellectual response to circumstances. In the very first pages of the book, she depicted her conversion to anarchism as a literally hysterical reaction to the execution of the Haymarket anarchists, as she tried to strangle one of their detractors, then fell to the floor in a swoon: "'The child has gone crazy,'" someone exclaims. She hadn't gone crazy: she had become an anarchist. And from then on in the story, impulses became the driving force for her political behavior—when she leapt to the stage to horsewhip Most, for example—and for the political behavior of others as well. Czolgosz, Berkman, and other practitioners of violence were always described as "sensitive souls" driven by uncontrollable emotions, not as men (or women) whose knowledge of the past or whose rational calculations led them, albeit mistakenly, to commit murder.[15] No wonder, then, that the *New Republic* remarked on her emotionalism, her *élan vital*, her "total lack of ideology," her "instinctivism": "Emma Goldman was an anarchist—and without having to think about it." And so the reviewer's inevitable conclusion: "Her failure to understand Russia is the anarchist failure to understand and hence to work upon the world."[16]

Similarly, the *New York Times* reviewer described Goldman as "often carried away by wild impulses. . . . Even those who differ most radically with her conclusions will find that they are dealing with a woman whose emotional reactions . . . are as normal as their next-door neigh-

bor's. . . . Her heart is all right whatever may be said of her dogma."
The implication was that anarchists were emotionally unbalanced: "A
psychologist could easily explain" why Goldman and others became anarchists, the reviewer pointed out.[17] The *Nation*'s Freda Kirchwey wrote,
"The emotion that drove her was a single force, whether it was directed
against the might of the government of Russia or toward the fulfillment
of personal passion. . . . Always she feels first and thinks later—and
less."[18]

Reviewers could afford to be generous, if condescending, to Goldman, for they saw as clearly as she did and without her help that anarchism was no longer a political movement to be taken seriously. The
New Republic's review was entitled "Elegy for Anarchism." Anarchism
was dead, the reviewer wrote, killed by communism and "by its [own]
eccentric emotionalism."[19] The *New York Times* review was also an obit-
uary. If there was to be a revolution, it would be a communist not an
anarchist revolution, the reviewer wrote. Unintentionally echoing Goldman's own words, the writer concluded: "The anarchist is nowhere at
home, and his numbers are dwindling."[20]

Goldman's publisher, Alfred A. Knopf, had given her a $7,000 ad-
vance. (*American Mercury*, which Knopf owned, had run two chapters
of the autobiography before its publication.[21]) Partly to make back the
advance and partly because the manuscript was very long, Knopf priced
the book at $7.50, more than Goldman had wanted it to cost and more
than most Americans were willing to pay during the hard times of 1931.
Although *Living My Life* may have had far more readers than buyers, it
did not make Goldman rich or financially secure.

In the spring of 1932, therefore, she left St. Tropez and began another lecture tour. The powerful regimes of Stalin, Mussolini, and Hitler,
and the imminence of another world war were an anarchist's nightmare,
and they became her chief lecture topics. In Copenhagen she spoke on
"Dictatorships: A World Menace." In Berlin, where a decade earlier
Goldman had spent two peaceful and productive years, Nazis threatened
her on the street. Even before Hitler took power, Germany was out of
bounds for the old Jewish radical.

Goldman's next base of operation was England. There she had
friends like Rebecca West and Paul Robeson, who celebrated with her
the publication of *Living My Life*. (In 1934 Robeson became a Communist after a visit to the Soviet Union.) But her lectures on dictatorship,
which now included Hitler as well as Stalin, could not stir the apathetic
British. In Holland, she was warned not to criticize the Dutch govern-

ment or the government of other countries such as Germany, as the Dutch tried to placate their neighbor, Hitler. Initially invigorated by the prospect of another free-speech battle, Goldman was summarily expelled from Holland in November 1933.

Although her British citizenship, courtesy of James Colton, guaranteed her political safety, Goldman was never free from police harassment. She had even been threatened with expulsion from France in March 1930, saved only by the intervention of an influential attorney.

Berkman, on the other hand, carried only a passport issued by the League of Nations for stateless persons. In May 1930 Berkman had been deported from France to Belgium. Given permission to return by the French government, he was nevertheless denied a visa and had to smuggle himself back into France. From that time on, Berkman's residence there was precarious. The United States government apparently wished him deported, or at least harassed, by the French. Only the efforts of a group of well-known intellectuals, including Albert Einstein, John Dewey, and Bertrand Russell, prevented his deportation in 1931. Berkman remained under police surveillance, however, and in 1935 was denied permission to move from Nice to St. Tropez. He was to remain in Nice under virtual house arrest until his death in 1936.

By 1933 Goldman was welcome almost nowhere in western Europe. She decided to return to Canada. There she could count on sympathetic anarchists, but of greater importance, from there she might more easily return to the United States. "America," she wrote Berkman, "is really a question of life and death to me. . . . It is my last resort to justify my life before myself." It was the place where she had spent most of her political life, had been most successful, and had enjoyed most personal happiness, she said. Understandably, she wanted to go back.[22] Goldman had enlisted the help of an influential liberal, Mabel Carver Crouch. Crouch organized a campaign for Goldman's return to the United States, supported by important political and literary figures including Dewey, Sinclair Lewis, and Amos Pinchot. Roger Baldwin received permission from U.S. Secretary of Labor Frances Perkins for Goldman to spend 90 days in the United States, provided that she speak only on literature and drama. After agreeing reluctantly to the conditions, Goldman arrived in the States on 1 February 1934. "Elderly Red Here to Pay Us 90-Day Visit," announced *News-Week*.[23]

A curious press and enthusiastic crowds greeted Goldman in her adopted hometown, New York. A welcoming dinner was oversubscribed and attended by liberal and leftist colleagues, including old friends Harry

Kelly, Henry Alsberg, and Leonard Abbott. As she had in 1914, she again refused an offer to appear on the vaudeville stage and was eagerly sought out as a speaker by Socialist and labor organizations. Her only critics were the Communist *Daily Worker*, which refused to carry the advertisements for her lectures, and the Daughters of the American Revolution, who refused to rent her a hall. FBI director J. Edgar Hoover kept her under surveillance.

Goldman drew good crowds in Chicago, Detroit, and Pittsburgh. These were her former stamping grounds, and lectures were arranged by political comrades. Elsewhere, however, her audiences were small and unenthusiastic. Goldman blamed it on the tour manager, James Pond, who had booked halls too large and too expensive to fill. Pond, in turn, claimed that the public was still hostile. More probably the public simply wasn't interested. Goldman was no longer a star, and Americans had short memories and did not recall the hysteria she had evoked 15 years earlier.

Goldman's opposition to both capitalism and communism put her nowhere on the political spectrum. Her libertarianism seemed quaint and outdated. In the face of the growing power of governments everywhere, the anarchism that had gotten Goldman deported in 1919 seemed not dangerous but nostalgic. Goldman's return prompted the *Nation*, for example, to reminisce about the American left: "In the old days Emma Goldman represented the extreme left; if you were more red than a Socialist, you might become an Anarchist. Today the Anarchists are a scattered handful of survivors, and the extreme left is divided among the various Communist groups. To them Emma Goldman is not a symbol of freedom in a world of tyrants; she is merely a wrong-headed old woman." The young and the working class were not interested in her or in anarchism, the article continued. "It is the middle-aged, middle-class liberals to whom she is a promise and a reminder . . . that freedom cannot be rolled under by the tanks and tractors of centralized power."[24]

For Goldman, her visit ended too soon, and she returned to Toronto. She remained a critic of the United States, as she reminded the readers of *Harper's Magazine*: it was a country in which the rich could acquire great wealth and power at the expense of the poor, where politicians manipulated votes, and where government stifled dissent and individuality.[25] But she saw hopeful signs, even in the New Deal. As she wrote Berkman, "America remains naive, childish in many respects in comparison to the sophistication of Europe. But I prefer its naïveté; there is youth in it, there is still the spirit of adventure. . . . The very experiment of Roosevelt, childish as it is, has the adventurous spirit of the country." No wonder she felt rejuvenated at being home: "In all the years in Europe I have not felt so vital or alive as I did while in the States and even in Canada."[26]

Goldman still hoped that American officials would have a change of heart. Baldwin made another application for her return, which was at first postponed and then rejected when a general strike of 100,000 workers in San Francisco broke out. Apparently someone in the federal government felt that she was still dangerous. Goldman made a last desperate attempt to use influential connections to change the Roosevelt administration's mind, but to no avail.[27] Since the war, she told the readers of the *Nation*, political dissenters were no longer given ready asylum in western European countries as they once had been. Instead, they wandered from country to country or were kept at the beck and call of local police. This, she wrote, was the "tragedy of the political exiles." She used Berkman as an example, but her own political exile too was tragic.[28]

Harper's had asked her to respond to the question, Was my life worth living? Goldman's public answer in December 1934 was an emphatic yes. She defined anarchism as she always had: "anarchism insists that the center of gravity in society is the individual—that he must think for himself, act freely, and live fully." She was careful to distinguish her position from that of the political right: her belief in freedom was not "'rugged individualism,' which at the first sign of danger runs to the armies and navies of the state for protection," she pointed out. The rise of dictatorships, the emergence of ever-stronger governments had temporarily put the anarchist movement on the defensive, she conceded. But dictatorships on the left and right had strengthened her own belief in anarchism. Eventually, the universal "love of freedom" would assert itself and anarchism would be vindicated, she predicted.[29]

As always, she was far less confident in her private correspondence with Berkman, which became more and more important to her as she found herself cut off from others on the left. Berkman himself was—as always—more despairing, for his situation was far more desperate. He could not leave France to lecture, as she could. He received no advances for his two books, *The Bolshevik Myth* and *What Is Anarchist Communism*, and he made so little money translating plays, fiction, and anarchist literature that he was close to destitution much of the time, rescued only by gifts from American comrades and sometimes from Goldman. When Goldman had complained in 1927 about the difficulties of lecturing in Canada, Berkman had replied: "there is either something wrong with our ideas (maybe they don't fit life) or with our mode of propaganda for the last forty years. . . . Why continue work that serves really no purpose?" In 1933 Berkman's analysis was even grimmer. "Fascism is growing," he wrote Mollie Steimer. "It is everywhere already, even if in some places still underground. And do not forget that this fascism, whether in black shirts, brown shirts, blue or red shirts, is supported by the masses. . . . There is a wave of reaction all through the world. . . . The truth is, our movement has accomplished nothing, anywhere."[30]

If the present looked bleak, the future of the anarchist revolution appeared bleaker. Goldman had never placed much faith in the people, and her elitism was now reinforced by the popular support for totalitarian governments. When Berkman was writing his *What Is Communist Anarchism*, intended to be a primer for workers, Goldman had advised him: "Hold the mirror of slavish acquiescence and willingness to follow any charlatan who can hoodwink the workers up before your readers." And as he watched the Russians, the Italians, and the Germans follow such "charlatans," Berkman became even more pessimistic. In 1931 Goldman had written him, "I am delighted to find that your attitude to the world situation is as mine. I too have come to the conclusion, bitter as it is, that hardly anything has come of our years of effort. And that the mass is really hopeless as far as real progress and freedom are concerned."[31] Goldman continued to hope that the individual could hold out against the dictatorship of the mob or the politician. But Berkman saw, as she did not, the implications of her elitism. "That means," he pointed out, "that we have no faith any more in the realization of our ideas. Or at least damned little. For if the masses cannot be relied on since they are so easily swayed by demagogues, then WHO is going to do it? The FEW exceptional individuals? They can't bring about a social change. Unless they do it as it has been done until now—by violence, political activity, by the state, in short. . . . THAT is just the reason why our movement makes little progress—in fact, practically none at all, as a movement."[32]

And the more prescient and pessimistic their predictions of the early 1930s proved to be, the more politically isolated the two anarchists became. As the Bolsheviks chased their former leader Trotsky across Europe and changed the brutal Cheka into the equally brutal political police, the GPU, and as the struggle to the death between international fascism and communism took shape, Goldman and Berkman felt vindicated: they had predicted this scenario for almost a decade, although few on the left would admit they were right. Charged with giving ammunition to the political right when a Hearst newspaper reprinted one of her articles critical of the Communist regime, Goldman responded, "if one is first going to consider the use reactionaries are going to make, one will always have to remain silent. And by silence, one becomes a party to the wrong." She had learned that sad lesson during her two years in Bolshevik Russia.[33]

While in Canada in summer of 1934, Goldman had one last romantic adventure. Her admirer was a blind sociologist whom she had met on tour in Chicago. Frank Heiner claimed to be infatuated with her work and with her. Needing the reassurance of this young lover—he was 36 and she was 65—she could not resist encouraging him. As always, she justified her attraction partly in terms of his politics: he was an anarchist. But he was also married; his wife, Mary, read Goldman's letters to her husband and his letters to Goldman. At his insistence, Goldman spent two love-filled weeks with Heiner in Toronto, but she had few illusions about their affair. It ended when she returned to St. Tropez, although they exchanged love letters for some months afterward.

Goldman had earned so little writing for American journals and lecturing in Canada that a friend had to buy her return ticket to France. Exiled both by political events and by nations, a heartsick Goldman left Canada on 3 May 1935. Back in St. Tropez, she wrote Roger Baldwin: "For a revolutionist and internationalist it is indeed disgraceful to be so rooted to the soil of one country. Perhaps one cannot adjust oneself easily in later years as one does in one's youth. Whatever the reason, I have to admit defeat. . . . I know now that I will remain an alien abroad for the rest of my life."[34]

As the pessimistic Goldman might have predicted, although the Depression persisted and worsened, there was no revolution in the United States. Hundreds of thousands of workers joined unions, and there were scattered outbursts of violence—for example, on Memorial Day 1937 when Chicago police fired on striking steelworkers. But most Americans blamed themselves or each other, not free-enterprise capitalism, for their financial problems. Liberal solutions to the long-running economic downturn, the second phase of the New Deal in 1935, included a more progressive income tax, social insurance in the form of the Social Security Act, and the National Labor Relations Act, or Wagner Act, which put the federal stamp of approval on unions and collective bargaining. None of these measures was revolutionary or even new. Most had been discussed since the Progressive period. But in the context of long-term unemployment and hunger, the legislation appeared at least reformist.

Also in 1935, liberal reformism became good enough for the CPUSA. Frightened by fascism on its borders and searching for allies among the western democracies, the Soviet Communist party ordered a reversal of its earlier demand for an immediate and exclusively Communist-led revolution. The new policy, announced at the Seventh World Congress of the Communist International, did an about-face: "instead of the class struggle, cooperation with the bourgeoisie. Instead of the Soviet system, eulogy of democracy."[35] In the United States, this policy meant a "Popular Front" against fascism, a cease-fire in the CPUSA's attacks on the "social fascist" Socialists, and collaboration with whatever liberal and leftist elements would go along. Communism, so the new slogan read, was "twentieth-century Americanism." The works of Marx and Lenin took a backseat to those of the American revolutionaries Jefferson and Paine. The American-born Earl Browder, former Socialist and former Wobbly, became the party leader. Communists formed or controlled a wide variety of "front organizations" with left-wing and liberal memberships, including the American Writers Congress, the National Negro Congress, and the American Student Union. The CPUSA remained mildly critical of the New Deal; in the 1936 presidential election, however, it attacked not Roosevelt but his Republican opponent, Alfred Landon.

The CPUSA also threw itself energetically into the organizing drives of the Congress of Industrial Organization (CIO). The CIO, encouraged by the passage of the Wagner Act, broke with the American Federation of Labor in 1935 and set out to form unions that had industrial rather than craft bases. Although slow to sense the significance of the CIO, the Communists, trained in the earlier dual unions of the Trade Union Unity League, were skillful and dedicated organizers. Communists led the United Auto Workers in the victorious sit-down strike against General Motors in Flint, Michigan, and Communists became officials in many industrial and white-collar unions, such as the United Electrical Union, the Radio and Machine Workers Union, the Transport Workers Union, and the American Newspaper Guild, as well as on the staff of the CIO itself.[36]

Thus the CPUSA, the ultraleft outcast of the 1920s, gained respectability and success in the mid-1930s by eschewing revolution. The new moderation of the Popular Front attracted union members, liberals, and intellectuals who had found William Z. Foster's talk of "open struggle by the toiling masses" foreign-sounding and abrasive. By 1939 the party had begun to support FDR for a third term. The CPUSA membership was estimated at 80,000 to 90,000, and for the first time the majority of members were American-born. The party also exerted influence over thousands of nonmembers through front groups and unions.[37]

The Socialist party generally viewed the Communist Popular Front with distaste or caution, still smarting from recent accusations of "social fascism" as well as from a Communist-inspired riot at a Socialist meeting in Madison Square Garden in February 1934. Its right wing had broken from the SP in 1936 to form the Social Democratic Federation, which had taken with it only a handful of members but some important financial contributors, including Abraham Cahan, editor of the *Jewish Daily Forward*. The Social Democratic Federation would not even vote for Socialist candidates. SP leader Norman Thomas joined in few Popular Front activities and remained critical of the New Deal, as well. After Roosevelt had co-opted some of the reforms advocated by the SP in 1932, Thomas's 1936 presidential campaign stressed the differences between socialism and the New Deal. The result was a disastrous defeat for the SP. The SP's most significant loss was organized labor, which almost completely deserted socialism for Roosevelt.

The few anarchists who remained interested in politics in the light of the failed Russian Revolution became friendly to Roosevelt—even if they did not vote for him. One of the last remaining English-language anarchist journals, *Road to Freedom*, had published an editorial in 1930 lamenting, "There is no single hopeful sign of an awakening spirit among the people of the West. . . . History has taught the masses nothing."[38]

Goldman made a last attempt at lecturing in London on the drama and on the increasingly ominous possibility of a European war. The lectures were not a financial success, and she returned to St. Tropez to sell the cottage and to be close to Berkman. He had asked that she return to care for him and Emmy Eckstein, since both faced operations. In March 1936, Berkman underwent a second prostate operation, which left him in considerable pain. Eckstein was also very ill, suffering from a disabling stomach disorder.

Eckstein and Goldman had never liked each other, and despite Berkman's invitations, Goldman had always been reluctant to visit them in Nice. Eckstein was from a conventional middle-class German background. She had continued to hope that Berkman would marry her, but although he contemplated it, he never did. More important, Eckstein was possessive and inordinately jealous of all the women Berkman knew and particularly of Goldman, who had shared most of Berkman's life. Goldman was jealous too, and she could be officious and interfering, qualities that do not generally moderate with age. The friction between Goldman and the younger woman could not have made Berkman's life easy.

Yet the friendship between the two aging exiles survived, even though, as always, they had their differences. From London Goldman wrote Berkman this touching message on his sixty-fifth birthday: "no one ever was so rooted in my being, so ingrained in every fiber, as you have been and are to this day. . . . Our common struggle and all it has brought us in travail and disappointment hardly explain what I feel for you. Indeed, I know that the only loss that would matter would be to lose you or your friendship." As Berkman was awaiting his second operation, he had left her instructions in the event of his death and in a rare sentimental moment, had spoken of her importance to him: "Dearest sailor mine, staunchest chum of my lifetime . . . I just want you to know that my thoughts are with you and I consider our life of work and comradeship and friendship . . . one of the most beautiful and dearest things in the world. . . . I embrace you with all my heart, you bravest, strongest, and truest woman and comrade I have known in my life." But he concluded pessimistically: "I have lived my life and I am really of the opinion that when one has neither health nor means and cannot work for his ideas, it is time to clear out."[39]

Berkman survived the surgery physically, but he could not survive the overwhelming depression that had dogged him for years. Overcome by pain and a diagnosis of cancer, by poverty, and, perhaps worst, by recurring despair over the failure of his lifework, Berkman shot himself on 27 June 1936, after first sending Goldman a birthday telegram. The bullet perforated his stomach but did not kill him. He concealed the wound from Eckstein until a doctor discovered it several hours later. When Goldman arrived at his bedside, Berkman was still conscious but in great pain, and he soon slipped into a coma. He died at 10 P.M. on 28 June and was buried on 30 June in a cemetery in Nice.

Goldman was shattered. Berkman had been her lover, teacher, and comrade, the emotional, moral, and intellectual center of her life for 46 years. Especially since their deportation from the United States, he had been her mainstay. On her birthday morning, she had written to him: "Whom else should I write on this day but you. Only there is nothing to tell. I keep thinking what a long time to live. For whom? For what? But there is no answer." With Berkman gone, there was no one even to ask. "The largest part of my life followed our comrade to his grave," she wrote in an open letter to friends in July. But she pledged herself to "continue the struggle for a new and beautiful world . . . the ultimate triumph of anarchism, the ideal Sasha loved passionately."[40]

Only two months later, Goldman had her last opportunity to fight for that ideal, in the Spanish civil war. In the 1930s the anarchist movement was probably stronger in Spain than anywhere else. It had a long and vigorous tradition there, dating back at least 70 years, nourished by the poverty of the peasants and industrial workers. Often persecuted by the Spanish monarchy, anarchism had produced its own martyr, Francisco Ferrer, who was executed in 1909. The movement had also created two organizations: in 1910, a confederation of trade unions, the Confederacion National del Trabajo (CNT) and in 1924 after the CNT was officially dissolved, a militant underground organization, the Federación Anarquista Ibérica (FAI), which surfaced as the CNT-FAI in 1936. Spanish anarchists had sporadically employed general strikes and terrorism as strategies of opposition; the movement was particularly strong in Catalonia.

In February 1936 a leftist coalition was elected to power, replacing a repressive conservative regime. Anarchists had participated in the election, but they continued to oppose the new Spanish republic for which they had voted. The anarchists' goal was a social revolution that would replace the government with workers' communes, such as anarchists had attempted to establish in various parts of Spain from 1931 to 1936. In July 1936, however, the troops of Nationalist leader Francisco Franco launched an attack to overthrow the republic.

The CNT-FAI joined in the fight against Franco with its own militia. The organization set up anarchist collectives in Catalonia and seized control of some cities, notably Barcelona. Anarchists saw their actions less as a defense of the republican government than as an effort to further their own revolution. (Anarchist literature still calls this conflict the "Spanish Revolution," not the Spanish civil war.)

In August the CNT-FAI invited Goldman to join the fight by directing a press bureau that would handle their English-language propaganda. The invitation saved Goldman from her despair over Berkman's death. Her interest in the Spanish anarchist movement dated back to the first decade of the century. She had protested the repression of anarchists in 1909 and had sponsored the Ferrer Modern School in New York City. She had met representatives from the Spanish anarchist organizations in the Soviet Union at meetings of the Red International of Trade Unions and had visited Spain as a tourist in December 1928. Made cautious by her bitter experience with the Bolsheviks, however, Goldman had been slower than some of her anarchist comrades to see the revolutionary potential in Spain. But at the invitation from the CNT-FAI, she plunged with enthusiasm into the battle. In the fall of 1936, at age 67, Goldman traveled to Barcelona, where the anarchist revolution had come closest to realization. There trade unions and socialist and anarchist groups owned and operated the shops and factories, and the flags and songs of revolution filled the streets. Goldman also visited the front lines, where she admired the courage of anarchist soldiers like Buenaventura Durruti and "the great heroes of the battle . . . the Spanish masses."[41] The factories, shops, and farms, managed as workers' collectives, were visible proof that anarchism was not just a lofty ideal but was practical and workable. Goldman's early misgivings about the backwardness of Spanish women were dispelled when she saw women fighting in the militia and met members of the feminist anarchist organization, Mujeres Libres (Emancipated Women). Goldman would make three short trips to Spain, the last in the fall of 1938. She did not speak the native language, however, and depended on guides from the CNT-FAI, who doubtless showed her what they wanted her to see.

Most of Goldman's work for the Spanish anarchists was done in London. There she used her skills as a writer and speaker to propagandize and to raise money for the relief of homeless Spanish women and children. Despite the weakness of the English anarchist movement and the lingering hostility toward Goldman herself because of her anticommunism, she held some large and successful public meetings and raised a significant amount of money. This is "our Revolution," she wrote fellow anarchist Harry Kelly, and indeed the events in Spain generated hope and excitement within the disheartened anarchist communities in the United States, as well.[42]

But the cause wasn't as simple as Goldman thought, for the Spanish civil war had almost immediately assumed international importance. Fascist Germany and Italy sent troops, guns, and planes to Franco in July 1936. The republican forces had hoped for aid from the western democracies, but those countries opted for neutrality and nonintervention. Instead, help for the republicans came from Soviet Russia, which sent arms and, later, technicians.

For the American left, the war in Spain pitted the armies of fascism—Franco, Mussolini, and Hitler—against the forces of liberty and democracy—the Spanish republicans and the Soviet Communists. The Soviet Union's sending aid also meant that the war became a Popular Front cause. Despite the U.S. government's neutrality, 3,200 Americans, mostly liberals and leftists, joined a fighting force that went to Spain. Under CPUSA influence, the unit was named the Abraham Lincoln Brigade, thus borrowing the aura of the president who had fought to save the American republic. Socialist efforts to organize a Eugene V. Debs brigade failed.

In November 1936, four Spanish anarchists became ministers in the embattled republican government. They made common cause with a coalition government that included Communists and was sustained by Soviet weapons and troops. Anarchist militiamen were turned into conventional brigades controlled by the central government. In May 1937, however, some government troops fought rebellious anarchists on the streets of Barcelona, leaving hundreds dead. The four anarchist ministers were removed from office, and a new coalition that was more responsive to Communists, because of the crucial Soviet military aid, took charge. The new government then proceeded to repress anarchists and other dissidents.

As a paid publicist for the CNT-FAI, Goldman had to defend the Spanish anarchists not only from leftists and liberals but also from other anarchists. The CNT-FAI's participation in the electoral process and in government, she wrote in an article for *Spain and the World*, was justified because it was motivated not by a desire for personal or political power but by the need to defend democracy against fascism. "One can still breathe in democratic countries, little democracy though they may have. . . . All of this is obliterated by Fascism. . . . I believe as fervently as I always have that affiliations with governments and political parties are inimical to Anarchism and harmful. I cannot, however, remain blind to the fact that life is more impelling than theories."[43]

Publicly she described the war as a revolution embodying Berkman's anarchist communism, a rebirth of his ideals. In actual fact, however, Berkman had supported the anarchist participation in the February 1936 elections only halfheartedly, and Goldman herself had spoken out against that participation in March 1936.[44] Privately, therefore, she anguished and doubted. In a letter to her old friend Ben Capes, she wondered "what Sasha would have done. Would he have refused to work for the CNT-FAI? . . . I sometimes doubt our dead comrade, such a stickler to every iota of our ideas, would have joined me in my stand." And yet, she concluded hopefully, "I rather think he would."[45] By 1938 the Spanish anarchists themselves divided over the issue of continued collaboration. Whatever her private misgivings, Goldman did not publicly oppose it.

Some anarchists, such as Mollie Steimer, were also pacifists, and Goldman herself had recently come to believe, in the light of the Bolshevik Revolution, that violence was destructive. And yet she had to defend this armed conflict and to admire seasoned terrorists and military heroes like Durruti. Spanish anarchists, she claimed, used violence only in defense of the social revolution. This was Berkman's old argument. And yet in private correspondence Goldman wrote, "More and more I come to the conclusion that there can be no anarchist revolution. By its very violent nature, revolution denies everything anarchism stands for."[46]

Anarchists had long debated the uses of violence and political action; these were familiar issues. Also painfully familiar to Goldman was her personal dilemma: her failure to make public her own criticisms of a revolution whose general goal she supported but whose strategies she opposed. Goldman had sadly regretted her silence about the Bolsheviks during her two years in Russia. Yet this time not only did she remain silent, but she also wrote and spoke on behalf of anarchists who betrayed her principles. When the CNT-FAI reprimanded her for writing about political persecution in Spain, she threatened to resign her position as CNT-FAI representative, but she never did. In May 1938, she wrote to friend and mentor Rudolph Rocker: "I am torn into a thousand directions. I want to help our comrades and yet I feel that my silence is a sign of consent to all the dreadful and useless compromises our comrades are making."[47]

Both the anarchist revolution and the republican war against fascism in Spain were lost. By the time Franco's forces took over Spain in April 1939, Communists within the republican government had destroyed the anarchist collectives and anarchists' influence.

Goldman's faith in anarchist revolution, badly shaken already, almost collapsed with the fall of republican Spain. Her faith in herself was shaken as well. "You do not know how frightfully cut off I am from everybody and everything I know in the States," she wrote Rocker. "I never felt that way so long as Sasha was alive. . . . I miss Sasha more since the Spanish struggle and defeat."[48] As the anarchists had abandoned Barcelona before the advancing Franco, Goldman had fled London and gone to Amsterdam to organize Berkman's papers, which she had donated to the International Institute for Social History. As Alice Wexler points out, Goldman attempted to sort out her past as her present collapsed.[49] In public, however, Goldman retained her faith in her Spanish comrades and blamed the loss of the war on Communist sabotage. In June 1939 she went again to Canada, this time to raise funds for Spanish relief.

Many on the American left had made even more costly compromises with conscience than Goldman had. Cooperation with the Communist Popular Front had meant collaboration with Stalin's regime, which from 1934 to 1938 had initiated the imprisonment and extermination of 8 million of its so-called political opponents. As news of the trials and purges reached the United States, some Americans immediately withdrew from the CPUSA or from Popular Front activities, and an investigation was initiated into the Moscow trials of Trotsky and other alleged traitors. Although the investigation, headed by philosopher John Dewey, established to its own satisfaction that Trotsky had not been a traitor, it proved to be a futile exercise. Trotsky was assassinated in Mexico in 1940.

For Goldman, there was bittersweet satisfaction in watching Americans' growing disillusionment with Communism, so similar to her own almost two decades earlier. Who could blame her for reminding Dewey that repression did not begin with Stalin's purges, but with the Bolshevik regime and Trotsky himself, "the butcher of Kronstadt"?[50]

Others on the left who had excused collaboration with Communists because the Soviet Union had held out against fascism finally gave up their last illusions when the Soviet and Nazi governments signed a non-aggression pact in August 1939. The CPUSA lost at least 15 percent of its membership, probably more, and many of its fellow travelers in the various front organizations. The party, which had vigorously opposed American neutrality during the Spanish civil war, now argued just as vigorously against American military intervention as Hitler invaded Poland and Russia invaded eastern Poland and Finland. The CPUSA's membership and influence would never recover from Stalin's shocking about-face.[51]

By this time Goldman was making her home with Dutch comrades in Toronto, and the Canadian Jewish anarchists again made her welcome. She had returned to her Jewish roots, which she had seldom acknowledged and about which she was still ambivalent. She was critical of Jews for not having resisted Hitler, for example, but at the same time she criticized countries like Britain that did not grant Jews political asylum. Still longing for the United States, Goldman nevertheless had rejected a possible return that was conditional upon her testifying before the Dies Committee of Congress, then investigating communism. She knew that the grounds for its opposition to communism were very different from her own. On 27 June 1939 Goldman celebrated her seventieth birthday in Toronto. She received a visit from her family and dozens of letters and telegrams from well-wishers around the world. Especially prized was the message from CNT-FAI leader Marino Vasquez: "'The Spanish militants admire and revere you, as Anarchists should admire and value those of a great heart and abiding humanism for all mankind. . . . We declare you our spiritual mother.'"[52]

In public Goldman remained as confident of her ideal as ever. In an open letter to friends and comrades, she reminisced: "August 15 [1939] will be exactly a half century since I entered our ranks and took up the battle for Anarchism. Far from regretting this step, I can say honestly I am more convinced than in August 1889 of the logic and justice of our ideal" despite the "blackest reaction in every country." In private, however, she despaired: "I feel so uprooted I do not belong anywhere," she wrote Rocker. "I know nearly everybody feels that way now. . . . [T]here is no movement anywhere. . . . The tragedy is that having dedicated fifty years to one thing, one becomes unfit for anything else."[53]

In September 1939, Great Britain and France declared war on Germany, and the conflict that Goldman had foreseen began. Although she loathed the fascism of Hitler's Germany (with which the Soviet Union was still allied), she opposed this war between nations, as she had opposed the First World War. She had come to believe—and certainly her own experience bore her out—that nothing good came of war.

In October, four Italian immigrants were arrested and charged with violating the Canadian War Measures Act because they possessed leftist literature. As she had two decades earlier in the United States, Goldman challenged what she saw as government repression of free speech. As tirelessly as a woman of 70 could, she threw herself into the effort to prevent the threatened deportation of Arthur Bortolotti to Italy, where she was confident that he would be executed by Mussolini's government. The young Italians were soon released from jail. When Bortolotti became ill, she used her own last physical reserves to nurse him.

Powerful states and powerful political leaders had made anarchism an anachronism, and collaboration and compromises with the left wing had proved futile. The Depression and the Spanish civil war had offered the left opportunities that it had not seized. The Second World War, like the first, would be followed by a wave of political reaction in western nations, but there would be no revolution.

On 17 February 1940, in the company of anarchist friends, Goldman suffered a massive cerebral hemmorhage. Her right side was paralyzed, and she could speak only with difficulty. When she appeared to be recovering, her niece Stella organized a Friends of Emma Goldman Committee to raise funds for her care and to press for her return to the United States.

Goldman died 14 May 1940. Only then was she permitted back into her adopted homeland. She was buried at Waldheim Cemetery in Chicago, near the Haymarket martyrs who had been the beginning of her journey, and near Voltairine de Cleyre, Mother Jones, and Bill Haywood, who had accompanied her along the way.

EPILOGUE

Goldman's self-portrait in *Living My Life* was not self-deception. She was often "nowhere at home," the wandering Jew, the marginal immigrant, the exiled radical, the "voice crying in the wilderness." But although both her personality and her political philosophy encouraged her to ignore it, Goldman was part of—indeed symbolic of—a larger community.

John Sayles's short story, "At the Anarchists' Convention," explores the passage of time and the American left: "old Mrs. Axelrod, who knew Emma Goldman from the Garment Workers, is dozing in her chair. . . . [A] museum piece, [a] link to the past." Deaf, arthritic, querulous, and quarrelsome, the elderly Jewish anarchists gather for their annual meeting at a fancy New York hotel. A college student circulates among them with a tape recorder, trying to preserve "the memories of anarchism," she explains. The young woman is astonished to meet an anarchist whose work she has read: "I didn't realize you were still alive," she exclaims. "It's a matter of seconds," he replies. Even before dinner the anarchists begin to bicker and argue, as old animosities and ancient grudges resurface. The tumult of their shouts and recriminations reveals their frustration, "born out of all the insults swallowed, the battles lost, out of all the smothered dreams and desires . . . the sound of a terribly deep despair. . . . Over an hour it lasts, the sniping, the shouting, the accusations, and countercharges." Then the hotel manager enters and tells the old people they must leave so that the Rotary Club can use the room. But the anarchists have paid already (in cash, they don't believe in checks), and they unite against the common enemy. When the manager returns with the police, he finds the anarchists "standing together, arms linked, the lame held up out of their wheelchairs, the deaf joining from memory . . . in 'We Shall Not Be Moved.'"[1]

With humor and compassion, Sayles tells us how the New Left of the 1960s saw the Old: alive, but barely. And Sayles's assessment is almost right. The Communist party of the United States was able to survive World War II by forging another popular front to support the United States' wartime alliance with the Soviet Union. But as that war ended and the Cold War against international communism began, the United States experienced a second "red scare." Scores of CPUSA leaders, including Elizabeth Gurley Flynn, went to prison. In 1956, Nikita Khrushchev's revelations of the enormity of Stalin's purges, and then the Soviet invasion of Hungary, cost thousands of American Communists their last illusions and the CPUSA much of its remaining membership.

The Socialist party had remained paralyzed between the New Deal welfare state on the right, which had stolen SP reform measures, and the CPUSA on the left, which had stolen many of its members. Pacifist Norman Thomas had first strenuously opposed the United States' entrance into World War II and had then given the enormously popular war only minimal support, further weakening his own leadership and the SP itself. As Socialist membership and votes declined, Thomas urged in 1950 that the party cease to run presidential candidates and concentrate on education rather than political action. Ignoring Thomas, the SP in 1952 ran a candidate who won fewer votes than the Socialist Labor or Prohibitionist candidates. This humiliation effectively ended the political career of the once-popular party of Eugene V. Debs.

The anarchist movement that Goldman and Berkman had led was almost gone too, done in by the failure of the Spanish revolution, the seductive appeals of a federal government whose powers were swollen by the Depression and by wartime emergencies, and an end to the influx of the southeastern European immigrants who had become the backbone of the movement. Anarchism lived on only as a cultural and social phenomenon, primarily among Yiddish-speaking Jews in New York, who appear in Sayles's story.[2]

Sayles calls the aging anarchists "old Lefties" because he sees anarchism not as a tiny peripheral movement but as representative of all American radicalism. He thus acknowledges in his fiction what historians seldom have: the importance of anarchism to the American left, an importance dramatized by Goldman's life. First, anarchists often made common cause with others on the left: together they organized unions and strikes, rescued Tom Mooney, fought for birth control and free speech, opposed the First World War, and supported the Spanish Republic. Second, the anarchists, who were visible, outspoken, often immigrants and therefore politically vulnerable, were the ritual scapegoats of the left—lightning rods who attracted and sometimes deflected the wrath of the American public and the government. Anarchists became targets of the first immigration law, which barred people for their political beliefs, and anarchists provided the American left with their few famous martyrs: the Haymarket eight, Joe Hill, and Sacco and Vanzetti.

Anarchism in fact experienced a kind of rebirth in the 1960s, for the youthful radicalism of that decade had common goals with the earlier movement: free speech, free love, women's liberation, and an end to the draft and to an unjust war. In addition, the movements shared a predilection for intellectual heterodoxy and dramatic gesture, a distrust of electoral politics-as-usual, and a preference for direct action and the communal lifestyle.[3] John Lennon's compelling lyric "Imagine" is the anarchist vision set to music. Whether they knew it or not, the New Lefties borrowed much from the anarchist "old Lefties."

When political radicalism was briefly reborn in the 1960s and early 1970s, so was scholarly and popular interest in the left and in Goldman. She began to appear in biographies, in plays, and in movies, most prominently in the 1981 film *Reds*.

Goldman was not homeless. She was an anarchist—an "old Lefty"—maybe the most famous and certainly the most dramatic of them all. Often (although not always) faced with the common enemies of injustice and repression, Goldman took her place with the others on the left: "standing together, arms linked . . . joining . . . in 'We Shall Not Be Moved.'"

CHRONOLOGY

1869   Emma Goldman born 27 June in Kovno, Lithuania.

1881   Assassination of Alexander II. Goldman family moves to St. Petersburg.

1886   Emma and sister Helene emigrate to the United States. Haymarket riot.

1887   Edward Bellamy publishes *Looking Backward*.

1889   Goldman moves to New York City and meets Alexander Berkman. Jane Addams opens Hull House in Chicago.

1892   The failed *attentat* at Homestead. Berkman is imprisoned in Western Penitentiary.

1893   Goldman goes to jail for one year for inciting to riot.

1895   Studies medicine in Vienna. Meets Kropotkin in London.

1897–1899   Makes cross-country speaking tours in United States.

1901   Leon Czolgosz assassinates President William McKinley. Socialist Party of America founded.

1905   Industrial Workers of the World founded.

1906   *Mother Earth* begins publication. Berkman is released from Western Penitentiary.

1908   Goldman meets Benjamin Reitman.

1909–1912   Free-speech fights.

1912   Strike at Lawrence, Massachusetts.

1915–1916   Birth control fight. Goldman goes to jail for two weeks for distributing birth control information.

1917   United States enters World War I. Goldman and Berkman organize No-Conscription League. Both are arrested and imprisoned for opposition to draft. Espionage Act. Bolshevik Revolution.

1918   Sedition Act. *Mother Earth* is shut down.

1919   Eugene V. Debs is imprisoned. John Reed publishes *Ten Days That Shook the World*. Goldman and Berkman are released from prison; both are deported. Socialist Party splits.

1920   Passage of the Nineteenth Amendment enfranchises women. Goldman and Berkman arrive in Soviet Russia. Both consult Lenin and Kropotkin. They go to work for the Museum of the Revolution.

1921   Goldman and Berkman leave the Soviet Union.

1922–1924   In Berlin, Goldman writes *My Disillusionment in Russia*.

1926   Marries James Colton and travels to Canada.

1928   Settles in St. Tropez, begins writing *Living My Life*.

1931   *Living My Life* is published. Lincoln Steffens publishes *The Autobiography of Lincoln Steffens*.

1933   Hitler comes to power in Germany.

1934   Goldman makes a 90-day visit to the United States.

1935   Communist Popular Front.

1936   Berkman commits suicide.

1936–1939   Goldman works for Spanish anarchists in support of the Spanish revolution.

1940   Emma Goldman dies in Toronto and is buried at Waldheim Cemetery in Chicago.

NOTES AND REFERENCES

PREFACE

1. The quote is from an undated letter excerpted in Richard and Anna Marie Drinnon, eds., *Nowhere at Home: Letters from Exile of Emma Goldman and Alexander Berkman* (New York: Schocken Books, 1975), xi. I have adapted the Drinnons' title for the subtitle of this book.

2. George Woodcock, *Anarchism: A History of Libertarian Ideas and Movements* (Cleveland: Meridian Books, 1962), is the best introduction to anarchism.

3. This standard classification is used by George Woodcock ("Anarchism," in Paul Edwards, ed., *The Encyclopedia of Philosophy* [New York: Macmillan, 1967], 113–14), Paul Avrich (*An American Anarchist: The Life of Voltairine de Cleyre* [Princeton, N.J.: Princeton University Press, 1978], xv–xvi), and others.

4. De Cleyre is quoted in Avrich, *An American Anarchist*, 11. Ascaso is quoted in James Joll, *The Anarchists* (Cambridge, Mass.: Harvard University Press, 1980), 231.

5. Emma Goldman, *Anarchism and Other Essays* (Port Washington, N.Y.: Kennikat Press, 1910); *My Disillusionment in Russia* (New York: Doubleday, Page and Co., 1923); *My Further Disillusionment in Russia* (New York: Doubleday, Page and Co., 1924); Drinnon and Drinnon, eds., *Nowhere at Home*; David Porter, ed., *Vision on Fire: Emma Goldman on the Spanish Revolution* (New Paltz, N.Y.: Commonground Press, 1985).

6. Emma Goldman, *Living My Life* (New York: Knopf, 1931).

CHAPTER 1

1. Frank Harris, *Contemporary Portraits* (London: Grant Richards Ltd., 1924), 223.

2. Mary Antin, *The Promised Land* (1912; reprint, Boston: Houghton Mifflin, 1969), 3, 5.

3. Nicholas V. Riasanovsky, *A History of Russia* (New York: Oxford University Press, 1984), 324–35.

4. Antin, *Promised Land*, 8.

5. Antin, *Promised Land*, 30.

6. Antin, *Promised Land*, 33.

7. Antin, *Promised Land*, 29.

8. Emma Goldman, *Living My Life* (New York: Dover Publications, 1970), 447. Hereinafter cited as *LML*.

9. *LML*, 59–60.

10. Alice Wexler, *Emma Goldman in America* (Boston: Beacon Press, 1984), 15–16.

11. Hippolyte Havel, "Introduction to Emma Goldman," in Goldman, *Anarchism and Other Essays* (Port Washington, N.Y.: Kennikat Press, 1910), 8–9.

12. Harris, *Contemporary Portraits*, 224–26.

13. *LML*, 21.

14. Harris, *Contemporary Portraits*, 225–26.

15. Havel, "Introduction to Emma Goldman," 9.

16. *LML*, 21.

17. *LML*, 116–17.

18. Havel, "Introduction to Emma Goldman," 10; Harris, *Contemporary Portraits*, 11.

19. *LML*, 39.

20. *LML*, 118.

21. Riasanovsky, *A History of Russia*, 381–84.

22. Harris, *Contemporary Portraits*, 229. See also Emma Goldman, *My Disillusionment in Russia* (New York: Doubleday, Page and Co., 1923), 11.

23. Havel, "Introduction to Emma Goldman," 11.

24. Alexander Berkman, *Prison Memoirs of an Anarchist* (1912; reprint, New York: Schocken, 1970), 5.

25. *LML*, 28.

26. Harris, *Contemporary Portraits*, 229.

27. *LML*, 15.

28. Havel, "Introduction to Emma Goldman," 13.

29. *LML*, 23–24.

30. *LML*, 370.

31. Goldman's penchant for disguise is not what Patricia Meyer Spack calls "selves in hiding" in women's autobiography—that is, an uncertainty about literary identity. See Spack, "Selves in Hiding," in Estelle C. Jelinek, ed., *Women's Autobiography: Essays in Criticism* (Bloomington: Indiana University Press, 1980), 112–32. Goldman knew who she was but sometimes preferred to be someone else.

CHAPTER 2

1. The phrase is borrowed from John Higham, *Strangers in the Land* (New Brunswick, N.J.: Rutgers University Press, 1955).

2. Edward Bellamy, *Looking Backward* (New York: New American Library, 1960), 32.

3. Bellamy, *Looking Backward*, 29.

4. Emma Goldman, *Living My Life* (New York: Dover Publications, 1970), 11. Hereinafter cited as *LML*.

5. *LML*, 20.

6. *LML*, 23.

7. *LML*, 43, 8–10.

8. *LML*, 23.

9. *LML*, 61.

10. Ira Kipnis, *The American Socialist Movement, 1897–1912* (New York: Columbia University Press, 1952), 22, 19.

11. Paul Avrich, *The Haymarket Tragedy* (Princeton, N.J.: Princeton University Press, 1984), 68–78, 83–89, 160, 432–33.

12. Abraham Cahan, *The Education of Abraham Cahan*. Leon Stein, Abraham P. Conan, and Lynn Davison, trans. (1926; reprint, Philadelphia: Jewish Publication Society of America, 1969), 228–29.

13. *LML*, 3.

14. *LML*, 5.

15. Alexander Berkman, *Prison Memoirs of an Anarchist* (New York: Schocken Books, 1970), 236.

16. Berkman, *Prison Memoirs*, 237.

17. *LML*, 49.

18. Berkman, *Prison Memoirs*, 8.

19. *LML*, 61.

20. *LML*, 56.

21. *LML*, 70–74.

22. *LML*, 85.

23. *LML*, 86.

24. *LML*, 87.

25. Alice Wexler, *Emma Goldman in America* (Boston: Beacon Press, 1984), 292. Wexler speculates that Berkman may have been just as interested in killing himself as in killing Frick. Berkman did end his own life in 1936, and he had fought off suicidal depressions several times. In his *Prison Memoirs*, the descriptions of the *attentat* are interspersed with references to his guilt at surviving his mother. Early in his imprisonment, Goldman was supposed to bring Berkman "the gift of Lingg," but for some reason she did not bring it. In November 1892, using his sister's name, she did visit him. It is not clear why she assumed this disguise, since she was not wanted by the police; nor is it clear why he felt compelled to pass a secret note into her mouth as they kissed, since the note only told her how to arrange a visit for the next day, which she had already been promised. See *LML*, 111–13.

26. Berkman, *Prison Memoirs*, 137, 83.

27. *LML*, 109.

28. *LML*, 131.

29. *LML*, 148.

30. *LML*, 168, 173.

31. *LML*, 205, 245.

32. *LML*, 193.

33. *LML*, 268.

34. David D. Van Tassel and John J. Grabowski, eds. *Encyclopedia of Cleveland History* (Bloomington: Indiana University Press, 1987), 327–28.

35. *LML*, 296; Cleveland *Plain Dealer*, 8 September 1901, 1. The Cleveland newspapers came down especially hard on Czolgosz, since he had embarrassed the city as well as assassinated the president.

36. *LML*, 304.

CHAPTER 3

1. Sidney Fine, "Anarchism and the Assassination of McKinley," *American Historical Review* (July 1955), 777–99. De Cleyre is quoted in Paul Avrich, *An American Anarchist: The Life of Voltairine de Cleyre* (Princeton, N.J.: Princeton University Press, 1978), 133–35.

2. Cleveland *Plain Dealer*, 9 September 1901, 1. (In the same speech, Howard, former head of the Freedmen's Bureau, opposed lynching.)

3. Emma Goldman, *Living My Life* (New York: Dover Publications, 1970), 302. Hereinafter cited as *LML*.

4. *LML*, 301.

5. De Cleyre was quoted in *Free Society*, 6 October 1901. Avrich, *An American Anarchist*, 134–35.

6. Cleveland *Plain Dealer*, 7 September 1901, 1.

7. Cleveland *Citizen*, 4 May 1901, 1; 11 May 1901, 1; 5 October 1901, 1.

8. Quoted in *LML*, 312.

9. *LML*, 318.

10. The letter is quoted in its entirety in Alexander Berkman, *Prison Memoirs of an Anarchist* (New York: Schocken Books, 1970), 412–17, and in part in *LML*, 322–24. In 1928 Emma wrote him that the letter as it appeared in *Prison Memoirs* was "historically not correct" because Sasha had not been willing to admit McKinley's "humanity" in 1901, although he did so later when when he wrote his *Memoirs*. See Richard and Anna Marie Drinnon, eds., *Nowhere at Home: Letters from Exile of Emma Goldman and Alexander Berkman* (New York: Schocken Books, 1975), 95.

11. *LML*, 324.

12. Berkman, *Prison Memoirs*, 418.

13. Proposed and popularized by reformer Henry George in *Progress and Poverty* (1879), the single tax was to be levied on real estate when its value had increased because of its location in the community—for example, on the main street of a growing city—rather than because of improvements made by its owner. George and his many followers believed that the single tax would discourage land monopoly and speculation. The moderation of the single tax won adherents in both major parties as well as among Socialists, as evidenced in George's good showing in the 1886 New York City mayoral race.

14. *LML*, 358.

15. Richard Drinnon, *Rebel in Paradise: A Biography of Emma Goldman* (New York: Bantam Books, 1973), 174. Irving Howe has described Emma as "one of the first intellectuals to 'graduate' from and then move out of their [immigrant Jewish] milieu." See Irving Howe, *World of Our Fathers* (New York: Harcourt Brace Jovanovich, 1976), 107.

16. Eugene V. Debs, in *Writings and Speeches of Eugene V. Debs* (New York: Hermitage Press, 1948), 46.

17. *LML*, 220.

18. Debs, in *Writings and Speeches*, 283–84, 267.

19. Ray Ginger, *The Bending Cross: A Biography of Eugene Victor Debs* (New York: Russell and Russell, 1949), 273; James Weinstein, *The Decline of Socialism in America, 1912–1925* (New Brunswick, N.J.: Rutgers University Press, 1984), 16–26.

20. Ira Kipnis, *The American Socialist Movement, 1897–1912* (New York: Columbia University Press, 1952), 156, 199.

21. *LML*, 375.

22. *LML*, 539.

23. Goldman, "A Rejoinder," *Mother Earth* (December 1910), 326–27.

24. Drinnon, *Rebel in Paradise*, 120.

25. Berkman, *Prison Memoirs*, 489.

26. *LML*, 384.

27. Berkman, *Prison Memoirs*, 493.

28. *LML*, 384; Berkman, *Prison Memoirs*, 512.

29. *LML*, 393.

30. *LML*, 415–16.

31. *LML*, 469. Elizabeth Gurley Flynn described Reitman as "an insufferable buffoon" whose management transformed Goldman from an agitator to "the idol of middleclass liberals." See Flynn, *The Rebel Girl: An Autobiography: My First Life (1906–1926)* (New York: International Publishers, 1973), 50.

32. Candace Falk, *Love, Anarchy, and Emma Goldman: A Biography* (New York: Holt, Rinehart & Winston, 1984), is the best treatment of their affair; see especially 85, 112. See also Alice Wexler, *Emma Goldman in America* (Boston: Beacon Press, 1984), 142–61.

33. *LML*, 420.

34. The letter is quoted in Wexler, *Emma Goldman in America*, 148.

35. *LML*, 432.

36. Wexler, *Emma Goldman in America*, 280.

37. Ben L. Reitman, "Three Years: Report of the Manager," *Mother Earth* (May 1911), 85.

38. *LML*, 469.

39. "On the Trail," *Mother Earth*, (February 1911), 388–89.

40. *LML*, 451–59.

41. Melvyn Dubofsky, *"Big Bill" Haywood* (New York: St. Martin's Press, 1987), 2.

42. *Mother Earth* (May 1912), 27.

43. Bernard K. Johnpoll and Lillian Johnpoll, *The Impossible Dream: The Rise and Demise of the American Left* (Westport, Conn.: Greenwood Press, 1981), 304.

44. *LML*, 513–14.

45. *Mother Earth*, (May 1912), 26–27, and (March 1911), 87.

46. *LML*, 481–82.

47. Emma Goldman, *Anarchism and Other Essays* (Port Washington, N.Y.: Kennikat Press, 1910), 82.

48. George Woodcock, *Anarchism: A History of Libertarian Ideas and Movements* (Cleveland: Meridian Books, 1962), 456.

49. *LML*, 402–403.

50. These two essays are reprinted in Alix Kates Shulman, ed., *Red Emma Speaks:*

Selected Writings and Speeches by Emma Goldman (New York: Vintage Books, 1972), 34–63.

51. Shulman, *Red Emma Speaks,* 73; See also Goldman, *Anarchism and Other Essays,* 73, 75.

52. Shulman, *Red Emma Speaks,* 75.

CHAPTER 4

1. Emma Goldman, "The Tragedy of Woman's Emancipation," in Goldman, *Anarchism and Other Essays* (1910; reprint, Port Washington, N.Y.: Kennikat Press, 1969), 219–32.

2. Jane Addams, *Twenty Years at Hull House* (New York: New American Library, 1961), 81–82.

3. Nancy Woloch, *Women and the American Experience* (New York: Knopf, 1984), 299–303.

4. Jane Addams, "Why Women Should Vote," *Ladies' Home Journal,* (January 1910), 22.

5. Nancy F. Cott, *The Grounding of Modern Feminism* (New Haven, Conn.: Yale University Press, 1987), 30.

6. Goldman, *Anarchism and Other Essays,* 223, 224.

7. *Mother Earth,* (August 1915), 195–96, and (November 1915), 291–92.

8. Goldman, *Anarchism and Other Essays,* 183–200.

9. Emma Goldman, *Living My Life* (New York: Dover Publications, 1970), 160. Hereinafter cited as *LML.*

10. Alix Kates Shulman, ed., *Red Emma Speaks: Selected Writings and Speeches by Emma Goldman* (New York: Vintage Books, 1972), 78–85.

11. Goldman, *Anarchism and Other Essays,* 213.

12. *Mother Earth,* (August 1915), 195–96.

13. *Mother Earth,* (May 1915), 111, and (November 1915), 291.

14. Goldman, *Anarchism and Other Essays,* 204.

15. Goldman, *Anarchism and Other Essays,* 210–11, 209, 203.

16. *LML,* 557.

17. Emma Goldman, *The Social Significance of the Modern Drama* (1914; reprint, New York: Applause Theater Book Publishing, 1987), 88.

18. Goldman, *Anarchism and Other Essays,* 230.

19. Goldman, *The Social Significance of the Modern Drama,* 12.

20. "Mary Wollstonecraft, Her Tragic Life and Her Passionate Struggle for Freedom," *Mother Earth,* (November 1911); quoted in Alice Wexler, "Emma Goldman on Mary Wollstonecraft," *Feminist Studies* 7 (Spring 1981), 114.

21. Goldman, *Anarchism and Other Essays,* 220, 223.

22. Goldman, *Anarchism and Other Essays,* 234, 242.

23. See Hal D. Sears, *The Sex Radicals: Free Love in High Victorian America* (Lawrence: University of Kansas Press, 1977), for a discussion of this tradition.

24. *LML,* 505.

25. *LML,* 557.

26. Candace Falk, *Love, Anarchy, and Emma Goldman: A Biography* (New York: Holt, Rinehart & Winston, 1984), 169–77, 424; the quotation is on p. 233. Alice Wexler (*Emma Goldman in America* [Boston: Beacon Press, 1984], 182–83) argues that while Goldman may have found lesbians attractive or interesting, she was heterosexual, not bisexual.

27. Jones is quoted in Dale Fetherling, *Mother Jones: The Miners' Angel, A Portrait* (Carbondale: Southern Illinois University Press, 1974), 148.

28. Mary Jones, *The Autobiography of Mother Jones* (Chicago: Charles Kerr, 1972), 293; *LML*, 521–22.

29. Mari Jo Buhle, *Women and American Socialism, 1870–1920* (Urbana: University of Illinois Press, 1981), 160.

30. Buhle, *Women and American Socialism*, 110, 246–48.

31. Buhle, *Women and American Socialism*, 320–21. See also *LML*, 459.

32. *LML*, 488–89. See also Elizabeth Gurley Flynn, *The Rebel Girl: An Autobiography: My First Life (1906–1926)* (New York: International Publishers, 1973).

33. Paul Avrich, *An American Anarchist: The Life of Voltairine de Cleyre* (Princeton, N.J.: Princeton University Press, 1978), 160. See also Margaret S. Marsh, *Anarchist Women, 1870–1920* (Philadelphia: Temple University Press, 1981).

34. *LML*, 702.

35. *LML*, 536.

36. *LML*, 538.

37. Frederic C. Howe, *Confessions of a Reformer* (Chicago: Quadrangle Books, 1967), 240.

38. Goldman, *The Social Significance of the Modern Drama*, 1–3.

39. Goldman, *The Social Significance of the Modern Drama*, 134.

40. Howe, *Confessions*, 243.

41. *LML*, 526.

42. Cott, *The Grounding of Modern Feminism*, 12–50.

43. *Mother Earth*, (March 1915), 435.

44. Goldman, *The Social Significance of the Modern Drama*, 125.

45. *Mother Earth*, (July 1915), 187.

46. Shulman, *Red Emma*, 176–85.

47. Sears, *The Sex Radicals*, 153–82; 107–17; 273–74.

48. *Mother Earth*, (April 1916), 469.

49. Goldman, *The Social Significance of the Modern Drama*, 95.

50. Goldman, *The Social Significance of the Modern Drama*, 95.

51. *Mother Earth*, (March 1916), 423.

52. *Mother Earth*, (October 1916), 643.

53. *LML*, 553.

54. *LML*, 552–53.

55. *Mother Earth*, (April 1915), 77–78.

56. Margaret Sanger, *An Autobiography* (New York: Dover Publications, 1971), 207; *LML*, 590.

57. *Mother Earth*, (April 1916), 492.

58. Quote from Richard Drinnon, *Rebel in Paradise: A Biography of Emma Goldman* (New York: Bantam Books, 1973), 209.

59. *LML*, 570.

60. *Mother Earth,* (February 1917), 766.

61. *Mother Earth,* (May 1915), 102.

62. *Mother Earth,* (August 1917), 197–98.

CHAPTER 5

1. Frederic C. Howe, *The Confessions of a Reformer* (New York: Quadrangle Books, 1967), 267, 277.

2. *Mother Earth,* (May 1915), 120–21.

3. Emma Goldman, *Anarchism and Other Essays* (Port Washington, N.Y.: Kennikat Press, 1910), 140–43.

4. Alix Kates Shulman, ed., *Red Emma Speaks: Selected Writings and Speeches by Emma Goldman* (New York: Vintage Books, 1972), 301, 305.

5. *Mother Earth,* (March 1917), 10.

6. *Mother Earth,* (June 1917), 113.

7. James Weinstein, *The Decline of Socialism in America, 1912–1925* (New Brunswick, N.J.: Rutgers University Press, 1984), 134–40.

8. *Mother Earth,* (July 1917), 140.

9. Emma Goldman, *Living My Life* (New York: Dover Publications, 1970), 620. Hereinafter cited as *LML.*

10. Shulman, *Red Emma,* 311–27.

11. Quoted in Richard Drinnon, *Rebel in Paradise: A Biography of Emma Goldman* (New York: Bantam Books, 1973), 242.

12. Quoted in Weinstein, *The Decline of Socialism,* 126.

13. Quoted in H. C. Peterson and Gilbert C. Fite, *Opponents of War, 1917–1918* (Madison: University of Wisconsin Press, 1957), 254.

14. *Mother Earth Bulletin,* (December 1917), 1.

15. *LML,* 581.

16. *LML,* 694.

17. *LML,* 652.

18. Quoted in Drinnon, *Rebel in Paradise,* 252.

19. *LML,* 691.

20. *LML,* 696–97.

21. Howe, *Confessions,* 274.

22. Elizabeth Gurley Flynn, *The Rebel Girl: An Autobiography: My First Life (1906–1926)* (New York: International Publishers, 1973), 255. Flynn was a charter member of the American Civil Liberties Union until the ACLU expelled her in 1940 for her membership in the Communist party. See also David D. Van Tassel and John J. Grabowski, eds, *The Encyclopedia of Cleveland History* (Bloomington: Indiana University Press, 1987), 667.

23. Drinnon, *Rebel in Paradise,* 259–67.

24. Quoted in *LML,* 703.

25. *LML,* 703–4.

26. *LML,* 708.

27. Howe, *Confessions,* 274.

28. *LML,* 714.

29. *LML*, 715.

30. Richard and Anna Marie Drinnon, eds., *Nowhere at Home: Letters from Exile of Emma Goldman and Alexander Berkman* (New York: Schocken Books, 1975), 13.

CHAPTER 6

1. Milton Cantor, *The Divided Left: American Radicalism, 1900–1975* (New York: Hill and Wang, 1978), 65.

2. John Reed, *Ten Days That Shook the World* (New York: New American Library, 1967), 19, 36.

3. Reed, *Ten Days*, 204, 270.

4. Quoted in Ray Ginger, *The Bending Cross: A Biography of Eugene Victor Debs* (New York: Russell and Russell, 1949), 402.

5. Cantor, *The Divided Left*, 71.

6. Patrick Renshaw, *The Wobblies: The Story of Syndicalism in the United States* (Garden City, N.Y.: Anchor Books, 1968), 198–99.

7. Irving Howe and Lewis Coser, *The American Communist Party: A Critical History (1919–1957)* (Boston: Beacon Press, 1957), 55.

8. Harvey Klehr, *The Heyday of American Communism: The Depression Decade* (New York: Basic Books, 1984), 4.

9. Emma Goldman, *Living My Life* (New York: Dover Publications, 1970), 684. Hereinafter cited as *LML*.

10. Paul Avrich, *Anarchist Portraits* (Princeton, N.J.: Princeton University Press, 1988), 194.

11. *LML*, 725.

12. Emma Goldman, *My Disillusionment in Russia* (New York: Doubleday, Page and Co., 1923), 12.

13. *LML*, 731.

14. *LML*, 780; Goldman, *My Disillusionment*, 88.

15. See Alice Wexler, *Emma Goldman in Exile: From the Russian Revolution to the Spanish Civil War* (Boston: Beacon Press, 1989), 44–46.

16. *LML*, 739.

17. *LML*, 739–40; Goldman, *My Disillusionment*, 143–44.

18. *LML*, 763–67.

19. *LML*, 768–71; Goldman, *My Disillusionment*, 53–56.

20. *LML*, 777.

21. *LML*, 782.

22. *LML*, 786, 800.

23. *LML*, 325.

24. *LML*, 854.

25. Goldman, *My Disillusionment*, 155–59.

26. *LML*, 882–83.

27. Quoted in Richard Drinnon, *Rebel in Paradise: A Biography of Emma Goldman* (New York: Bantam Books, 1973), 293.

28. Wexler, *Emma Goldman in Exile*, 33–35.

29. *LML*, 913.

30. Daniel Aaron, *Writers on the Left* (New York: Avon Books, 1961), 156.

31. Renshaw, *The Wobblies,* 209–12.

32. Avrich, *Anarchist Portraits,* 196–98.

33. James Weinstein. *Ambiguous Legacy: The Left in American Politics* (New York: Franklin Watts, 1975), 40.

34. Wexler, *Emma Goldman in Exile,* 58–60. See also Drinnon, *Rebel in Paradise,* 297.

35. *LML,* 938.

36. Goldman, *My Disillusionment,* vii.

37. Goldman, *My Disillusionment,* ix–x.

38. Goldman, *My Disillusionment,* xvii–xviii.

39. Goldman, *My Further Disillusionment in Russia* (New York: Doubleday, Page and Co., 1924), 171, 163.

40. "Emma Goldman's Russia," *Nation* (18 February 1925), 190–91.

41. Quoted in Drinnon, *Rebel in Paradise,* 315.

42. Richard and Anna Marie Drinnon, eds., *Nowhere at Home: Letters from Exile of Emma Goldman and Alexander Berkman* (New York: Schocken Books, 1975), 32.

43. Drinnon and Drinnon, *Nowhere,* 128.

44. Drinnon and Drinnon, *Nowhere,* 131.

45. *LML,* 987.

46. *LML,* 990.

47. Drinnon and Drinnon, *Nowhere,* 85.

48. "Questionnaire," *The Little Review* (May 1929), 37.

49. Drinnon and Drinnon, *Nowhere,* 82.

50. Emma Goldman, "Johann Most," *American Mercury* (June 1926), 165–66.

51. Alexander Berkman, *What Is Communist Anarchism* [*Now and After: The ABC of Communist Anarchism*] (New York: Dover Publications, 1972), 177, 223–27.

52. Drinnon and Drinnon, *Nowhere,* 90.

53. Drinnon and Drinnon, *Nowhere,* 90.

CHAPTER 7

1. Lincoln Steffens, *The Autobiography of Lincoln Steffens* (New York: The Literary Guild, 1931), 856, 828.

2. Steffens, *Autobiography,* 825, 827.

3. Steffens, *Autobiography,* 865.

4. Steffens, *Autobiography,* 844. After reading the autobiography, Berkman described Steffens as "a moron," and Goldman agreed. See Richard and Anna Marie Drinnon, eds., *Nowhere at Home: Letters from Exile of Emma Goldman and Alexander Berkman* (New York: Schocken Books, 1975), 47.

5. Patrick Renshaw, *The Wobblies: The Story of Syndicalism in the United States* (Garden City, N.Y.: Anchor Books, 1968), 214.

6. William Z. Foster, *Toward Soviet America* (New York: Coward-McCann, 1932), 212.

7. Harvey Klehr, *The Heyday of American Communism: The Depression Decade* (New York: Basic Books, 1984), 60, 66–68.

8. Joseph R. Conlin, ed., *The American Radical Press, 1880–1960*, vol. 2 (Westport, Conn.: Greenwood Press, 1974), 407–19.

9. Emma Goldman, *Living My Life* (New York: Dover Publications, 1970), vii. Hereinafter cited as *LML*.

10. Herbert Leibowitz, *Fabricating Lives: Explorations in American Autobiography* (New York: Knopf, 1989), 195. Leibowitz also criticizes Goldman's literary style, referring to it as "ludicrous," "mawkish," "corny," for example (162–64).

11. Alice Wexler finds Goldman "uncertain" about her literary identity, torn between feminine self-sacrifice and masculine self-actualization. Wexler, *Emma Goldman in Exile: From the Russian Revolution to the Spanish Civil War* (Boston: Beacon Press, 1989), 131–56. See also Patricia Meyer Spack, "Selves in Hiding," in Estelle C. Jelinek, ed., *Women's Autobiography: Essays in Criticism* (Bloomington: Indiana University Press), 112–32.

12. *LML*, 179, 120.

13. Drinnon and Drinnon, *Nowhere*, 145, 167.

14. *New York Times*, 25 October 1931, Book Reviews, 1.

15. *LML*, 10.

16. "Elegy for Anarchism," *New Republic* (30 December 1931), 193–94.

17. *New York Times*, 25 October 1931, Book Reviews, 1.

18. "Emma Goldman," *Nation* (2 December 1931), 612–13.

19. "Elegy for Anarchism," *New Republic* (30 December 1931), 193–94.

20. *New York Times*, 25 October 1931, Book Reviews, 1.

21. Emma Goldman, "Voyage of the Buford," *American Mercury* (July 1931), 276–86; "The Assassination of McKinley," *American Mercury* (September 1931), 53–67.

22. Drinnon and Drinnon, *Nowhere*, 230–31.

23. *News-Week* (20 January 1934), 20.

24. "Emma Goldman," *Nation* (21 March 1934), 320–21.

25. "Was My Life Worth Living," reprinted from *Harper's Magazine* (December 1934) in Alix Kates Shulman, ed., *Red Emma Speaks: Selected Writings and Speeches by Emma Goldman* (New York: Vintage Books, 1972), 387–90.

26. Drinnon and Drinnon, *Nowhere*, 234–35.

27. Richard Drinnon, *Rebel in Paradise: A Biography of Emma Goldman* (New York: Bantam Books, 1973), 359.

28. "Tragedy of Political Exiles," *Nation*, (1 October 1934), 401–2.

29. "Was My Life Worth Living," in Shulman, *Red Emma*, 386–98.

30. Drinnon and Drinnon, *Nowhere*, 79, 105.

31. Drinnon and Drinnon, *Nowhere*, 82, 49.

32. Drinnon and Drinnon, *Nowhere*, 112–13.

33. Drinnon and Drinnon, *Nowhere*, 51, 52, 54.

34. Drinnon and Drinnon, *Nowhere*, 59.

35. Quoted in Irving Howe and Lewis Coser, *The American Communist Party: A Critical History (1919–1957)* (Boston: Beacon Press, 1957), 319.

36. Klehr, *Heyday of American Communism*, 232–40.

37. Howe and Coser, *The American Communist Party*, 386. See also Klehr, *Heyday of American Communism*, 381.

38. Paul Avrich, *Anarchist Portraits* (Princeton, N.J.: Princeton University Press, 1989), 136. The quote is in Conlin, *The American Radical Press*, vol. 2, 410.

39. Drinnon and Drinnon, *Nowhere*, 246, 258.

40. Drinnon and Drinnon, *Nowhere*, 259, 267–68.

41. David Porter, ed., *Vision on Fire: Emma Goldman on the Spanish Revolution* (New Paltz, N.Y.: Commonground Press, 1983), 38–39.

42. Porter, *Vision*, 30. See also Conlin, ed., *The American Radical Press*, vol. 2, 418–19.

43. Porter, *Vision*, 32.

44. Preface to 1937 edition of Alexander Berkman, *What Is Communist Anarchism* [*Now and After: The ABC of Communist Anarchism* (New York: Dover Books, 1972), xx. See also Drinnon and Drinnon, *Nowhere*, 255–56.

45. Porter, *Vision*, 120.

46. Porter, *Vision*, 234.

47. Porter, *Vision*, 123.

48. Drinnon and Drinnon, *Nowhere*, 320.

49. Wexler, *Emma Goldman in Exile*, 228.

50. Drinnon and Drinnon, *Nowhere*, 269, 51.

51. Klehr, *Heyday of American Communism*, 401–9.

52. Quoted in Drinnon, *Rebel in Paradise*, 386–87.

53. Porter, *Vision*, 322, 320.

EPILOGUE

1. John Sayles, *The Anarchists' Convention* (Boston: Little Brown, 1979), 23–34.

2. Joseph R. Conlin, ed., *The American Radical Press*, vol. 1 (Westport, Conn.: Greenwood Press 1974), 177–79. See also Laurence Veysey, *The Communal Experience: Anarchist and Mystical Counter-cultures in America* (New York: Harper & Row, 1973), 36–39. The *Freie Arbeiter Shtime*, which Goldman and Berkman had read eagerly in their early days on the East Side, finally folded in December 1977, the last foreign-language anarchist newspaper in the United States. See Paul Avrich, *Anarchist Portraits* (Princeton, N.J.: Princeton University Press, 1989), 197–99.

3. Veysey, *The Communal Experience*, 36–37. See also William O. Reichert, *Partisans of Freedom: A Study in American Anarchism* (Bowling Green, Ohio: Bowling Green University Popular Press, 1976), 487–580. See Maurice Isserman, *If I Had a Hammer* (New York: Basic Books, 1987) for a discussion of the links between the Old and the New Left.

BIBLIOGRAPHIC ESSAY

Preface

The best introduction to international anarchism is the scholarly and balanced work by George Woodcock, *Anarchism: A History of Libertarian Ideas and Movements* (Cleveland: World Publishing, 1962). Paul Avrich has written several fine books on American anarchism and American anarchists, including *An American Anarchist: The Life of Voltairine de Cleyre* (Princeton, N.J.: Princeton University Press, 1978).

Chapter 1

This biography is much indebted throughout to Richard Drinnon, *Rebel in Paradise* (New York: Bantam Books, 1973) and to Alice Wexler, *Emma Goldman in America* (Boston: Beacon Press, 1984), both of which provide excellent accounts of Goldman's youth and adolescence. Goldman's own account of her youth in *Living My Life* (New York: Knopf, 1931), is highly selective, and it is useful to compare it with a somewhat earlier version that appears in *Contemporary Portraits*, Fourth Series (London: Grant Richards, 1924), by her friend Frank Harris. In addition, I have referred to the autobiography of Mary Antin, another Russian Jewish woman, also an immigrant and also an author, although not a radical: Mary Antin, *The Promised Land* (Boston: Houghton Mifflin, 1969), originally published in 1912, describes growing up within the Jewish Pale in circumstances much like Goldman's. See also Louis Greenberg, *The Jews in Russia: The Struggle for Emancipation* (New York: Schocken Books, 1976).

Chapter 2

Edward Bellamy was the most influential reformer-author of the late nineteenth century, and his *Looking Backward* (New York: New American Library, 1960) provides a revealing picture of the massive economic, social, and political problems of the period. In *The Haymarket Tragedy* (Princeton: Princeton University Press, 1984) Paul Avrich gives a sympathetic and detailed account of immigrant anarchism and especially of the famous incident, revered by the political left. The beginnings of American socialism are most completely described in Ira Kipnis, *The American Socialist Movement, 1897–1912* (New York: Columbia University Press, 1952). *Living My Life* contains little on Goldman's years in Rochester, since she claimed that her life "began" when she came to New York City. Irving Howe, *World Of Our Fathers* (New York: Harcourt Brace Jovanovich, 1976) provides a descriptive and analytical history of Jews on New York's Lower East Side. Alexander Berkman's *Prison Memoirs of an Anarchist* (New York: Schocken Books, 1970), originally published in 1912 by Mother Earth Publishing, provides insight into Goldman and Berkman in their early years together and was written at a time much closer to those events than was Goldman's autobiography. The psychological approach taken by Alice Wexler in *Emma Goldman in America*, Chapters 5 and 6, is particularly interesting on this period.

Chapter 3

On the terrorist tradition within anarchism, see James Joll, *The Anarchists* (Cambridge, Mass.: Harvard University Press, 1980). Excellent accounts of the founding of the Socialist Party of America are found in Kipnis, *The American Socialist Movement*; Ray Ginger, *The Bending Cross: A Biography of Eugene Victor Debs* (New York: Russell and Russell, 1949); and David A. Shannon, *The Socialist Party of America: A History* (New York: Macmillan, 1955). Melvyn Dubofsky, *We Shall Be All: A History of the Industrial Workers of the World* (Chicago: Quadrangle Books, 1969) and Patrick Renshaw, *The Wobblies: The Story of Syndicalism in the United States* (Garden City, N.Y.: Anchor Books, 1968) are standard histories of the Industrial Workers of the World. Candace Falk, *Love, Anarchy, and Emma Goldman: A Biography* (New York: Holt, Rinehart & Winston, 1984), based on a newly discovered cache of letters written by Goldman and Ben Reitman to each other, provides insight into their sexual relationship, which Goldman, constrained by literary convention or perhaps good taste, could only hint at. William O. Reichert, *Partisans of Freedom: A Study in American Anarchism* (Bowling Green, Ohio: Bowling Green University Popular Press, 1976), is an interesting but partisan account of the American anarchist movement. The issues of *Mother Earth*, 1906–1912, describe the events and concerns of those on the political left, and Goldman's *Anarchism and Other Essays* (Port Washington, N.Y.: Kennikat Press, 1910) illustrates her thinking at that time. Several of the essays are reprinted in *Red Emma Speaks: Selected Writings and Speeches by Emma Goldman*, edited by Alix Kates Shulman (New York: Vintage Books, 1972), which also includes a good biographical essay.

Chapter 4

Jane Addams's *Twenty Years at Hull House* (New York: New American Library, 1961) is a wonderful introduction to the Progressive period, especially to the unique analysis of its problems and solutions by women reformers. Addams, the most famous woman of her time, did not speak for all American women, but she did speak *to* many of them. Excellent general histories of American women include *Women and the American Experience* by Nancy Woloch (New York: Knopf, 1984) and *Women's America: Refocusing the Past*, edited by Linda K. Kerber and Jane DeHart Mathews (New York: Oxford University Press, 1987). Histories of women on the American left include Mari Jo Buhle, *Women and American Socialism, 1870–1920* (Urbana: University of Illinois Press, 1981) and Margaret S. Marsh, *Anarchist Women, 1870–1920* (Philadelphia: Temple University Press, 1981). On the fight for legal birth control, see Linda Gordon, *Woman's Body, Woman's Right: A Social History of Birth Control in America* (New York: Penguin, 1988) and on the ideas of the suffragist movement and early twentieth-century feminists, see Nancy F. Cott, *The Grounding of Modern Feminism* (New Haven, Conn.: Yale University Press, 1987). Goldman's own ideas about women's issues are best expressed in the pages of *Mother Earth*, in Goldman's *The Social Significance of the Modern Drama* (New York: Applause Theater Book Publishing, 1987), and in essays found in Shulman, *Red Emma Speaks*. Wexler, *Emma Goldman in America*, Chapter 12, offers a thoughtful analysis of Goldman's version of feminism. Blanche Weisen Cook, in "Female Support Networks and Political Activism: Lillian Wald, Crystal Eastman, Emma Goldman," *Chrysalis* 1977: 43–61, has also pointed out that Goldman had few female friends.

Chapter 5

Frederick C. Howe, *The Confessions of a Reformer* (New York: Quadrangle Books, 1967) is a useful account of the period from the perspective of a political activist who shared some of Goldman's interests. The legal complexities of Goldman and Berkman's trial and deportation are best analysed in Drinnon,

Rebel in Paradise, Chapters 20–25. On the peace movement before World War I, see Charles Debenedetti, *The Peace Reform in American History* (Bloomington: Indiana University Press, 1980) and Charles Chatfield, *For Peace and Justice: Pacifism in America, 1914–1941* (Knoxville: The University of Tennessee Press, 1971). *Opponents of War, 1917–1918*, by H. C. Peterson and Gilbert C. Fite (Madison: University of Wisconsin Press, 1957), describes the wide spectrum of opposition to American involvement. Goldman provides the best account of her stay in the Jefferson City prison in *Living My Life*, Chapters 47–49. On the "red scare," see William Preston, Jr., *Aliens and Dissenters: Federal Suppression of Radicals, 1903–1933* (New York: Harper & Row, 1963).

Chapter 6

John Reed's classic, *Ten Days That Shook the World*, originally published in 1919, (New York: Signet, 1967) can still arouse enthusiasm, as it did at the time. Goldman's *My Disillusionment in Russia* (New York: Doubleday, Page and Co., 1923) and *My Further Disillusionment in Russia* (Doubleday, Page and Co., 1924) provide an entirely different perspective on the Bolsheviks than Reed's. These two accounts, in turn, do not exactly mesh with a later version of Goldman's activities in Soviet Russia, in *Living My Life*, Chapter 52. Paul Avrich, *The Russian Anarchists* (Princeton: Princeton University Press, 1967) puts Goldman's descriptions of anarchists in context. On the impact of the "cult of Russia" on the American left, see Milton Cantor, *The Divided Left: American Radicalism, 1900–1975* (New York: Hill and Wang, 1978), Chapter 5, and Daniel Aaron, *Writers on the Left* (New York: Avon Books, 1965). Admittedly more partisan is Irving Howe and Lewis Coser, *The American Communist Party: A Critical History (1919–1957)* (Boston: Beacon Press, 1957). Alice Wexler, *Emma Goldman in Exile* (Boston: Beacon Press, 1989) is a full and fascinating account of Goldman's life after her deportation. This book is even more psychologically oriented than *Emma Goldman in America*, however, and Wexler suggests on several occasions that Goldman's fervent anti-communism stemmed from her emotional stress and psychological disorientation rather than from her reasoned political assessment: for examples, see pages 73, 98, and 110.

Chapter 7

Lincoln Steffens, *The Autobiography of Lincoln Steffens* (New York: The Literary Guild, 1931) was published the same year as Goldman's, and it describes a political odyssey that, in some ways, was representative of the intellectual journey of the American left. *Living My Life* ends Goldman's own version of her life in

1928. The best source on Goldman during the last years of her life is *Nowhere at Home: Letters from Exile of Emma Goldman and Alexander Berkman*, edited by Richard and Anna Marie Drinnon (New York: Schocken Books, 1975); Richard Drinnon's *Rebel in Paradise* relies on these revealing personal and political letters, but they are here printed in their entirety and fully cited. Goldman's public and private writing on the Spanish civil war are collected in *Vision on Fire: Emma Goldman on the Spanish Revolution*, edited by David Porter (New Paltz, N.Y.: Commonground Press, 1985). James Joll, *The Anarchists*, Chapter 9, provides another perspective on the war in Spain. On the Popular Front, see the detailed and lively account by Harvey Klehr, *The Heyday of American Communism: The Depression Decade* (New York: Basic Books, 1984), and Howe and Coser, *The American Communist Party*. On American anarchism in the decades between the wars, see Paul Avrich, *Anarchist Portraits* (Princeton: Princeton University Press, 1989), Chapters 12 and 13.

SELECTED BIBLIOGRAPHY

Primary Sources

Anarchism and Other Essays. 1910. Reprint. Port Washington, N.Y.: Kennikat Press, 1969.

Living My Life. 2 vols. New York: Knopf, 1931. Reprint. New York: Dover Publications, 1970. See also the 1-vol. edition edited by Richard and Anna Marie Drinnon (New York: New American Library, 1977).

Mother Earth. (1906–1918) Reprinted by Greenwood Press (Westport, Conn.), 1968. This journal carries many of Goldman's essays.

My Disillusionment in Russia. New York: Doubleday, Page and Co., 1923.

My Further Disillusionment in Russia. New York: Doubleday, Page and Co., 1924.

Nowhere at Home: Letters from Exile of Emma Goldman and Alexander Berkman, edited by Richard and Anna Marie Drinnon. New York: Schocken Books, 1975.

Red Emma Speaks: Selected Writings and Speeches by Emma Goldman, edited by Alix Kates Shulman. New York: Vintage Books, 1972.

The Social Significance of the Modern Drama. Boston: Richard G. Badger, 1914. Reprint. New York: Applause Theater Book Publishing, 1987.

Vision on Fire: Emma Goldman on the Spanish Revolution, edited by David Porter. New Paltz, N.Y.: Commonground Press, 1985.

Secondary Sources

BIOGRAPHIES OF EMMA GOLDMAN

Chalberg, John. *Emma Goldman: American Individualist.* New York: Harper-Collins, 1991. A sympathetic and readable narrative that interprets Goldman as primarily an American phenomenon.

Drinnon, Richard. *Rebel in Paradise: A Biography of Emma Goldman.* New York:

Bantam Books, 1973. A lively, excellent biography, particularly good on political context; based on Drinnon's doctoral dissertation, "Emma Goldman: A Study in American Radicalism" (University of Minnesota, 1957).

Falk, Candace. *Love, Anarchy, and Emma Goldman: A Biography.* New York: Holt, Rinehart & Winston, 1984. This sympathetic and well-documented biography focuses on Goldman's relationship with Ben Reitman.

Shulman, Alix Kates. *To the Barricades: The Anarchist Life of Emma Goldman.* New York: Thomas Y. Crowell, 1971. A juvenile biography.

Solomon, Martha. *Emma Goldman.* Boston: Twayne Publishers, 1987. An analysis of writing and speaking styles and an exhaustive bibliography of her published writings.

Wexler, Alice. *Emma Goldman in America.* Boston: Beacon Press, 1984. Reprint. Originally published as *Emma Goldman: An Intimate Life.* New York: Pantheon Books, 1984. A political and psychological biography, notable for its imaginative use of primary sources.

————. *Emma Goldman in Exile: From the Russian Revolution to the Spanish Civil War.* Boston: Beacon Press, 1989. An excellent sequel in which, however, the psychological and political dimensions become too closely intertwined.

BOOKS ON THE AMERICAN LEFT

Aaron, Daniel. *Writers on the Left.* New York: Avon Books, 1965. An analysis of the impact of communism on American writers, from the Bolshevik Revolution to the 1940s.

Avrich, Paul. *An American Anarchist: The Life of Voltairine de Cleyre.* Princeton, N.J.: Princeton University Press, 1978. A biography of the other leading woman anarchist in the United States.

————. *Anarchist Portraits.* Princeton, N.J.: Princeton University Press, 1988. Biographical essays on both European and American anarchists.

————. *The Haymarket Tragedy.* Princeton, N.J.: Princeton University Press, 1984. A biographical approach to this famous incident; useful on the anarchist movement in the late nineteenth century.

————. *The Russian Anarchists.* Princeton, N.J.: Princeton University Press, 1967. The history of the anarchist movement from 1905 through 1919.

Berkman, Alexander. *Prison Memoirs of an Anarchist.* 1912. Reprint. New York: Schocken Books, 1970. A fascinating account of Berkman's 14 years in prison for his attempted assassination of Henry Frick in 1892; also includes information about his youth and his relationship with Goldman.

————. *The Bolshevik Myth.* New York: Boni and Liveright, 1925. Berkman's version of their years in Bolshevik Russia.

————. *What Is Communist Anarchism [Now and After: The ABC of Communist Anarchism].* 1929. Reprint. New York: Dover Publications, 1972. Designed as an introduction to anarchism for the worker and still useful.

Buhle, Mari Jo. *Women and American Socialism, 1870–1920.* Urbana: University of Illinois Press, 1981. A scholarly discussion of native-born and immigrant women and their place within the Socialist Party of America.

Cantor, Milton. *The Divided Left: American Radicalism, 1900–1975.* New York: Hill and Wang, 1978. A provocative overview that reexamines the perennial question of the failure of the American left.

Conlin, Joseph R., ed. *The American Radical Press, 1880–1960.* 2 vols. Westport, Conn.: Greenwood Press, 1974. Brief descriptions of dozens of leftist journals, including an excellent section on anarchist publications.

Diggins, John P. *The American Left in the Twentieth Century.* New York: Harcourt Brace Jovanovich, 1973. The emphasis is on the theoretical underpinnings of the several leftist traditions.

Dubofsky, Melvyn. *We Shall Be All: A History of the Industrial Workers of the World.* Chicago: Quadrangle Books, 1969. An analysis of the Industrial Workers of the World as a radical political movement.

Flynn, Elizabeth Gurley. *The Rebel Girl: An Autobiography. My First Life (1906–1926).* Originally published in 1955 as *I Speak My Piece.* New York: International Publishers, 1973. Flynn is probably the best known woman on the American left, after Goldman. Her autobiography is a good source of information on the left, because she knew everybody and was involved in many labor and left-wing activities.

Gordon, Linda. *Woman's Body, Woman's Right: A Social History of Birth Control in America.* New York: Penguin, 1977. A sophisticated treatment of the various efforts to legalize birth control, from the late nineteenth century to the present.

Howe, Irving. *World of Our Fathers.* New York and London: Harcourt Brace Jovanovich, 1976. An elegant analysis of Jewish life and culture from the European *shtetl* to New York's East Side.

Howe, Irving, and Lewis Coser, *The American Communist Party: A Critical History (1919–1957).* Boston: Beacon Press, 1957. An interesting and provocative analysis.

Joll, James. *The Anarchists.* Cambridge, Mass.: Harvard University Press, 1980. An intellectual and political history of international anarchism.

Kipnis, Ira. *The American Socialist Movement, 1897–1912.* New York: Columbia University Press, 1952. A detailed study of the Socialist Labor party and the Socialist Party of America.

Klehr, Harvey. *The Heyday of American Communism: The Depression Decade.* New York: Basic Books, 1984. A lively and exhaustive treatment of the Communist Party of the United States during the 1930s.

Marsh, Margaret S. *Anarchist Women, 1870–1920.* Philadelphia: Temple University Press, 1981. An analysis of the feminists and feminism within the anarchist movement.

Peterson, H. D. and Gilbert C. Fite. *Opponents of War, 1917–1918.* Madison:

University of Wisconsin Press, 1957. A detailed account of the harassment and repression of the political left.

Reichert, William O. *Partisans of Freedom: A Study in American Anarchism.* Bowling Green, Ohio: Bowling Green University Popular Press, 1976. Traces American anarchism back to Thomas Paine and forward to Paul Goodman.

Renshaw, Patrick. *The Wobblies: The Story of Syndicalism in the United States.* Garden City, N.Y.: Anchor Books. 1968. A scholarly history that discusses the Industrial Workers of the World as a labor organization.

Sanders, Ronald. *The Downtown Jews: Portraits of an Immigrant Generation.* New York: Harper & Row, 1969. A good discussion of the Jewish immigrant left: its origins in Russia and its activism on New York's East Side in the early twentieth century.

Sanger, Margaret. *An Autobiography.* Originally published in 1938 by W. W. Norton. New York: Dover Publications, 1971. Sanger is best known for her birth control activities, but she was active for other left-wing causes as well.

Sears, Hal D. *The Sex Radicals: Free Love in High Victorian America.* Lawrence: The Regents Press of Kansas, 1977. The story of the men and women who advocated free love and legal birth control before Goldman.

Shannon, David A. *The Socialist Party of America: A History.* New York: Macmillan, 1955. An even-handed discussion of the Socialist party from 1900 to 1950.

Sorin, Gerald. *The Prophetic Minority: American Jewish Immigrant Radicals, 1880–1920.* Bloomington: Indiana University Press, 1985. A biographical study of 170 Jewish radicals, including Goldman, that argues there is an affinity between Jewishness and political radicalism.

Weinstein, James. *Ambiguous Legacy: The Left in American Politics.* New York: Franklin Watts, 1975. An interpretive overview of the left from the Socialist Party of America to the women's movement of the 1960s.

———. *The Decline of Socialism in America, 1912–1925.* New Brunswick, N.J.: Rutgers University Press, 1984. A discussion of the disintegrating impact of communism on the Socialist Party of America.

Woodcock, George. *Anarchism: A History of Libertarian Ideas and Movements* (Cleveland: World Publishing, 1962). A scholarly history of anarchism focusing on its international development.

INDEX

ABOUT THE AUTHOR

Marian J. Morton received her doctorate in American Studies from Case Western Reserve University and is a professor of history at John Carroll University. She is co-editor with Sylvia Frey of *New World, New Roles: A Documentary History of Women in Pre-Industrial America* (Westport, Conn.: Greenwood Press, 1986) and author of *The Terrors of Ideological Politics: Liberal Historians in a Conservative Mood* (Cleveland: Case Western Reserve University Press, 1972), *And Sin No More: Social Policy and Unwed Mothers in Cleveland, 1855–1990* (Ohio State University Press, forthcoming), and articles in *Ohio History, Journal of Urban History, Social Service Review,* and *The Encyclopedia of Cleveland History* (Bloomington: Indiana University Press, 1987).